Building an

Antislavery

Wall

Building an
Antislavery
Wall

=========

*Black Americans in the
Atlantic Abolitionist
Movement, 1830–1860*

R. J. M. Blackett

Louisiana State University Press
Baton Rouge and London

Copyright © 1983 by Louisiana State University Press
All rights reserved
Manufactured in the United States of America

Designer: Barbara Werden
Typeface: Linotron Fournier
Typesetter: G & S Typesetters, Inc.
Printer and Binder: Thomson-Shore, Inc.

Library of Congress Cataloging in Publication Data

Blackett, R. J. M., 1943–
    Building an antislavery wall.

    Bibliography: p.
    Includes index.
    1. Afro-Americans—Great Britain—History—19th
century. 2. Abolitionists—Great Britain. 3. Slavery—
United States—Anti-slavery movements. 4. Slavery—
United States—Public opinion. 5. Public opinion—
Great Britain. I. Title.
DA125.N4B54   1983   941'.00496073   82-21724
ISBN 0-8071-1082-5

Publication of this book has been assisted by a grant
from the Andrew W. Mellon Foundation.

To my grandmother
Mrs. Dorothy Blackett
my first teacher

Contents

Preface

My interest in this subject was stimulated soon after my arrival in Pittsburgh by the large number of studies on Martin R. Delany, a local black hero, who was heralded as the "Father of Black Nationalism." Tracing his activities in Britain in 1860, I kept stumbling across references to a score of other black Americans who, for one reason or another, had also visited Britain. Why did they come? Were they simply refugees from American slavery and discrimination joining other more prominent exiles from European revolutions in London, or did they come, like Delany, to win support for specific projects? These were just some of the questions for which I had no clear-cut answers. This study was undertaken, therefore, in an attempt to answer some of these questions and describe the activities of black Americans in Britain during the years 1830 to 1860.

There were Nathaniel Paul, James McCune Smith, Robert Purvis, and Moses Roper in the 1830s; Charles Lenox Remond, J. W. C. Pennington, Frederick Douglass, William Wells Brown, Henry Highland Garnet, and Alexander Crummell in the 1840s; Josiah Henson, William and Ellen Craft, William G. Allen, Henry "Box" Brown, John Brown, Martin Delany, Sarah Parker Remond, Robert Campbell, and Samuel Ringgold Ward, to mention only a few, in the 1850s. This group included almost all of the leading figures in antebellum black America, men and women who had committed themselves to the destruction of slavery and discrimination. They were joined by hundreds of unknown fugitive slaves, particularly in the years following the enactment of the Fugitive Slave Law. There were also those like Jesse Glasgow who came to study at British universities either because, like McCune Smith, they had been refused entry to American universities or because the British schools were more prestigious.

Standard histories of the abolitionist movement make few references to the activities of black Americans in Britain. The history of the movement has traditionally been viewed as almost synonymous with the history of organized abolitionist societies, and analyses have been almost entirely limited to accounts of contacts between and activities of such societies. These studies have understandably placed great emphasis on the personal correspondence, minutes, reports, and newspapers of organized societies, which give the distinct impression that few blacks, with the possible exception of Douglass, Charles Remond, and William Wells Brown, played major roles in the international movement. It is an approach that has limited our understanding of the complexity of the abolition movement and of the important contributions blacks made to it.

In fact, established abolition societies became less important in the international movement as divisions broadened following the split in the American movement in 1840 and as white abolitionists on both sides of the Atlantic spent considerable energy on sectarian disputes. Starting with Charles Remond, however, black visitors attempted to ignore these differences where possible and to bridge them where practical, in the hope of marshaling the full weight of British opinion in their favor. Their objective, as Douglass and others consistently stated, was to harness British support for the abolition of slavery, not to participate in the disputes that greatly undermined the international movement. In this they were relatively successful. They did a great deal to keep the movement unified, but the relative ease with which they moved between the contending parties, while initially lending some semblance of cohesion to the international effort, in the long run may have further divided the movement. The trend, starting with Douglass' successful visit from 1845 to 1847, grew more pronounced in the 1850s, and blacks came to be viewed by many British abolitionists as a "third alternative" to the old contending groups.

Concentration on established abolitionist organizations has also resulted in the underestimation of British working-class support for American abolition. This is not to suggest that blacks ignored or avoided contact with organized abolitionist societies, for they did not. But the evidence does suggest that these societies became less crucial to their plans after 1840 and were replaced by *ad hoc* groups of local sympathizers who may or may not have been affiliated with established abolitionist societies but who were responsible for organizing local meetings that were always well attended by the working classes. For thirty years blacks took their message to cities, towns, and villages, drawing large crowds to their lectures. This in itself was a major success, for they were concerned not only to win financial support for specific projects at home but more importantly to inform international opinion about the nature of American slavery and discrimination in the hope that informed world opinion would somehow persuade America to grant blacks the full rights of citizenship. There is no way to definitively measure the success of these efforts, except to say that at the outbreak of the Civil War the British public was knowledgeable about the nature of American slavery and that each belligerent in the conflict desperately sought to influence British opinion in its favor.

A number of people and institutions contributed to the completion of this study. The University of Pittsburgh's Provost Office and the Center for International Studies kindly gave me some assistance that allowed me to take a leave of absence to start work on the project, and when the wolves were baying at the door in London, Curtiss Porter, Chairman of Black Studies, sent sufficient support to rescue the family. The Cropper family of Kendal and Kenneth Charlton of King's College, University of London, allowed me to review the papers of James Cropper in their possession. The late Thomas Hodgkin invited me to his home to consult the papers of his great-uncle and plied me all day and into the early hours of the morning with his fine home-brewed cider. I'm not quite sure how much I got out of those papers, but I enjoyed every minute of it.

I am grateful to the New York Public Library, Birmingham Public Libraries, the British Library, the John Rylands University Library of Manchester, the Houghton Library at Harvard University, the Historical Society of Pennsylvania, the Amistad Research Center, the Rare Book and Manuscript Library at Columbia University, Dr. Williams's Library in London, the Mitchell Library in Glasgow, the Rhodes House Library, the Royal Geographical Society, the Church Missionary Society, and the Boston Public Library for permission to quote from manuscript materials in their possession. Portions of this book were originally published as articles in the *Journal of American Studies*, the *Historian*, and the *Canadian Journal of History*.

I could not record the names of all those who helped by guiding me to sources that proved to be gold mines or the host of librarians in Britain and America who never failed to amaze me with their enthusiasm for my work. I would like to thank Barry Scott, a former student who spent many hours sorting out my chaotic references and putting them on index cards. This study owes much to the seminal works of Betty Fladeland, C. Duncan Rice, and Douglass C. Riach who inspired me to take this drastic step. I also owe thanks to Larry Glasco, Fladeland, and Rice for reading parts of the manuscript when they could have been doing something much more pleasurable. My wife, Cheryl, was kind enough to spend her free time typing and listening to my interminable complaints. She has been a tower of strength. Finally I must thank my two daughters who could never quite understand why but very rarely complained that their father spent most of his time locked up in a room tinkering.

Abbreviations Used

in the Notes

=====

ACS   American Colonization Society Papers. Manuscript Division, Library of Congress.

AMA   American Missionary Association Papers. Amistad Research Center, New Orleans.

ASB   American Anti-Slavery Society Papers. Boston Public Library. Used by courtesy of the Trustees of the Boston Public Library.

BFASS   British and Foreign Anti-Slavery Society Papers. Rhodes House Library, Oxford University, Oxford.

CMS   Church Missionary Society Papers. Church Missionary Society Archives, London.

FDP   Frederick Douglass Papers. Library of Congress.

FOD   British Foreign Office Documents. Public Record Office, London.

HCW   English, Irish, and Scottish Letters Addressed to Henry C. Wright, 1843–47. Houghton Library, Harvard University, Cambridge. Used by permission of the Houghton Library.

HP   Thomas Hodgkin Papers. In possession of Hodgkin family, Warwickshire.

JF   Jay Family Papers, etc. Rare Book and Manuscript Library, Columbia University, New York.

RED   Raymond English Deposit. John Rylands University Library of Manchester, Manchester, England.

Building an

Antislavery

Wall

.

Chapter 1

Building a
Moral Cordon

One important feature of movements for social and political change is the attempt to influence international opinion in favor of and to generate material and financial support for the cause at home. The success of such efforts usually results from the work of small cadres of committed and competent individuals, who make use of personal contacts, lectures, letters to the editor, posters, pamphlets, and other means in the drive to win international support. As is to be expected, the oppressed—those who have suffered most and are, therefore, knowledgeable witnesses against the system they are attacking—usually play a major role in this effort.

Black Americans are no exception; they have historically placed great store in the belief that favorable international opinion could influence developments at home. When international organizations have existed, as they do today, blacks have used them as vehicles for condemning America's refusal to grant them the full rights of citizenship. In the nineteenth century, before such organizations had been formed, blacks made every effort to win British support through direct appeals to the British public. Almost every major black leader visited Britain during the thirty years before the Civil War, some of them to raise money for projects at home, others as fugitive slaves fearful of possible recapture, and yet others as students. But all, irrespective of their immediate objectives, went as representatives of their people, determined to influence British opinion against American slavery and racial discrimination.

By the late 1830s Britain was already attracting large numbers of

exiles from Europe. London in the early 1850s was home for many
European democrats—men such as Lajos Kossuth, Giuseppe Maz-
zini, Giuseppe Garibaldi, Alexandre Ledru-Rollin, Felice Orsini, Arnold Ruge, Aleksander Herzen, and Karl Marx—who had fled the
Continent. There were Poles escaping repression following the
Cracow uprising of 1846, Italian proletarians, Turks, Russians,
Scandinavians, and Dutch. Newly formed organizations conducted
meetings in all the major cities to promote the causes of Poles, Ital-
ians, Hungarians, and other refugees. By 1840 Britain's support of
these exiles had so enhanced her image abroad that she was viewed
as the "moral arbiter of the western world." [1] To the black Americans
who formed an important part of this community of exiles in the
years after 1830, Britain's moral prestige was a direct consequence
of her decision to abolish slavery in the West Indies. Once the
source of American civilization had ceased to endorse slavery and
many of her citizens had committed themselves to its total extirpa-
tion, it was not unreasonable to hope, as many black Americans did,
that America would follow Britain's lead and emancipate her slaves.

Black Americans visited Britain in significant numbers in the
thirty years before the Civil War. There was the young James Mc-
Cune Smith who arrived in 1831 to attend the University of Glasgow after he was refused entry to an American university, the Reverend Nathaniel Paul who arrived soon after to raise funds for the
newly established Wilberforce Settlement of free blacks in Canada
and stayed to lead the opposition to the American Colonization Society in Britain, and there was the towering fugitive slave, Moses
Roper, six feet, five inches tall, who came to escape possible recapture and later became a popular lecturer on the antislavery circuit.
They were the first exiles from American oppression, the harbingers
of a group of representatives whose numbers increased significantly
over the next three decades. They came also as an integral part of
the transatlantic abolitionist movement, which was entering a new
phase of international cooperation.

1. William Woodruff, *Impact of Western Man: A Study of Europe's Role in the World
Economy, 1750–1960* (London, 1966), 46; Merle E. Curti, "Young America," *American Historical Review*, XXII (1926), 48–49; Asa Briggs, *Victorian People* (London,
1965), 64.

There were no black communities in England from which these early arrivals could gain support. London's black population had all but disappeared by the 1830s as a result of emigration and intermarriage. Most of the few blacks still to be seen in London and Liverpool were servants. Over the years, their numbers were augmented by a steadily increasing flow of blacks from America. The trickle of fugitives and students in the thirties and forties became almost a flood after the passage of the Fugitive Slave Law in 1850. Their numbers were significant enough to prompt the formation of societies to aid them in finding jobs and to facilitate their settlement in other countries. Henry Mayhew in his 1851 survey of London found a few black American beggars who, he reported, relied "on the abject misery and down-trodden despair of their appearance" in order to survive.[2] The fugitives themselves formed a short-lived association, American Fugitive Slaves in the British Metropolis, to promote their own interests. But not all were destitute, nor did all emigrate to other British colonies. Some like William North found permanent jobs; others like John Brown took temporary jobs at the end of the lecturing season; and still others like William Watson enrolled as students. William Powell, a free black from New York City who was disgusted with the Fugitive Slave Law and determined to raise his children in a free environment, moved his family to Liverpool, where he worked as a clerk in a local merchant house until the Civil War, when he returned to America.[3]

All these American blacks, whether fugitives, students, or anti-slavery lecturers, were living refutations of America's boasted freedom, representatives of their oppressed brethren at home. Moreover, they were aware of their position and determined to exploit it. Those who proposed to visit Britain were usually given grand farewells at meetings that endorsed them as official representatives of black America. Even those who were not officially endorsed were viewed as unofficial emissaries, regardless of their immediate ob-

2. Henry Mayhew, *London Labour and the London Poor* (4 vols.; 1851–64; rpr. London, 1967), II, 425–26; James Walvin (ed.), *Black and White: The Negro and English Society, 1555–1945* (London, 1973), 190.

3. Warrington *Guardian*, February 12, 1859; *Ladies Society for the Aid of Fugitive Slaves in England* (London, 1857).

jectives. A meeting in Troy, New York, for example, passed resolutions welcoming the upcoming World Antislavery Convention to be held in London in the summer of 1843 and accepted the Reverend J. W. C. Pennington as the "representative of the Colored People of the United States." The Reverend Alexander Crummell, on a mission to raise funds for his church in New York, was recommended to the British public as an emissary of his people.[4]

Unlike European exiles in Britain, blacks, as part of the wider Anglo-American abolitionist movement, were constrained by the limits of a nonviolent ideology. They were interested not in raising arms and men to combat oppression, but in erecting a moral cordon around America that would isolate her from the international community. This cordon of antislavery feeling, as Frederick Douglass called it, would be bounded by "Canada on the North, Mexico in the west, and England, Scotland and Ireland on the east, so that wherever a slaveholder went, he might hear nothing but denunciation of slavery, that he might be looked down upon as a man-stealing, cradle-robbing, and woman-stripping monster, and that he might see reproof and detestation on every hand."[5] As an aggressive system, slavery had to be attacked, William Wells Brown told his readers, through "the cultivation of a correct public sentiment at home and abroad." But, Douglass warned, America had in large measure succumbed to this system of wrong that blinded all around it, hardening their hearts, corrupting their morals and religion, and sapping their principles of justice to the point where the country lacked the "moral stamina necessary to its removal." The United States had to be isolated, therefore, by all who were committed to the principle of the unity of the human family. The international community, in the words of Sarah Parker Remond, had to act as a jury, had to listen to the facts and "render a verdict in behalf of her suffering countrymen and women."[6]

4. Alexander Crummell to John Jay, April, 1849, in JF; William Rich et al. to [?], n.d., Mss. Brit. Emp. 522 G85, in BFASS.

5. Glasgow Argus, n.d., in Liberator, May 15, 1846.

6. Bolton Chronicle, November 1, 1859; Philip Foner (ed.), The Life and Writings of Frederick Douglass (6 vols.; New York, 1950–78), I, 154–55; William Wells Brown, Narrative of William Wells Brown, an American Slave (London, 1850), iv.

The cordon, in their view, would be cemented by the principles of the brotherhood of man and the universal rejection of all forms of oppression. Oppression in one part of the world, they pointed out, destroyed freedom in another and had to be attacked wherever it existed if freedom was to be guaranteed. "When any part of that brotherhood is trampled in the dust," Douglass warned his listeners, "all, all, should spring at once to the rescue, and for their instant deliverance." Theirs was not the cause of the black man alone, but of "universal man," for no man, warned Alexander Crummell, "is fully in possession of freedom . . . while there exists one slave beneath the lash in any quarter of the globe." This principle made the issue of American slavery an international question in spite of those who argued to the contrary. By violating this "universal law of morals," as Pennington called it, America had abrogated her right to insist that slavery was a domestic institution free from international scrutiny.[7] It was on these principles that blacks and white abolitionists aimed to erect the moral cordon, win support for their efforts at home, and keep the issues of American slavery and racial discrimination alive in the minds of the British public.

In the United States, August 1, the anniversary of British West Indian emancipation, was widely celebrated by most blacks and by white abolitionists, replacing the Fourth of July, which, they argued, was nothing more than a symbol of American hypocrisy. Throughout northern black communities parades and picnics were held to commemorate the freeing of West Indian slaves. At these gatherings blacks compared the "energy" and "purity" of British abolitionists who spared no efforts to free the slave to the determination of southern slaveholders and their northern apologists who did everything in their power to maintain a system that violated the established principles of freedom and the precepts of Christianity. Meetings passed resolutions commending Britain "for her Clarksons, her Wilberforces, her Buxtons, her Thompsons, men who fought for the

7. J. F. Johnson, *Proceedings of the General Anti-Slavery Convention Called by the Committee of the British and Foreign Anti-Slavery Society, Held in London from Tuesday, June 13th to Tuesday, June 20th, 1843* (London, 1844), 55; *British Banner*, May 24, 1848; *British India Advocate*, August 16, 1841; Newcastle *Guardian*, January 2, 1847.

rights of *man*, as *men*—who were the friends of human nature."[8]
Speeches and resolutions were carefully worded to embarrass the
United States through unfavorable comparisons to a nation American nationalists saw as a threat and a major competitor. The Reverend Samuel Ringgold Ward captured the significance of this comparison when he told a Southampton audience that "the British
people were looked upon by the Negro as his especial friends and
guardians, and surely the actions and sacrifices of the British people
in the Negro's behalf fully justified this idea." Americans, by comparison, were the greatest enemies of black people.[9]

Those who went to Britain to gain support for projects at home
and for fugitive slave communities in Canada took the critical comparison one step further. They argued that the removal of inequalities in the United States would largely depend on whether free
blacks were allowed to alter their condition through education; the
establishment of viable independent institutions, such as churches,
orphan homes, alms houses, and businesses; and participation in
politics. What success they had attained so far had been won in the
face of vigorous opposition at home. Adequate schools were denied
them, as was the right to vote; ministers found it impossible to attend the needs of their congregations and to make ends meet because of continuing opposition from local communities; and universities and seminaries consistently refused to accept blacks. Those
who came to Britain, therefore, were symbols of determination and
hopes destroyed, and Britain received them with open arms. James
McCune Smith was a success at Glasgow University, as was Crummell at Cambridge, and so too was Robert Douglas who attended
the Royal Academy of Arts. Books were contributed to fledgling
schools, money was raised to establish schools for fugitives and to
purchase fugitive slaves, and donations were sent to antislavery
bazaars.

The money was needed, of course, to finance particular projects
in America and Canada. But for blacks, the money was far more
important as evidence of British endorsement of their fight against

8. *Colored American*, September 26, 1840, September 15, 1838.
9. *Hampshire Independent*, January 20, 1855.

American oppression. Crummell, in Britain to raise funds to build a chapel for his congregation, which for ten years had been struggling to survive, worshiping in rented rooms and often without a minister, told an audience in Bath that their aid would show America that they "disavowed the system of caste; they would show that the cry of the Negro had been heard on earth as well as in heaven; they would enter their protest against oppression; and would show that the bond of Christian love transcended all earthly distinction."[10] When he finally decided to delay his return home in order to attend Cambridge, he wrote his mentor John Jay, who had expressed some concern that a long stay in Britain would hurt the cause in America, that in light of his denomination's refusal to accept him at its seminary his acceptance at Cambridge would have a "lively and a startling influence among the prejudiced and pro-slavery at home, especially in our church."[11] The significance of contributions to antislavery bazaars was not in their monetary value, Douglass contended, "but on account of the sympathy they displayed. Every stitch, every painting, embodied and shadowed forth a spirit of freedom and spoke of the power of English sympathy; and against that sympathy all opposition was fruitless."[12]

This sympathy and support had to be protected against visitors to America who either openly supported American slavery or who lent legitimacy to it through their silence. Both support and silence enhanced America's image; condemnation kept up the international pressure and reassured slavery's opponents of continuing support. Where open condemnation was impossible or impolitic, statements comparing foreign freedom to American oppression had the desired effect of tarnishing America's image. Throughout the period, therefore, blacks and white abolitionists kept a vigil over foreign visitors to America. When the Reverends F. A. Cox and J. Hoby, British representatives to the American Baptist convention in 1835, refused to openly condemn American slavery, they were accused of undermining abolitionists' efforts to overthrow slavery. When Sir Lionel Smith, former governor of Jamaica, visited New York in 1839, a

10. Bath and Cheltenham *Gazette*, July 5, 1848.
11. Crummell to Jay, August 9, 1848, in JF.
12. Bridgewater *Times*, September 3, 1846.

committee of blacks headed by McCune Smith took the opportunity to meet with him and to publicly commend him for his "equity, justice and firmness" in supervising the transition from slavery to freedom. The fact that Governor Smith's commitment to black freedom was highly questionable was largely immaterial; he was the representative of a nation whose emancipation of her slaves provided a stark contrast to America's refusal to free hers.[13] Blacks vigorously pursued this line throughout the period. During the 1860 American visit of the Prince of Wales, Boston blacks used the opportunity to express their "profound and grateful attachment and respect for the Throne . . . under whose shelter so many thousands of their race, fugitives from American slavery, find safety and rest; and of their love for that realm which . . . first struck off the fetters of her slaves; under whose law there is no race whose rights every other race is bound to respect; and where the road to wealth, education and social position, and civil office and honors is as free to the black man as to the white."[14] At the end of a decade that saw the passage of the Fugitive Slave Law and the Kansas-Nebraska Act, the Supreme Court's decision in the *Dred Scott* case, and the furor created at the International Statistical Congress, blacks were particularly concerned to continue to address their problems to the outside world.

By far the most prominent visitor, from the point of view of blacks and white abolitionists, was Lajos Kossuth, the Hungarian nationalist. Kossuth visited America in 1851 hoping to win support for Hungarian independence from Austria. During his earlier visit to Britain, abolitionists had warned him against American slavery and had provided him with a copy of the Fugitive Slave Law and Theodore Weld's *Slavery as It Is*, a catechism of abolitionism. Hoping to avoid any controversy, Kossuth tried to steer clear of the slavery issue but without success. Five days after his arrival in New York a delegation of blacks presented him with a memorial expressing both optimism for the "speedy disenthrallment" of Hungary and hope that "not Hungary alone, but with her the world—man-

13. *Colored American*, November 23, 1839; William L. Burn, *Emancipation and Apprenticeship in the British West Indies* (London, 1937), 319–25.

14. *Anti Slavery Advocate*, February, 1861.

kind" would be free from oppression. Kossuth's purpose, they declared, was "too high to be allied with party or sect"; it was nothing
less than "the common cause of crushed, outraged humanity." The
address placed Kossuth in an untenable position: endorsing it would
undoubtedly have provoked zealous American nationalists to accuse
him of meddling in domestic affairs; ignoring it would only have
won him the ire of abolitionists on both sides of the Atlantic. Caught
in this rather prickly dilemma, Kossuth chose to issue a statement of
neutrality that, under these circumstances, was seen as tantamount
to support for the South.[15] There were some differences among
blacks concerning the efficacy of their address to Kossuth, but there
was universal agreement among blacks and abolitionists that Kossuth's refusal to condemn American slavery on the grounds that it
was a purely domestic problem was mere dissembling. Slavery, like
any other form of oppression, they argued, should concern all moral
men irrespective of their nationality. William G. Allen, the second
black to be appointed to a professorship at a predominantly white
college, observed in condemning Kossuth that those fighting oppression "must have a heart not circumscribed by national lines, and
sympathies which can grasp the entire human family." Allen accused Kossuth of issuing false statements that "he could not, by any
possibility, have failed to know were such." Kossuth, he concluded,
was not being asked to forego Hungary's cause for that of the
American slave, only to be "a Philanthropist, not a Politician—a
Christian, not a Patriot."[16] The brotherhood of man demanded universal opposition to oppression, not cynical pragmatism; a catholic
philanthropy, not political expediency. In spite of the failure to win
Kossuth to the cause, the controversy generated by his refusal
to condemn slavery heightened awareness of the contradiction in
American democracy. How, blacks, abolitionists, and many others

15. Herbert Aptheker (ed.), *A Documentary History of the Negro People in the
United States* (2 vols.; Syracuse, 1951), I, 324–26; Donald S. Spencer, *Louis Kossuth
and Young America: A Study of Sectionalism and Foreign Policy, 1848–1852* (Columbia,
Mo., 1977), 71–77.
16. *Pennsylvania Freeman*, October 16, 1852. For differences among blacks over
the merits of the address to Kossuth, see *Liberator*, January 9, 1852, and Carter G.

asked, could a country support democratic struggles abroad while it continued to hold three million people in slavery?

All of this adverse criticism did not mean that blacks unequivocally repudiated the United States; there were places, people, and institutions of which they were as proud as any other American. What they did reject, however, was her slavery and discrimination, and they saw their missions to Britain as attempts to return America to her rightful place in the comity of nations, free of the debilitating cankers of slavery and racism. The Reverend Henry Highland Garnet observed as he left New York for Liverpool that he was "very forcibly reminded . . . that I hate nothing in America but Slavery and its associated evils. Even to me my country is lively—how much more so it must be to those of her sons around whom she throws her arms of protection." Many like Garnet greatly admired American enterprise and industry and were well aware of their contributions to her development. Robbed, however, of their nationality, freedom, and dignity, they were determined to expose America's shortcomings. International condemnation of this oppression, was viewed by many blacks as an important weapon in the battle to free America from slavery and discrimination. "Can I have any thing to say in favor of a country that makes me a chattel," William Wells Brown asked a London audience, "that renders me a saleable commodity, that converts me into a piece of property?" Being a man, with God-ordained rights, Douglass agreed, was more important than mere nationality. "To be a human being is to have claims above all the claims of nationality," he observed.[17] Love and hope for America, therefore, was not inconsistent with open and stern condemnation of her crimes against blacks.

In response to those who accused them of advocating foreign intervention in America's domestic affairs, blacks pointed out that Britain had certain responsibilities in the matter of slavery because

---

Woodson (ed.), *The Mind of the Negro as Reflected in Letters Written During the Crisis* (Washington, D.C., 1926), 290–92.

17. *Renfrewshire Advertiser*, April 25, 1846; *Liberator*, November 2, 1849; *Non-Slaveholder*, October 1, 1850; *Colored American*, December 2, 1837.

of her historical association with America. Slavery had been introduced to North America under British rule, and even though America was now independent and responsible for her present actions, Britain could not escape the responsibility for the establishment of slavery in her American colonies. Britain had done much by abolishing slavery in the West Indies. She had set a standard for all to follow. But Britain was also obligated to lend assistance to those who opposed slavery in her former colonies, "for Englishmen were the first to introduce it there, and now did a great deal to support it, not only by purchasing the produce of the slave's labour but in forging the very chains which manacled their limbs."[18] In addition, Douglass told a Belfast audience, the fact that America was indebted to Britain for her literature, religion, judicial system, and social institutions lent a certain historical authority to British law and custom. History dictated that Britain should do all within her power to alter America's policies towards her black "citizens."[19] Continuous criticism of American slavery and discrimination, blacks hoped, would impress on Britain, the fount of American civilization, its historical and moral obligation to assist in the fight for the elimination of slavery, the success of which would provide blacks with the freedom to become full and productive members of the Atlantic "community."

Over the decades blacks developed a well-oiled and pretty efficient propaganda machine, which they employed to "modify opinion" by exposing the shortcomings of American society and to re-educate potential allies to approve and accept the condemnations leveled against slavery and discrimination.[20] The machine involved extensive lecture tours covering most of the British Isles and personal contacts with people from all walks of life. Slave narratives were published and sold, and fugitives recounted their moving and dramatic escapes at public meetings. Blacks showed panoramas that depicted the barbarity of slavery and used special events like the Great Exhibition of 1851 to dramatize the plight of the slaves.

18. Newcastle *Chronicle*, March 21, 1840.

19. Belfast *Banner*, December 9, 1845, in *Liberator*, February 6, 1846.

20. Jacques Ellul, *Propaganda: The Formation of Men's Attitudes* (New York, 1965), xiii.

Wherever possible they also used other philanthropic movements, such as temperance, to bring information about slavery to a wider audience.

They touched almost all of Britain through their lectures. Wales, with the exception of areas around Wrexham, northern Wales, and Cardiff, attracted little attention. In southern Ireland their efforts were limited to the major cities and their environs; in northern Ireland they lectured mainly in the east, although Garnet got as far west as Dromore and Clogher and Allen to Enniskillen. In Scotland the black lecturers concentrated on the areas between Glasgow, Dundee, and Edinburgh with some visits to Aberdeen, Montrose, Arbroath, Ayrshire, and the southern counties of Berwick, Selkirk, Roxburgh, and Dunfries. Some seem to have carved out an area of concentration, making trips to other towns and cities when requested. Crummell, for example, worked in the West Country with his headquarters at Bath and Cheltenham; Pennington, during his second visit, worked in Roxburgh, Berwick, and Selkirk in Scotland; Garnet lectured in the area around Newcastle and Belfast; John Brown worked in Cornwall; and Allen spent his time in Dublin and Clogher. Others like Douglass, William Wells Brown, and William and Ellen Craft covered vast areas with equal success. Their combined efforts meant that most areas of Britain were at one time or another visited by these lecturers.

The activities of these black abolitionists were not restricted to the major cities; in fact, they often lectured in small towns and villages, many of which are still not found on a good road map. William Wells Brown, for instance, used a major city like Ayr as a base from which he could make regular visits to the outlying small towns of Kilwinning, Irvine, and Scaltcoats. In Hampshire and the Isle of Wight he lectured at Ventor, Havant, Emsworth, Melksham, and Ledbury—all small towns. Garnet was particularly successful in the small communities of Ballymena, Newtownards, and the town of Bangor in eastern Ulster. Even the relatively unknown James Watkins, a fugitive slave from Maryland, was popularly acclaimed in the Midlands where he lectured extensively. For example, in the Potteries and surrounding towns he gave one lecture at Congleton and Kidsgrove, three at Leek, four at Longton and Turnstall, five at

Newcastle, and six at Hanley.[21] Lectures were held in the largest available halls, which in small communities were usually attached to churches. According to his opponent Elliott Cresson, the Reverend Nathaniel Paul, a Baptist minister, used Baptist chapels throughout the country to condemn the work of the American Colonization Society. But overall, there appears to have been no denominational bias, and even those who were not ministers gave a considerable number of their lectures in church halls and from church pulpits. In addition, particularly after 1840 when British abolitionism came to reflect the division in America between "old" and "new" organizations, blacks opposed to the Garrisonian wing of the movement were as successful in cities with a strong Garrisonian society as they were in other places.

It is quite possible that many came to these lectures to be entertained or out of mere curiosity. Undoubtedly, many people were anxious to get a glimpse of Moses Roper, the fugitive slave who stood six feet, five inches tall. Some exploited this curiosity to great effect. Henry "Box" Brown, for example, had himself crated in the box in which he had escaped from slavery and sent from Bradford to Leeds, emerging, one would suspect, somewhat worse for wear after a journey of an hour and a half.[22] It is reasonable to assume that over the years this sort of attraction would have lost its appeal, especially in larger towns and cities where alternative entertainment became increasingly available, but the evidence suggests no diminution in their popularity. Blacks were still drawing large audiences at the outbreak of the Civil War. Whatever the reason, the crowds flocked to hear and see these representatives of black America.

Each lecturer followed his own distinct pattern, but all aimed to evoke revulsion against American oppression. Frederick Douglass, for example, usually began by pleading ignorance, the result of an untutored youth spent in slavery. Once he had stirred the sympathy of his audience, he would proceed to deliver a devastating and highly organized lecture replete with wit, humor, and pathos that, as

21. James Watkins, *Narrative of the Life of James Watkins, Formerly a Slave in Maryland, United States* (Manchester, 1859), 58–60. The itineraries of other lecturers were pieced together from a host of different sources.

22. *Liberator*, July 11, 1851.

one paper observed, "called forth the applause, laughter, and the tears of the assembly." At one lecture he "buttoned up his coat, twisted his countenance into a grave and canting aspect, and with a most inimitable tone of voice, and a genuine Yankee twang," gave a sermon on the text "Servants obey your Masters."[23] It was not unusual for him to speak for three hours. Brown used an introduction similar to Douglass', which was followed by analyses of slavery and its laws, the domestic slave trade, church support of slavery, and the destruction of family life under slavery, ending on many occasions with a slave song.[24] Songs were introduced not only to entertain audiences but also to demonstrate how they were used for communication by slaves determined to undermine the system as best they could. Garnet was very fond of telling how some slaves went about protesting their inadequate food supply. At harvesttime one master gave his slaves only buttermilk and whey to eat. To protest, the slaves made up a work song, which they sang at a very slow tempo: "But-ter-milk and whey / Th-ree times a-day." The master, concerned that his crop would not be harvested in time, decided to give them bacon and eggs instead. The slaves responded by quickening the tempo of the song and of the corresponding work rate, singing, "Bacon and eggs / Take care of your legs."[25] Some lecturers displayed the machines of human torture. Roper showed his Welsh audience a "negro flopper" and paddle. In the north of England, Garnet and Pennington displayed neck chains made in Birmingham and a whip that, one local newspaper reported, was "stained with human gore." This form of sensationalism always had the desired shock effect.[26]

The common theme of all these lectures was resistance: the oppressed, facing apparently insuperable odds, continued to resist and to improve themselves where possible. And the lectures were very effective in exciting revulsion against American slavery. What sort

23. *Western Times*, September 5, 1846; Gateshead *Observer*, January 16, 1847.

24. Good examples are to be found in the Essex *Standard*, October 19, 1849, and Newcastle *Guardian*, December 15, 1849.

25. *Banner of Ulster*, January 24, 1851.

26. Carlisle *Journal*, November 22, 1850; *Non-Slaveholder*, November 1, 1850; Carnarvon and Denbigh *Herald*, November 6, 1841.

of country, newspaper reports asked, could enslave such articulate and obviously intelligent people? More important, if these were a sample of the sort of person enslaved, what a destruction of talent! Following a visit to Aberdeen by William Wells Brown and the Crafts, a local newspaper captured the effect of their lectures: "Their visit to Aberdeen will be the means, we doubt not, of giving many a more vivid idea of the evils of slavery, and also, of leading them more forcibly to realize the enormous inconsistency and criminality of a professed land of liberty and Christianity holding 3 millions of intelligent and immortal beings in bondage."[27]

The number and frequency of these lectures provide some indication of their success. Douglass delivered fifty lectures in the first four months of his visit, the number rising by the end of his nineteen-month tour, to three hundred. William Wells Brown estimated that he had traveled twenty thousand miles and given over a thousand lectures in five years. In early 1841 Remond spoke twenty-three nights out of thirty on slavery, prejudice, and colonization and lost his voice for his pains.[28] In many instances their visits resulted in the formation of local societies or the reactivation of defunct ones. Remond's "eloquent lectures," it was reported to Boston, were directly responsible for an increase in antislavery activity in Cork.[29]

Equally popular in Scotland, Remond found himself in some rather bizarre and embarrassing situations. One speaker at a public breakfast in Edinburgh suggested that he should stand in the middle of the hall so that all those present could shake his hand. Understandably embarrassed, Remond politely declined, only to have everyone shake his hand anyway. Even the otherwise staid and reserved Dr. Ralph Wardlaw took the hand-shaking gesture to un-

27. Aberdeen *Journal*, February 12, 1851.

28. *Liberator*, May 21, 1841, September 22, 1854; Belfast *News Letter*, n.d., in *Liberator*, March 20, 1846; Bristol *Mercury*, April 3, 1847; William E. Farrison, *William Wells Brown: Author and Reformer* (Chicago, 1969), 244; Charles Lenox Remond to William Smeal, February 15, 1841, in ASB.

29. Cork Ladies Anti Slavery Society to Secretary, Boston Female Anti Slavery Society, November 15, 1841, in ASB. Both Richard Allen and Douglass confirmed this. See *Liberator*, September 10, 1841, November 28, 1845.

usual ends. At a public meeting in Glasgow, Wardlaw, with tears in his eyes, took Remond's hands and thundered: "I feel as a man, a Christian, and a Briton, the greatest pride in giving to you the right hand of fellowship. . . . I now declare that we enter our united protest against the execrable prejudice." Wardlaw's performance was contagious, and others followed his lead, much to the amazement of Remond. While he preserved his voice on this occasion, Remond was fortunate to leave the meeting with his arm intact.[30]

Other lecturers were as popular but fortunately never had to run a similar gauntlet. Following his success in Ulster, Garnet was asked by the Reverend J. L. Rentoul's church in Ballymoney to assist in raising money to pay off its debts. In less than a month Garnet raised fifty-three pounds, and he had similar success raising money for the Reverend M'Kees' church in Dromore. His popularity prompted his friends in Ulster to arrange for a second tour of the province, and again large crowds flocked to his lectures and sermons throughout the area.[31]

The large number, frequency, and popularity of these lectures suggest that they must have reached a large segment of the British population, bringing home to their audiences the horrors of slavery and discrimination. During their tours, the lecturers built upon and used local societies, and where these did not exist, the residue of antislavery sentiment dormant since the popularity of the cause in the thirties was revived.[32] It is safe to assume that their appeal reached far beyond the middle-class "respectables" of local communities. Paul established a tradition in 1833 when almost four thousand turned out to hear him lecture on the Wilberforce Settlement. Throughout the Free Church controversy and after, Douglass attracted large audiences wherever he lectured: there were an estimated twenty-five hundred at Edinburgh; twelve hundred at Dundee; crowds of three thousand and fifteen hundred at two Paisley

30. *Liberator*, August 28, 1840.
31. *Banner of Ulster*, February 18, August 12, September 19, 1851.
32. Howard Temperley estimates that there were twelve hundred local auxiliaries of the Agency Society, an offshoot of the London Emancipation Society, in 1833. See Temperley, "Anti-Slavery," in Patricia Hollis (ed.), *Pressure from Without in Early Victorian England* (London, 1974), 50.

meetings (the smaller crowd due to a four-pence entry fee); twelve hundred at Newcastle; and a thousand at South Shields. Garnet attracted fifteen hundred to his Bangor meeting in August, 1851, and when he and Pennington lectured together in Sunderland, the turnout was so large that two adjacent churches had to be used to accommodate the crowd. As late as 1860, Sarah Parker Remond drew an audience of two thousand to her Edinburgh lecture, and in Warrington a local editor openly lamented the fact that the organizers of her lecture did not insist on entry by ticket so as to ensure a few seats "for the better class of people who were almost entirely excluded." Only William G. Allen of the major lecturers failed to attract large audiences partly because he preferred the academic to the popular lecture. But even he spoke to audiences made up "almost exclusively of the working classes."[33] These were not uncommon attendance figures; they varied in some areas but there is very little evidence of poor turnouts.

The editors of the Cork *Examiner*, observed that the city's poor, who were thronging to hear Douglass' exposure of American slavery, could now recognize that "slavery—and such slavery that America inflicts on its victims—is an evil of a magnitude that outweighs the most abject poverty."[34] It was undoubtedly a comforting thought for the *Examiner*'s editors, but the large audiences of workingmen would not allow the matter to rest there. They called on their visitors to address the problem of oppression in Britain; and interestingly, although views were expressed that were not always favorable, free exchange was permitted and encouraged. Following Garnet's lecture to almost two thousand at Newtownards in County Down, Dr. Coulter, moderator of the Presbyterian General Assembly made a motion stating that there were similarities between black slavery in America and "tenant slavery" in Ireland. "Was there

33. Bradford *Observer*, December 15, 1853; Warrington *Times*, January 1, 1859; *Scotsman*, October 9, 1860; Sunderland *Herald*, October 4, 1850; *Liberator*, June 12, 1846, April 12, 1834; Dundee *Courier*, March 17, 1846; Newcastle *Guardian*, August 8, 1846; Gateshead *Observer*, January 16, 1847; Norwich *Mercury*, December 14, 1833; Austin Steward, *Twenty-Two Years a Slave and Forty Years a Freeman* (1856; rpr. New York, 1968), 352–53.

34. Cork *Examiner*, October 27, 1845.

not," he asked, "a feudal power in our land which exercised arbitrary authority over its vassals—beggared, enslaved, harassed, dispossessed, murdered the people, forced them to act contrary to their rights, interests and convictions of duty as citizens and freemen—rooted them up out of their homes and inheritances, and dismissed them to workhouses—the wild winter waves of the Atlantic—Canada—the grave?" Coulter, supporter of the Irish tenants, many of whom were in the audience, called on Garnet and the Belfast Anti-Slavery Society to examine landlord laws and usages in Ireland so that they could all cooperate more efficiently in working for the elimination of all forms of oppression. Accepting Coulter's analysis, Garnet rather evasively agreed "to keep his eyes and his ears open."[35] He was caught in a "Kossuth bind." But while Garnet, fearful of alienating other groups of supporters in Ulster, did not openly endorse the Tenant League, his lectures did provide an opening for the discussion of domestic problems, American slavery, and the issue of the commonality of oppression. Remond had a similar experience in Ipswich. When he pointed out that America was willing to use blacks in her wars but refused to grant them the full rights of citizenship, a workingman in the audience observed that the same situation existed in Britain. Remond agreed, commenting that the experiences of free blacks were similar to those of the British worker with whose struggles he totally sympathized.[36]

It is interesting to note that while this free exchange occurred between blacks and their working-class audiences, the same courtesy was not usually extended to visiting white abolitionists, as James Mott and others found out during their visit to Scotland in 1840. Although Chartists took over their Glasgow meeting, refusing to allow George Thompson to speak and denying Lucretia Mott's request to address the meeting on the grounds that women should not be allowed to speak in public, Remond was listened to without interruption. James Mott observed that, while the Chartists were opposed to "listening to the expostulations or exhortations of women,

35. *Banner of Ulster*, February 7, 1851.
36. Ipswich *Express*, January 5, 1841.

they had not the unholy prejudice against color."[37] His conclusion, though perhaps overly simplistic, points up an interesting phenomenon of the period: at meetings where blacks were the main speakers, there was an open exchange of views with no interruptions from workers in their audiences. Furthermore, no black visitor met with the kind of protest that greeted the appearance of Harriet Beecher Stowe's *Sunny Memories*, which praised the Sutherland family's policies toward its tenants, many of whom were forced to leave the lands they had cultivated for decades.[38] Even Ward, who of all the black visitors seemed to have been most partial to the British aristocracy, gained significant support from poor and working-class people. He informed the *British Banner* that at his meetings in Poplar and Ramsgate "many donations were made by poor persons, widows and others," who, he observed, "generally do much more in proportion to their means, than the rich do."[39] He went even further at a meeting in Dr. Wardlaw's chapel when he called on his two thousand listeners to identify themselves with the poor and work for their improvement. Worried, the Glasgow *Examiner* wondered if Ward were suggesting that Christians should associate themselves with the "paupers and vagabonds which crowd our great city. Any approach to them is found to be sufficiently dangerous both to the person and property of those who would befriend them." Ward, the editorial continued, must have been referring to the "virtuous poor . . . and not to those who make themselves poor through their own misconduct."[40]

Ward and other blacks would have agreed; like the editors of the Glasgow *Examiner*, Ward meant the "respectable poor," not the many who in William Wells Brown's view were responsible for their own degradation. Intemperance, Brown told his friend Sydney Howard Gay, was the main cause of impoverishment in Britain. "The

37. James Mott, *Three Months in Great Britain* (Philadelphia, 1841), 64; *Liberator*, October 2, 1840.

38. Donald MacLeod, "Gloomy Memories of the Highlands," in Alexander Mackenzie (ed.), *The History of the Highland Clearances* (Inverness, 1883), 139.

39. British *Banner*, February 22, 1854, September 28, 1853.

40. Glasgow *Examiner*, November 12, 1853.

best comment upon that fact," he observed, "is found in statistics of poverty, crime, and disease which have been most clearly proven to have sprung from intemperance. The only enjoyment that many of the lower classes know is the song, the drink, and the pipe. It is enough to horrify any one to go amongst these people, who seem abandoned to the varied evils that neglect, ignorance and vice have induced."[41] Douglass agreed with Brown's assessment. He, too, attributed the "human misery, ignorance, degradation, filth and wretchedness" of the Irish poor to intemperance. Nine-tenths of Scotland's crime, misery, disease, and death, he told a Paisley audience, was "occasioned by intemperance."[42]

If all this sounds very much like white America's views of the causes of black poverty, we should not be too surprised, for such views of the origins and consequences of poverty were part of the conventional wisdom of the century, and blacks were products of their time. These views do not denote an insensitivity to the plight of the British worker. Clare Taylor has argued that blacks, "most used to poverty and hardship," almost without exception "betrayed little sympathy for working-class problems. In general indebted to wealthy patrons, they tended to follow upper-class practice and shut their eyes to, or gloss over, industrial poverty."[43] However, the evidence in no way suggests that this was the case. On the contrary, throughout the period blacks continued to emphasize the common experiences of oppressed peoples. Doubtless, the widespread interest among British workingmen in the plight of the slave, reflected in attendance at the lectures, encouraged visiting blacks, already sensitive to the destructiveness of oppression, to examine and comment on the issue of "wage slavery." Speaking of Irish poverty, Douglass declared that "he who really and truly feels for the American slave, cannot steel his heart to the woes of others; and he who thinks him-

41. William Wells Brown to Sydney Howard Gay, in *National Anti Slavery Standard*, September 20, 1853.
42. Foner (ed.), *Life and Writings of Frederick Douglass*, I, 138–42, V, 40; Frederick Douglass to Eliza Nicholson, August 1, 1846, in FDP.
43. G. Clare Taylor, "Some American Reformers and Their Influence on Reform Movements in Great Britain from 1830 to 1860" (Ph.D. dissertation, University of Edinburgh, 1960), 152.

self an abolitionist, and yet cannot enter into the wrongs of others, has yet to find a true foundation for his antislavery faith."[44] Most lecturers evinced deep sympathy for working-class problems, and they tried to understand and address these problems as part of their general effort to eliminate all forms of oppression. They saw their movement not as competing with that of the British workers, but as complementing it.

Despite their sympathy for the working poor, however, all blacks did insist that slavery was the most destructive form of oppression and that it should therefore be the concern of all freedom-loving people, including the British working class. Unanimously, blacks maintained that there was a fundamental difference between chattel slavery and other forms of oppression. As early as 1832 James McCune Smith wrote in his diary that the artisan, master of his own person, "knows whilst the sweat pours from his hard-wrought frame, that his distant cot is safe, and is protected by the invisible but all-pervading power of the British law. He knows that when the evening comes and his toil is at an end, he may return to his humble but happy abode, and find it not robbed of the wife of his bosom, or the children of his love."[45] The slave had no such assurance, as speaker after speaker pointed out. Garnet thought that it was nothing short of insulting to the British worker to compare him to the American slave. It was true, he wrote, that "the poorman of Great Britain may be compelled to toil hard for a livelihood; but he toils for himself. He may not own an inch of soil; but he owns himself. He may dwell in a humble tenement; but it is his home—sweet home! and no tyrant dares to separate his family or to intrude upon his domestic rights." Oppression there was, a debilitating and dehumanizing oppression, but one that should in no way be confused with chattel slavery.[46]

The analogy with slavery became an integral part of the analysis of working-class struggle. Slavery had come to imply, as David

44. Foner (ed.), *Life and Writings of Frederick Douglass*, I, 141.

45. *Colored American*, February 3, 1838.

46. Carlisle *Journal*, November 22, 1850; North and South Shields *Gazette*, December 13, 1850.

Brion Davis has argued in another context, "the ultimate in dependence, disability, powerlessness, sinfulness and negation of autono-
mous self-consciousness."[47] In 1838, for instance, the Working
Men's Association of Northampton organized a demonstration on
August 1 to call for implementation of *The People's Charter*, "to denounce their own slavery to the rich, and to express a resolve to
burst the shackles which held them in a state of bondage." Some
Chartists, Bronterre O'Brien among them, argued that of the two
kinds of slavery chattel slavery was the lesser of the evils. O'Brien
claimed that such strong mutual attachment often developed between owner and slaves that the owner "will not part with the slaves
so long as he lives, or can retain them." No similar attachments,
O'Brien insisted, were developed under wage slavery. Moreover,
marriage for love was encouraged among slaves in America, according to O'Brien, while in Britain marriage was not encouraged among
the "pesantry" and many landlords would not lease to married
tenants.[48]

This line of argument ignored the salient feature of American
slavery, the "chattel principle," and in the minds of many blacks,
broadening the notion of slavery only allowed the slaveholder to escape the full force of international revulsion. According to Douglass, those who continued to apply the term *slavery* to all forms of
oppression were merely confusing the issue and offering few solu-
tions for the removal of either. Such arguments removed "in some
measure the horror with which the system had hitherto been contemplated." Some people, he told his listeners, pushed the analogy
to the point where it lost all its meaning, so that "intemperance was
slavery; working hard was slavery. If they allowed these persons to
go on they would suppose that to eat or work or have any necessity
at all was slavery." Douglass declared that he hated slavery, oppression, and tyranny and that all such forms of bondage should be
destroyed, but he concluded, there was no slavery in Britain.[49] It was

47. David Brion Davis, *The Problem of Slavery in the Age of Revolution, 1770–1823*
(Ithaca, N.Y., 1975), 40.
48. *Reynolds Political Instructor*, November 10, 1849–May 11, 1850; R. C. Gam-
mage, *History of the Chartist Movement, 1837–1854* (1894; rpr. London, 1969), 36.
49. Bridgewater *Times*, September 3, 1846; Bristol *Mercury*, August 29, 1846.

a conclusion to which all black visitors subscribed. Slavery was, they argued, the worst and most destructive form of oppression. If Roydon Harrison is correct, by the outbreak of the Civil War, at least the "labour aristocracy," without "offering anything in extenuation of" wage labor, would have agreed with Douglass and others that it represented an advance over slavery.[50]

Like the lecture, slave narratives were popular in Britain in the decades before the Civil War, and they were an integral part of the propaganda employed in the fight to win international support. The narratives were informative and persuasive attempts to win adherents to the cause. Through vivid descriptions of the inhumanity and barbarity of slavery, the authors of slave narratives tried to counter the view that in slavery there were "kind masters" or "Christian masters" and "well fed and clothed slaves." As William Craft observed in the introduction to his narrative, "This book is not intended as a full history of the life of my wife, nor of myself; but merely as an account of our escape; together with other matters which I hope may be the means of creating in some minds a deeper abhorrence of the sinful and abominable practice of enslaving and brutifying our fellow-creatures." Many narratives included chapters or appendices describing life on the plantation, references to southern slave laws, and newspaper advertisements for escaped slaves as evidence of the accuracy of their accusations. Pennington, for instance, gave an entire chapter to the feeding and clothing of the slaves; John Brown, extensive information on cotton cultivation; Box Brown, information on laws restricting the rights of slaves; and Josiah Henson, an analysis of the Fugitive Slave Law of 1850. Some narratives, Pennington's for example, were particularly concerned to influence the young reader.[51]

Although it is difficult to definitively measure the impact and influence of the slave narratives, it is certain that they were very popu-

50. Roydon Harrison, "British Labor and American Slavery," *Science and Society*, XXV (1961), 311.

51. J. .W. C. Pennington, "The Fugitive Blacksmith," and William Craft, "Running a Thousand Miles to Freedom," both in Arna Bontemps (ed.), *Great Slave Narratives* (Boston, 1969), 196, 270.

lar in this era of rapidly expanding literacy and likely that they left their mark on the minds of readers. It was easy to identify the fugitive's odyssey from slavery to freedom with Oliver Twist's ascent from rags to riches. Moreover, the slaves' stories had all the nightmarish qualities of Grimm's fairy tales. They sold faster than they could be printed. Pennington's quickly sold six thousand copies and ran through three editions between August, 1849, and July, 1850. William Wells Brown's went through three British, two American, one French, and one German edition. In 1844 Roper estimated that he had sold twenty-five thousand copies of the English edition that first appeared in 1837 and five thousand of the Welsh, printed in 1841; by 1856 the English edition had gone through ten printings. Douglass' narrative sold forty-five hundred between May and September, 1845, and was also translated into French.[52] Those who could not afford to buy their own copies borrowed them from others, and they were read in churches, Sunday schools, mechanics institutes, and working-class associations. Their success in large measure paved the way for *Uncle Tom's Cabin*. Speaking for most readers, one American reviewer observed, "This fugitive slave literature is destined to be a powerful lever. We have the most profound conviction of its potency. We see in it the easy and infallible means of abolitionizing the free states. Argument provokes argument, reason is met by sophistry. But narratives of slaves go right to the hearts of men."[53]

The narratives could all have been subtitled "The Progress of the Poor Fugitive," for they employed the traditions of the odyssey so popular in nineteenth-century literature. Like the pilgrims in Bunyan's *The Pilgrim's Progress*—a literary staple of the century—the fugitives were continually confronted by obstacles that tested their resolve, strength of will, and character. Worldly Wiseman's words

52. Josephine Brown, *Biography of an American Bondsman* (Boston, 1856), 5; Charles A. Nichols, *Many Thousands Gone: The Ex-Slaves' Account of Their Bondage and Freedom* (Leiden, 1963), xiv–xv; Gwynne E. Owen, "Welsh Anti Slavery Sentiments, 1795–1865: A Survey of Public Opinion" (M.A. thesis, University of Wales, 1964), 94; Moses Roper to Committee of BFASS, May 9, 1844, in BFASS.

53. Boston *Chronotype*, n.d. in *Anti Slavery Bugle*, November 3, 1849.

to Christian amply describe the plight of the fugitive who also had to confront and conquer "wearisomeness, painfulness, hunger, perils, nakedness, swords, lions, dragons and darkness." The fugitive wholeheartedly shared Christian's *cri de coeur*, "Whither shall I fly to be safe?" and his answer, "If I go back to mine own country, that is prepared for fire and brimstone; and I shall certainly perish there. If I can get to the Celestial City, I am sure to be in safety there. I must venture: to go back is nothing but death, to go forward is fear of death, and life everlasting beyond it. I will yet go forward." Many narratives describe this initial uncertainty, which is finally overcome by a combination of personal resolve and fear of the consequences of recapture. When the moment came to leave after months of careful preparations, Craft wrote, "we rose and stood for a few moments in breathless silence—we were afraid that someone might have been about the cottage listening and watching our movements. So I took my wife by the hand, stepped softly to the door, raised the latch, drew it open, and peeped out. Though there were trees all around the house, yet the foliage scarcely moved: in fact everything appeared to be as still as death." At this point his wife faltered, but after she regained her courage, they pushed on, convinced that there was no turning back.[54]

Fugitives were faced with a whole series of obstacles—the "furnaces of trial" Ward called them—any of which could have led to recapture or death. When his box was turned upside down, Henry "Box" Brown reported, "I felt my eyes swelling as if they would burst from their sockets." Death seemed near, but since he feared that less than slavery, he "resolved to submit to the will of God."[55] These obstacles produced periods of uncertainty and lack of resolve that also had to be overcome. William Wells Brown commented that throughout his escape there were periods of joy followed by bouts

54. Craft, "Running a Thousand Miles," 292–93; John Bunyan, *The Pilgrim's Progress* (1678; rpr. New York, 1964), 25, 46.

55. Henry "Box" Brown, *Narrative of the Life of Henry "Box" Brown, Written by Himself* (Manchester, 1851), 54; Samuel Ringgold Ward, *Autobiography of a Fugitive Negro: His Anti Slavery Labours in the United States, Canada, and England* (1855; rpr. Chicago, 1970), 116.

of despair, but "when I thought of slavery with its Democratic whips—its Republican chains—its evangelical bloodhounds, and its religious slaveholders—when I thought of all this paraphernalia of American Democracy and Religion behind me, and the prospect of liberty before me, I was encouraged to press forward, my heart was strengthened and I forgot that I was tired or hungry."[56] Having overcome, as Christian did, the Slough of Despond, Doubting Castle, Giant Despair, and many other hazards—the "improving process" Ward called it—the fugitive had, in the words of F. R. Leavis, "the assurance of being one of the elect." John Brown, for one, felt that something divine had intervened on his behalf. "When I look back upon the events of my life," he wrote, "I fancy I can perceive the directing hand of Providence in all that befell me."[57]

Most of the narratives also tried to describe the horrors of slavery in concrete terms. Many described the poor living conditions on the plantations in great detail. They told of huts with mud floors and wattle-and-daub walls, clothes that barely covered the body, workdays that in some cases ran from four o'clock in the morning until eleven or twelve o'clock at night, and food rations that could only be described as appalling. They also described the brutal punishment inflicted on slaves. One of Roper's masters gave him five hundred strokes with a perforated paddle when he attempted to escape, and each blow caused huge welts to appear. John Brown reported that a slave was flogged with a cowhide and a paddle. As he lay bleeding, salt and pepper were applied to his wounds. The narratives exposed the horrors of slave auctions too, where families were separated and individuals sold to the highest bidder. All of this, they pointed out, was condoned and sanctioned by southern churches, which, in the words of Douglass, acted as "a mere covering for the most horrid crimes—a justifier of the most appalling barbarity,—a sanctifier of the most hateful frauds,—and a dark shelter under which the darkest,

56. William Wells Brown, "Narrative," in Gilbert Osofsky (ed.), *Puttin' on Ole Massa* (New York, 1969), 205.

57. L. A. Chamerovzow (ed.), *Slave Life in Georgia: A Narrative of the Life, Sufferings, and Escape of John Brown, a Fugitive Slave Now in England* (London, 1855), 99; Samuel Ringgold Ward, *Autobiography*, 153; F. R. Leavis, Afterword, in Bunyan, *Pilgrim's Progress*, 288.

foulest, grossest, and most infernal deeds of slaveholders find the strongest protection."[58]

But by far the most emotive aspect of the narratives were the very graphic descriptions of the treatment meted out to female slaves. Every narrative depicted the traumas of family separations, caused in many cases by the resistance of strong-willed fathers who, as in the case of Henson's father, were determined to protect their wives and children. With the father sold away, the family would be held together by an enterprising, shrewd, and strong mother or grandmother who taught her children the values of religion and, as Box Brown observed, the "principles of morality."[59] They were the sole source of affection and protection for the young slaves. When William Wells Brown thought of escaping he could not bring himself to leave his mother, for he remembered how "she had often taken me upon her knee, and told me how she had carried me upon her back to the field when I was an infant—how often she had been whipped for leaving work to nurse me—and how happy I would appear when she would take me into her arms."[60] Unprotected, the women faced the licentious advances and the brutality of masters and overseers. Many female slaves were bought at auction especially for the purpose of satisfying the lust of slaveholders. Douglass' description of scenes at Taunton were typical of those in the narratives. He had seen his master "take up a young woman, and cause her to stand like this (the speaker displayed a painful position) for four hours at a time. I have seen him make bare her back and lash her until the warm blood trickled at his feet.[61] In a century during which the role of women in society was idealized and sentimentalized, the descriptions of southern licentiousness were guaranteed to both titillate and horrify readers.

58. Frederick Douglass, *Narrative of the Life of Frederick Douglass* (1845; rpr. Cambridge, Mass., 1960), 110; Moses Roper, *A Narrative of the Adventures and Escape of Moses Roper from American Slavery* (London, 1837), 13; Chamerovzow, *Slave Life in Georgia*, 5, 65–67.

59. Henry "Box" Brown, *Narrative*, 3; Francis Fedric, *Life and Sufferings of Francis Fedric, While in Slavery: An Escaped Slave After Fifty One Years in Bondage. A True Tale Founded on Facts Showing the Horrors of the Slave System* (Birmingham, 1859), 1.

60. William Wells Brown, "Narrative," 187.

61. *Somerset County Gazette*, September 5, 1846.

The licentiousness of slaveholders also raised the hoary question of miscegenation, a theme that has continued to interest modern commentators. I do not wish to suggest that the issue was not important, for blacks, determined to win support, were quick to portray the demonic powers of slavery and, as Ronald Walters has argued, to attack the South at its most sensitive point, "its image of itself and its women." The octoroon, beautiful, genteel, and vulnerable to sexual outrage, as was William Wells Brown's Clotel, offered readers and audiences "accustomed to idealized and sentimentalized heroines, a perfect object for tearful sympathy combined with moral indignation" and destroyed the proslavery argument that abolitionists were the amalgamationists.[62] However, blacks, in their lectures and narratives, were concerned to emphasize the sexual exploitation of all female slaves, not just the octoroon. Such exploitation had wider implications than miscegenation, they reiterated, for it showed the clear dangers of unrestrained power. One also suspects that the theme of sexual exploitation of female slaves was used to win the support of British women, who played a pivotal role in nineteenth-century British philanthropy.

The issue stressed in lectures and narratives was the destruction of human dignity. These gruesome tales of the punishment inflicted on female slaves and of their stoicism under adversity, had great impact on nineteenth-century audiences and readers. The female slave became a potent symbol, for she was "the most deplorably and helplessly wretched of human sufferers," as Sarah Parker Remond pointed out. "For the male slave, however brutally treated, there was recourse; but for the woman slave there was neither protection nor pity." She was the victim of "the heartless lust of her master, and the children she bore were his property."[63] Douglass' description of his feeble grandmother's banishment to a lonely hut is worth quoting in full, for it also refutes, in no uncertain terms, those who argued that, unlike factory owners who ignored the needs of old and

62. Ronald G. Walters, "The Erotic South: Civilization and Sexuality in American Abolitionism," *American Quarterly*, XXV, 182, 185; Jules Zanger, "The 'Tragic Octoroon' in Pre–Civil War Fiction," *American Quarterly*, XVIII, 64.

63. *Anti Slavery Advocate*, April, 1859; *Anti Slavery Reporter*, July 1, 1859.

retired workers, masters protected their slaves on the plantation. In her lonely hut, Douglass wrote:

> The hearth is desolate. The children, the unconscious children, who once sang and danced in her presence, are gone. She gropes her way, in the darkness of age, for a drink of water. Instead of the voices of her children, she hears by day the moans of the dove, and by night the screams of the hideous owl. All is gloom. The grave is at the door. And now, when weighted down by the pains and aches of old age, when the head inclines to the feet, when the beginning and ending of human existence meet, and helpless infancy and painful old age combine together—at this time, this most needful time, the time for the exercise of that tenderness and affection which children only can exercise towards a declining parent—my poor old grandmother, the devoted mother of twelve children, is left all alone, in yonder little hut, before a few dim embers.[64]

Such treatment, Pennington told the ladies of Edinburgh, was the product of "a system of barbarism." He appealed to their maternal affections: "Ladies of Scotland! mothers and sisters, *slave children are saleable at eight years old.* Can the mothers of Scotland let their children go from them at the tender age of eight years? Do little Scottish brothers and sisters separate willingly at that age, even to go away to boarding-school for a few years?"[65] Moving descriptions, followed by appeals for condemnation of this barbarism and support to isolate it, were the narratives' contribution to the building of the cordon. The narrative was, in the view of Dr. Drew of Belfast, "the stone in the sling to overthrow the Goliath of slavery."[66]

Over the years, as transportation and communication improved, the numbers of American visitors to Britain increased dramatically. Fraternal organizations began to send representatives to meetings across

64. Douglass, *Narrative*, 77–78.
65. *Report of the Proceedings at a Public Meeting of the Edinburgh Ladies Emancipation Society Held at Queen's Hall, Friday the 28th December, 1849* (Edinburgh, n.d.), 5.
66. Drew's remark given in James Stanfield to Henry C. Wright, December 12, 1845, in HCW.

the Atlantic, and these exchanges led to attempts to forge international alliances. In 1846, for example, evangelicals tried, though with little success, to form the Evangelical Alliance, there were international peace and temperance congresses and attempts to pool the knowledge of social scientists at international statistical congresses. These international gatherings, in which Americans played prominent roles, provided blacks and their British allies with opportunities to raise the issue of American slavery. Douglass successfully did so at the World Temperance Convention in 1846, provoking a flutter of protest from some American delegates. Subsequently, blacks used the increasing number of international gatherings as forums from which to attack American slavery.

In February, 1851, Henry C. Wright, the American abolitionist, wrote James Haughton of Dublin to suggest that British abolitionists take advantage of the presence of many foreign visitors at the Great Exhibition to protest American slavery. He thought that samples of the whips, chains, and other tools of punishment and control used by slaveholders would make a very effective display. In order to dramatize the issue, he suggested that William and Ellen Craft be exhibited on an auction block, Box Brown appear with his box, and William Wells Brown show his panorama.[67] On a visit to York in March, William Wells Brown and the Crafts announced their intention of raising the question of American slavery at the exhibition in the hope of counteracting the façade of philanthrophy and goodwill that Americans would present. "They would tell us," Brown argued, "of their efforts to spread the gospel, by sending missionaries and bibles to the heathen, whilst they forget the 3 or 4 millions of slaves perishing for lack of knowledge at their own doors."[68] Such duplicity had to be exposed. The Crafts and Brown were joined at the exhibition by some of the leading British abolitionists, among them George and Jenny Thompson, Richard and Maria Webb, and William Farmer. They walked arm in arm through the grounds, openly discussing slavery, in the hope that some irate

67. Wright to James Haughton, in *Liberator*, February 28, 1851.
68. *Yorkshire Gazette*, March 29, 1851.

American visitor would take up the challenge; but none did. William Farmer reported, "The gauntlet, which was unmistakably thrown down by our party, the Americans were too wary to take up. We spoke among each other of the wrongs of Slavery; it was in vain." William Craft and Brown kept up the effort for a few more days with little apparent effect.[69]

An incident occurred at the International Statistical Congress in 1860, however, that had much greater significance because of the prominence of the individuals involved. The congress, a meeting of the leading minds in the scientific world, had the approval and support of the United States and most European governments. In fact, delegates to the congress were selected by their respective governments. During the opening session, at the end of his speech of thanks to the Prince Consort, Lord Brougham, the famed abolitionist, turned to the American minister, George Mifflin Dallas, and commented on the presence of the black American Dr. Martin R. Delany. The comment and Delany's reply created an absolute sensation in the meeting. As the Manchester *Weekly Advertiser* reported it:

> Lord Brougham, seeing Mr. Dallas, the American Minister, present said: I hope my friend Mr. Dallas will forgive me reminding him that there is a negro gentleman present, a member of the congress. (Loud and vociferous cheering.) After the cheering had subsided, Mr. Dallas made no sign; but the negro in question, who we understood to be a Dr. Delany, rose amid the cheers, and said: I pray your royal highness will allow me to thank his lordship, who is always a most unflinching friend of the negro, for the observation he has made, and I assure your royal highness and his lordship that I also am a man. This unexpected incident elicited a round of cheering very extraordinary for an assemblage of sedate statisticians.[70]

69. Quoted in William Still, *The Underground Rail Road: A Record* (Philadelphia, 1872), 275.

70. Manchester *Weekly Advertiser*, July 21, 1860. The accounts of exactly what Brougham said vary, but it appears that this report comes closest to the truth. See

Dallas kept his seat and remained silent, but Judge Augustus Long-street of South Carolina, America's official delegate to the meeting, walked out in protest.

Longstreet was a well-known defender of southern slavery. During commencement exercises at the University of South Carolina in 1859, he had railed against abolitionists—these "mitered vandals, these frolicsome priests, these recruiting professors, these Jezebel women," who were bent on destroying the Union "for the sake of an abject race of Negroes, who never knew freedom and never can maintain it." Of the British, he also spoke harshly. "Standing upon the graves of their sires, with the profits of the slave trade in their pockets," he said, "they send forth their maledictions against us with as much self-satisfaction as the Pharisee felt in comparing himself with the publican." Brougham's remark and Delany's reply, it can well be imagined, flew in the face of all of Longstreet's cherished beliefs. In a letter to the *Morning Chronicle*, he defended his decision to walk out of the congress, repeating the arguments developed in his commencement address. And he told Howell Cobb, secretary of the treasury, "I regard this incident as an ill-timed assault upon our country, a wanton indignity offered to our minister and a pointed insult offered to me."[71]

George Sydney Fisher, a prominent Philadelphian, wrote a speech that he thought Dallas ought to have made at the congress. In it he defended the institution of slavery on the grounds that Africans had no intellectual endowments, no culture, no arts or science. "The race," he observed, "is not gifted with the force of character or intellect that fits it to originate or sustain a native, independent civilization." Slavery, in Fisher's view, was a logical outgrowth of this African deficiency that left the Christian American no alternative but to order the life of the Negro. The institution of slavery provided care, guidance, just control, and protection for the slave and security, order, enterprise, wealth, and progress for

also Frank A. Rollin, *Life and Public Services of Martin Delany* (Boston, 1883), 102; *Morning Chronicle*, July 23, 1860.

71. O. P. Fitzgerald, *Judge Longstreet: A Life Sketch* (Nashville, 1891), 97–105; *Morning Chronicle*, July 21, 1860; Rollin, *Life and Public Services*, 105.

whites. Fisher was hard put to understand how Britain, which had introduced slavery into America and which continued to benefit and grow rich from its cotton, could so brazenly criticize the institution.[72]

Newspapers in both countries joined the debate over the implications of the incident. American newspapers in most cases condemned Brougham and praised Dallas for his diplomatic silence. A number of them attributed Brougham's comments to senility. The demonstration, the Philadelphia *Press* editorialized, made Brougham appear ridiculous "and by the follies of his declining years obscures the bright fame of his vigorous manhood." Others saw Brougham's actions as part of a larger attack on the United States. *Harper's Weekly* offered a defense of American traditions: "There are points concerning slavery and the negro race about which we are agreed. We are all agreed that it does not suit our tastes to sit at a table with colored persons, or to mix with them in society on equal terms."[73] Frederick Douglass disagreed. Brougham's comment, he pointed out, told America through its minister, "Mr. Dallas, we make members of the International Statistical Congress out of the sort of men you make merchandize of in America. Delany, in Washington, is a *thing*; Delany, in London, is a man. You despise and degrade him as a beast: we esteem and honor him as a gentleman. Truth is of no color, Mr. Dallas, and to the eye of science a man is not a man because of his color, but because he is a man and nothing else."[74]

In Britain the *Morning Star* waxed poetic, seeing Delany's presence at the meeting as symbolic of changes for the better: "The metaphor of the lion lying down with the lamb must henceforth be regarded as weak and inexpressive; when poets wish to typify the highest triumph of humanizing influences over evil tendencies, they will point to the day when the Negro Dr. Delany, took his place in the same Congress with Mr. Dallas, the representative of the slaveholding Republic of the West, and was greeted with a cordial shout

72. *North American and U.S. Gazette*, August 18, 1860; "The Diary of George Sydney Fisher," *Pennsylvania Magazine of History and Biography*, LXXXVIII (1963), 344–45.

73. *Harper's Weekly*, August 11, 1860; Philadelphia *Press*, August 4, 1860; *Journal of Commerce*, n.d., in *Liberator*, August 17, 1860.

74. *Douglass Monthly*, September, 1860; *Liberator*, August 17, 1860.

of welcome." It was, the editors said, an outburst of sympathy, "a vigorous protest and a timely warning to those who still outrage Christianity by grinding the African under their heel." *Punch* remarked satirically that Brougham's comments would have little effect on Americans, for "they no more cared about being twitted on the subject of slavery than Thugs would mind being 'chaffed' about murder."[75] But not all English newspapers supported Brougham. The *Morning Chronicle* called his statement a pointed insult "thrown at the head of Mr. Dallas" and observed that such an insult, coming from a member of the House of Lords who was once a lord chancellor, and directed at the American minister, was sure to have some detrimental effect on relations between the two countries.[76]

In light of the long-standing jealousies between the United States and Britain, the situation was indeed explosive. The invitation to attend the congress had come directly from the British government.[77] Now a former official of that government, in the presence of the Prince Consort, had flouted protocol to openly confront the American minister. Brougham's remarks must have appeared to be a sanctioned attack on the American government. Even the London *Times* called his comments "ill-timed."[78]

Lord Brougham tried to defuse the situation by making a private apology through Dr. Edward Jarvis, the Massachusetts delegate, but Dallas insisted on a public retraction. Brougham then visited the American legation twice in the hope of offering his apologies, but Dallas refused to see him. Lord Shaftesbury also visited Dallas to discuss the incident and expressed the hope that no official word would be sent to Washington. Dallas called this idea "as silly as Lord Henry's act and perhaps much less excusable." In the end, Brougham was forced to make a public apology, but his apology was full of innuendos even more biting than the original remark.[79]

75. *Punch*, July 28, 1860; *Morning Star*, July 18, 1860.

76. *Morning Chronicle*, July 18, 1860.

77. Lord Russell to Lord Lyons, January 27, 1860, Lyons to Russell, April 23, 1860, Lyons to George Hammond, June 23, 1860, all in FOD.

78. London *Times*, September 29, 1860.

79. London *Times*, July 21, 1860; George M. Dallas to Lewis Cass, July 10, 1860, in Dispatches from U.S. Ministers to Great Britain, 1791–1906, Department

The incident was extremely awkward for Dallas, whose position in London was already difficult. He was not on good terms with President Buchanan, against whom he had campaigned for the Democratic presidential nomination in 1856. Buchanan was aware that his opponent could gain considerable political mileage in such a sensitive post. Dallas had been sent to London primarily to negotiate a treaty with Britain on Central America—something the U.S. government had not allowed Buchanan to handle when he was minister to London—but soon after Buchanan's election, Secretary of State Cass had stripped Dallas of all powers to continue negotiation on Central American matters. Dallas was vulnerable to recall at the slightest hint of diplomatic impropriety, and his problems were made worse by the negative reports sent home by the secretary of the legation, Benjamin Moran, a Buchanan protégé who had set his sights on becoming minister to the Court of St. James.[80] It was, therefore, with obvious concern that Dallas wrote Lewis Cass to explain his actions and ask for his government's approval. Soon after, he wrote to his friend Francis Markoe at the State Department to learn what the cabinet's reactions were to his handling of the incident; but Markoe could offer little comfort.[81]

The initial reaction of the American government had been a strongly worded protest to the British Foreign Office, but by September the mood had turned critical of Dallas. Cass's reply to Dallas made it quite clear that the government expected a different strategy from its minister. While agreeing with Dallas' views of Brougham, Cass thought that the minister should have lodged an official complaint to the Foreign Office once it became clear that the British government had no intention of apologizing. "I should probably have

of State Diplomatic Instructions, Great Britain, National Archives, Washington; Susan Dallas (ed.), *Diary of George Mifflin Dallas* (Philadelphia, 1892), 408–409; Sarah A. Wallace and Frances E. Gillespie (eds.), *The Journal of Benjamin Moran, 1857–1865* (2 vols.; Chicago, 1948), I, 697.

80. Theresa A. Donovan, "Difficulties of a Diplomat: George Mifflin Dallas in London," *Pennsylvania Magazine of History and Biography*, XCII (1968), 427–30.

81. Dallas to Cass, July 10, 1860, Francis Markoe to Dallas, August 8, 10, 1860, all in George Mifflin Dallas Collection, Historical Society of Pennsylvania, Philadelphia.

pursued that course," Cass wrote, "had it been free from embarrass-
ment. You did not make it, at the moment which, if it were made at
all, would have been the most appropriate." But while giving guarded
support to Dallas for his silence, Cass observed that both the president and the cabinet thought Dallas should not have remained at the
meeting: "What you should have done is a subject about which there
may well be a difference of opinion. But I am strongly under the
impression that your true proceeding would have been immediately
to address the Prince President and to announce to him that finding
your Country through you exposed to insult, without any effort for
your protection you would quit the meeting, and to have followed
this annunciation by an immediate departure. This course would
have been a merited and dignified rebuke befitting the occasion."[82]

The obvious censure galled Dallas, and he considered resigning.
But first he tried to vindicate his position, telling Cass that all suggestions of ways he might have reacted were based on deliberation
and all came too late. To have made a speech in reply to Brougham
would have been "to disturb the complacency of a proceeding so
perfectly understood in monarchical countries, would have been
rash, where not peremptorily necessary." To have walked out would
have been to give Brougham's statement an importance it did not
deserve. Silence was, therefore, the only alternative left open to
him. "In one of the most conspicuous theatres of public life, at a
Congress of Nations, and in the presence of Princes, Peers, Parliamentary statesmen and Sages without a word uttered, or a gesture
permitted, canting, meddling foreign Abolitionism, so long at work
to undermine the independence and destroy the Union of America,
has been dealt a blow, intolerable to its illustrious champion."[83] By
October, however, the issue was effectively dead, and as Moran observed, Dallas' defense of his actions came too late to gain any open
support from the Buchanan administration. It is quite possible that
Washington's handling of the situation may have been dictated by a
desire not to embarrass the Prince of Wales who was then on tour of

82. Cass to Dallas, September 11, 1860, in Department of State Diplomatic
Instructions, Great Britain.
83. Dallas to Cass, October 2, 1860, in Dispatches from U.S. Ministers, Department of State Diplomatic Instructions, Great Britain.

the United States at the suggestion of his mother. The consequences of offending the British royal family could have been serious. For its part, the British government played down the affair by studiously avoiding any discussion of the matter, even in its diplomatic dispatches to Washington.[84]

Probably Brougham had intended nothing more than a diplomatic rap on American knuckles, but unlike the demonstration at the Great Exhibition, his comments, directed at prominent Americans, had wide repercussions. As Douglass' comments suggest, blacks saw in Brougham's remarks, whatever his motives, a gesture of international solidarity in their fight against American injustice. White Americans were also aware that blacks and their British allies had traditionally used every opportunity to embarrass their country. American refusal to grant passports to blacks and ships that restricted black passengers to the steerage class had long been publicly condemned in Britain. When Frederick Douglass was attacked by a mob while walking along Broadway in the company of two white women, the London *Times* took the opportunity to castigate Brother Jonathan by comparing Douglass' reception in Britain with the treatment he received at home. Douglass, never one to miss an opportunity to prod his country into mending its ways, graciously accepted the concern of the *Times*, mouthpiece of the British establishment.[85]

The popularity of blacks in Britain rankled American nationalists who were conscious of the contradictions between their lauded principles of equality and the existence of slavery and discrimination. A correspondent for the New York *Express* attributed it to Albion's fickleness. American blacks had replaced the formerly lionized Asiatic and the Turk, and "nothing goes down now with her so well as the genuine black," he reported. They were seen in every public place in London and were so much in vogue that white men and women were "coloring their faces and hands, and going about London, imitating their sable visitors," who were reaping a harvest "bringing off their pockets full of money." This popularity could depopulate American plantations, he warned facetiously, as the "de-

84. Benjamin Moran to James Buchanan, October 9, 1860, in James Buchanan Collection, Historical Society of Pennsylvania, Philadelphia.

85. London *Times*, June 11, July 18, 1850.

mand for the 'article' of Ethiopian lions in the London market" increases.[86]

There was an element of truth in the account. From the early thirties, blacks were aware that their color had become an asset. Nathaniel Paul, for example, quickly found this out in his disputes with Elliott Cresson and used it to maximum effect. "The colour of his skin," the secretary of the Edinburgh Antislavery Society told George Thompson, "was an excellent introduction to him, something surely to surprise brother Jonathan. . . . Here there is no prejudice about the colour of a man's skin. The darker he is, the more likely is he to receive kind attention and support." Cresson, quick to recognize this fact, pleaded with the leaders of the American Colonization Society to find a black man who could counteract Paul's impact.[87]

Blacks were indeed lionized and in some instances with some very bizarre results, but even more significant was the fact that for the first time in their lives blacks were treated as equals by most of those they met. Paul spoke for every black visitor when he told William Lloyd Garrison, "Here if I go to church, I am not pointed to a 'negro seat' in the gallery; but any gentleman opens his pew door for my reception. If I wish for a passage in a stage, the only question that is asked me is 'Which do you choose, sir, an inside or an outside seat.' If I stop at a public inn no one would ever think of setting a separate table for me; I am conducted to the same table with other gentlemen. The only difference I have ever discovered is this, I am generally taken for a stranger, and they therefore seem anxious to pay me the greater respect."[88] After being "Caricatured, scorned, scoffed, mocked and maltreated with impunity" in America, Douglass found himself welcomed with open arms wherever he went in Britain and no one to shout "we don't allow niggers here." Having experienced perpetual villification in his own country, he was happy to be in Ireland where, he told Garrison, he had spent

86. Quoted in *National Anti Slavery Standard*, July 1, 1847.
87. R. J. M. Blackett, "Anglo-American Opposition to Liberian Colonization," *Historian*, XLI (1979), 285.
88. Paul to Garrison, in *Liberator*, June 22, 1833.

"some of the happiest moments" of his life. "I seem to have undergone a transformation," he observed; "I live a new Life."[89]

This transformation must have occurred in nearly all of the blacks who visited Britain, giving them a new self-confidence and allowing them to dream of real freedom at home. There is, for instance, a sense of serenity and calm, a relaxed quality in William Wells Brown's account of his travels in Europe that is reflected in his descriptions of the grand homes and other buildings in Paris and in Britain. After the Paris Peace Congress, John Lee invited Brown to visit Hartwell House, an event commemorated by an inscription on a brick under the observatory. The serenity of the house and the warmth of his reception offered a marked contrast to conditions in America where Brown had to live with constant anxiety. There were innumerable contrasts between American prejudice and British acceptance, but nothing enhanced his view of the British so much as to be accepted, admired, and feted by the first families of the realm.[90] Few would have gone as far as Brown in calling Britain the "fatherland," but many would have agreed with the sentiments of an old Methodist hymn:

> A Country I've found,
> Where true joys abound
> To live I'm determined on that happy ground.[91]

Popularity and acceptance in no way produced dependence, however. Some did come, as we have seen, to raise money for particular projects at home and in Canada, but once they had gathered enough money, they generally returned to America to continue the struggle. Most refused to depend on the generosity of their British friends. William Wells Brown, for instance, supported himself from proceeds of the sale of his narrative, and the *Anti-Slavery Harp* (a book of slave songs) and from fees charged to attend his lectures and view his panorama. He accepted some donations, but they were

89. Foner (ed.), *Life and Writings of Frederick Douglass*, I, 125–29.

90. William Wells Brown, *The American Fugitive in Europe: Sketches of Places and People Abroad* (London, 1855), 104.

91. Quoted in William Powell to Maria Chapman, January 21, 1859, in ASB.

hardly large enough to foster dependence. For example, he received twelve pounds from the ladies of Little Bolton and twenty sovereigns at a soiree in Newcastle. Other blacks worked for brief spells as paid lecturers for antislavery societies.[92] As one would expect, there were a few imposters and some questionable dealings. Nathaniel Paul was accused of using money contributed for the Wilberforce Settlement for his own purposes, and Samuel Ringgold Ward was suspected of swindling a Canadian colleague out of his savings before leaving for Jamaica. By the early fifties, the British and Foreign Anti-Slavery Society (BFASS) and others were warning the public against imposters and recommending the formation of committees to supervise the collection of money.[93] Given the situation, one is surprised that there were so few instances of fraud.

Their independence and popularity not only enhanced the image of blacks as the major proponents of American abolitionism but also made them, especially after the split in abolitionist ranks in 1840, the crucial unifying factor among British abolitionists. Generally, their position was straightforward and uncomplicated. Ideological or sectarian issues were secondary for them. They had come to Britain to win support for American abolitionism, and they were willing to work with everyone who could promote the cause. John Collins' visit to Britain in 1840 provides an illustration of the role blacks played in smoothing over the differences among abolitionists. Collins, a white abolitionist, had been sent to Britain by the American Anti-Slavery Society (AASS), which had sided with the Garrisonians when the movement split. The society was in financial trouble, and Collins was sent to raise money in Britain, where the schism in American abolitionism had already had repercussions. The BFASS

92. *Liberator*, February 8, April 26, August 9, 1850.
93. *Anti Slavery Reporter*, April 1, 1853, August 1, 1854, September 1, 1855, March 2, 1857; Steward, *Twenty-Two Years a Slave*, 262. See series of letters between Canadian abolitionists and BFASS in 1855, C115/105, C32/39, C156/19, all in BFASS; Alexander Lowell Murray, "Canada and the Anglo-American Anti Slavery Movement: A Study in International Philanthropy" (Ph.D. dissertation, University of Pennsylvania, 1960), 275–77.

had refused to accredit the female members of the AASS as full participants at the World Anti-Slavery Convention in London. In protest, Garrison, Remond, and others had refused to take their seats and had sat instead with the women in the gallery. The protest openly identified Remond with Garrison and the "old" organization, a fact that James G. Birney, a member of the "new" organization delegation, lamented. He explained to his friends at home that Remond, although he was being warmly received, could have done much more for the antislavery cause had he not associated himself so closely with Garrison.[94]

Remond made no apologies for his association with Garrison, but he quickly recognized that these bitter disputes seriously threatened the future of the international movement. When Collins arrived, spoiling for a fight, Remond counseled moderation, and when his advice was rejected, he refused to accompany Collins on his tour of Britain. He tried to persuade Collins to avoid "open warfare" with "new" organization supporters by "reserving explanations of differences for when particularly asked." As George Thompson reported, Remond believed that the "line of conduct . . . he has hitherto pursued in this country—that of independence and freedom from partisanship, with the opportunity of vindicating his friends whenever unjustly treated, was that which was most likely to lead to usefulness." Thompson realized that Collins had little chance of success without Remond, a judgment in which Elizabeth Pease, a British supporter of Garrison, concurred. Every effort had to be made to persuade Remond to accompany Collins.[95] After lengthy discussions with Thompson and much pleading, Remond consented to the proposal. But Collins was unable to avoid conflict, and exactly as Remond had predicted, confrontation worked against the Garrisonians. Collins returned home with little to show for his

94. Dwight L. Dumond (ed.), *Letters of James Gillespie Birney, 1831–1857* (2 vols.; New York, 1938), II, 584.

95. George Thompson to Elizabeth Pease, October 27, 30, 1840, both in RED; Pease to John Collins, November 16, 1840, George Thompson to Richard Webb, November 21, 1840, Remond to "My Esteemed Friend," November 27, 1840, all in ASB.

efforts, and Remond was left to mend fences. He set about this almost immediately, attending meetings of and holding private discussions with those sympathetic to the "new" organization and criticizing them when he disagreed with their position. Douglas Riach
has argued that Remond's ability to confine his speeches in Dublin,
Cork, Waterford, and Belfast "to simple and highly effective denunciations of slavery" won over a number of supporters who had earlier refused to have anything to do with Collins.[96]

But not everyone was as successful as Remond in steering a delicate course of neutrality. Not long after his arrival in Britain, William Wells Brown ran afoul of the cantankerous John Scoble, a secretary of the BFASS, who apparently maliciously started the rumor
that Brown had abandoned his wife in America and was traveling
with another woman in Britain. Pennington, Garnet, Henson, and
Ward, those "coloured ministers" as they were derisively called,
won the ire of British Garrisonians in Glasgow and Bristol. Even the
Crafts were soon at loggerheads with their supporters in Bristol for
refusing to toe the Garrisonian line. These were independent but
pragmatic men and women who refused to bow to others when they
believed that to do so would be against the interest of the cause but
who always remained open to rapprochement. Brown, for example,
who seems to have remained at odds with the BFASS even after the
departure of Scoble, continued to attend their meetings and to associate with many who were openly hostile to Garrison. Moreover,
blacks carefully avoided public discussion of differences between
themselves while in Britain. With the exception of a dispute between William Wells Brown and Josiah Henson, who, Brown as-
serted, intended to encourage fugitives in Canada to emigrate as laborers to Jamaica, blacks throughout the period and especially in
the early 1850s worked together for the promotion of their cause.
Refusal to participate in sectarian squabbles and the generally united
front that blacks presented to their British supporters reinforced
their independence and increased their influence. Although by the

96. Douglas C. Riach, "Ireland and the Campaign Against American Slavery"
(Ph.D. dissertation, University of Edinburgh, 1975), 138–41; Remond to Richard
Allen, January 7, 1841, in BFASS.

mid-1850s some British Garrisonians were inveighing against the "coloured ministers" who were attracting support away from their society, by maintaining communications with both wings of the movement, blacks were able to give the cause some semblance of unity.

Blacks knew that the major battles against American slavery and discrimination had to be fought at home. Social acceptance abroad was not only a factor in the growth of self-esteem but also a useful weapon in the fight against slavery and discrimination at home. James McCune Smith told his Glasgow friends who had gathered to say good-bye that he looked forward to his return to New York with some trepidation but felt strengthened by his reception in Britain:

> Amid the many insults, which I go, perhaps, to meet in my own country—insults which harm not the body, but which 'enter the soul,' the memory of the evening will be a pleasing and cheerful recollection. And whether it be the prejudice of the public walk, or the prejudice of the public conveyance, or that other more frightful and fiend like form of it, which stalks unbidden into the American sanctuary—be it anyone of them, or all of them combined, that shall at any time distress or embitter my mind—be assured that this happy moment will cross my recollection . . . and will cheer me on, not only to endure with patience the 'proud man's contumely,' and the 'oppressor's scorn,' but also invigorate me to struggle for the downfall, the total extirpation of that prejudice, and its parent slavery, from the otherwise glorious Republic of the West.

On his return home he told a reception organized by New York blacks that the refusal to admit him to college in America was his introduction to Scotland where he won "immediately and entirely, the society of those noble-minded men, amongst whom I went a young and friendless exile, by whom I was received and treated as a brother and equal." Smith returned, like many others, to the jolting realities of Jim Crow cars, segregated churches, and other forms of discrimination. He devoted the rest of his life to the struggle against slavery and discrimination, for to have done otherwise would have been to "commit suicide of the absurd."[97]

The international effort of blacks consisted of three elements: a protest against American inhumanity, a theory of rights, and a dream of a different and more egalitarian American society.[98] By depicting America as a nation devoid of moral values, blacks aimed to create international revulsion not against her free institutions, of which they were all proud, but against her slavery and discrimination, which violated all the stated principles of American democracy and the accepted precepts of Christianity. A nation that boasted of its freedom and continued to hold three million souls in slavery was a danger to all mankind, was, as Charles Lenox Remond observed, "an asp in a basket of flowers."[99] Such a nation had to be condemned by the outside world, and those who openly espoused slavery and discrimination or, by their silence, condoned them had to be refused communion in the international comity of Christians. Such isolation would be a continuing reminder to America that the outside world opposed her policies and would give succor to those at home fighting for the destruction of slavery and discrimination. This moral cordon of antislavery sentiment was not designed to foster foreign governmental action against America. It was an attempt to keep alive, through continuous appeal, international revulsion against and isolation of American slavery.

97. *Colored American*, October 28, September 9, 1837; Glasgow *Chronicle*, June 21, 1837, in *Colored American*, September 9, 1837.

98. Asa Briggs, *The Age of Improvement, 1783–1867* (London, 1959), 245, discusses this issue in relationship to radical views on reform.

99. Belfast *News Letter*, October 15, 1841.

Chapter 2

Colonization's Nemesis

The issues of black expatriation and the separation of the races have been persistent themes in American history. At one time or another, both blacks and whites have recommended such schemes: blacks, on the grounds that America has consistently violated its claims to equality by its failure to reconcile the contradictions between the principles of the Declaration of Independence and the persistence of racism and oppression; and whites, in the belief that America, as a "white man's country," could hold few hopes for blacks. It was one of these schemes, a proposal to colonize black Americans in Africa, that provided the initial impetus for the transatlantic abolitionist movement in the early thirties. Throughout the antebellum period blacks continued to play a central role in efforts to sway British opinion against colonization. Colonizationists, for their part, never desisted from attempts to win British approval for their projects. They first tried in the period 1831 to 1834, again from 1840 to 1841, and once more from 1849 to 1851. As a result, colonization remained a major concern of the international movement. The issue was further complicated by the emergence in the fifties of a black-inspired, black-led emigrationist movement that also sought the endorsement of British philanthropists. Its proponents viewed emigration as one option in their battle against American racism. They proposed a selective emigration of skilled men and women and took great pains to differentiate their objectives from those of white-inspired colonization schemes, which aimed to effect the total expatriation of all free blacks.

The principal proponent of African colonization was the American Colonization Society (ACS). Founded in December, 1816, the ACS aimed to remove, with their own consent, the entire population of free blacks and manumitted slaves to a colony on the west coast of Africa. The society hoped in this way to resolve the problems of growing racism in the North and the expansion and consolidation of slavery in the South, which, they argued, made it impossible for black Americans to achieve full equality in America. The society maintained that racism among whites, not an inherent inferiority of blacks, was the cause of poverty and destitution among the free-black population. Further, because southern slavery was cushioned and jealously guarded by state laws, it was impossible for the federal government to interfere to significantly stem the tide of its expansion. The ACS contended that the problem of prejudice in the North could be solved by providing blacks with a country of their own, an environment in which racism could not exist. At the same time, an African colony would provide a place where freed slaves could be settled, reassuring those slaveholders who were interested in the eventual abolition of slavery but afraid of the social impact of millions of free blacks. The colonization argument was well summed up by a Philadelphia colonizationist, John P. Kennedy. "If we cannot *remove* the evil," he argued, "it would be wise to remove *from* it."[1]

Through the first decade of its existence the society was able to maintain a delicate balance between those supporters who saw it as a means of achieving gradual abolition and those who advocated noninterference with southern slavery by issuing simultaneous statements advocating emancipation on the one hand and affirming the property rights of slaveholders on the other. This expediency contained the seeds of future conflict, however. As northern abolitionists moved from gradual to immediate abolitionism in the 1820s, they began to question the sincerity of the colonizationists' desire for emancipation.

From the beginning, blacks vigorously opposed all forms of colonization. At a Philadelphia meeting held in January, 1817, three thousand blacks roundly condemned the proposals of the ACS, and

1. *Freedom's Journal*, September 28, 1827.

subsequent efforts to promote African colonization met with quick and unequivocal condemnation. It was one of the few issues on which blacks consistently presented a united front, and opposition to the ACS and its scheme laid the foundations for the creation of national black organizations. In the years leading up to the Civil War every national and state meeting of the Negro Convention Movement reaffirmed its opposition to the ACS. The society, William Hamilton told the fourth annual meeting of the convention, was "the great Dragon of the land, before whom the people bow and cry, Great Jehovah, and to whom they would sacrifice the free people of colour." It was a view to which the vast majority of blacks subscribed. A resolution adopted by black Pittsburghers in 1831 was typical of free-black opposition to the society: "We the colored people of Pittsburgh and the citizens of these United States view the country in which we live as our only true home. We are just as much natives here as members of the Colonization Society. Here we were born—here bred—here are our earliest and most pleasant associations—here is all that binds men to earth, and makes life valuable. And we do consider every colored man who allows himself to be colonized in Africa, or elsewhere, a traitor to our cause."[2]

Throughout the 1820s blacks led the charge against the society. The publication of the first black newspaper, *Freedom's Journal*, in 1827 provided black opponents of the society with a medium through which they were able to disseminate their views to a much wider audience. Between 1827 and 1829, *Freedom's Journal* and its successor, the *Rights of All*, provided a forum for an examination of the issues involved in colonization. The newspapers opened their columns to a thorough discussion of the merits of colonization in Liberia. For the colonizationists, John P. Kennedy argued that the society was an association of concerned philanthropists, not slaveholders. These men, recognizing the extent of racism in the North and the nature of American slavery and concerned for the elevation of blacks, were trying through persuasion, rather than criticism, to

2. William Lloyd Garrison, *Thoughts on African Colonization* (1832; rpr. New York, 1969), Pt. II, 35; "Minutes of the Fourth Annual Convention for the Improvement of the Free People of Colour," in Howard H. Bell (ed.), *Minutes of the Proceedings of the National Negro Conventions, 1830–1864* (New York, 1969).

win support for the colony in Liberia. "When a respectable colony is established," Kennedy argued, "and the coloured merchant shall visit our shores, argument in the case will be superseded. The coloured man at home, will imperceptibly rise in influence and respectability, through the indirect influence of those in the Colony." As Liberia expanded, it would increasingly undermine the slave trade since it controlled much of the slave-trading coast. Arguing that there were many slaveholders who abhorred slavery but were more afraid of the "inundation" of free blacks that would follow emancipation, Kennedy maintained that colonization would provide "a dyke . . . for their slaves gradual removal." It was, he believed, a practicable scheme for the elimination of slavery.[3]

The editors of *Freedom's Journal* and some of its correspondents, such as William Watkins, who signed himself "Colored Baltimorian," attacked what they saw as the fallacy of the colonizationist argument. While they acknowledged that Liberia was a useful missionary station for the spread of Christianity in Africa, they opposed the idea that blacks should leave the country of their birth, a country for which they had given so much. "They [the ACS] had no right to meddle with the free men of color," he pointed out, "who are as truly Americans as the President of the United States, and as much entitled to the protection, rights and privileges of the country as he, while they behave themselves." Bishop Richard Allen of the African Methodist Episcopal church agreed, arguing that blacks, the "first tillers" of America, should be given precedence over recently arrived European immigrants, who were welcomed with opened arms.[4] The editors of the newspaper wondered why, if free blacks were as destitute and "vicious" as colonizationists had suggested, they should be used as a missionary vanguard, for surely a mere change in environment would not improve their character. Improvement of blacks in America and those who chose to emigrate voluntarily could be achieved only through the provision of an adequate education. This would necessitate an attack on prejudice by all those who acknowledged that the plight of blacks was a direct result of racism. William

3. *Freedom's Journal*, September 28, October 5, 12, 1827.
4. *Freedom's Journal*, September 7, October 26, 1827.

Watkins insisted that the concerned had to tackle the cause of black poverty rather than remove the object of white prejudice. Those who did not, he wrote "were without the moral courage to denounce those prejudices, or the benevolence to attempt a reformation of those morals." Only the total and unconditional abolition of slavery and the destruction of white racism, he declared, would improve the condition of black Americans.[5] This was the message blacks took to Britain in their attempt to broaden the base of opposition to the society.

The contributions of black Americans to the international anticolonization movement have generally been underestimated.[6] Historians have concentrated on the series of pamphlets published by Captain Charles Stuart, the British abolitionist, and on William Lloyd Garrison's *Thoughts on African Colonization*. However, a cursory examination of Garrison's and Stuart's major anticolonization tracts shows the extent to which they were influenced by the views of blacks that had earlier been published in *Freedom's Journal* and the *Rights of All*. This is not to suggest that Garrison and Stuart had nothing original to say on the subject or that they had no impact on the thinking of abolitionists. Through the wide circulation of their works, they were able to reach and influence a much larger audience than the two black newspapers could ever have done. The evidence does suggest, however, that by 1830 many leading British abolitionists were already aware of the depth of free-black opposition to the ACS through the limited circulation of both newspapers among British abolitionists.[7]

This awareness assumed greater significance as colonization became a crucial issue in the early years of the transatlantic abolitionist movement. In 1831 the ACS commissioned Elliott Cresson, a Philadelphia colonizationist, to visit Britain in the hope of winning financial support from British humanitarians. The ACS had good reason to believe that Cresson would be successful. Britain had al-

5. *Liberator*, March 23, 1833; *Freedom's Journal*, July 18, 1828, October 5, 1827.
6. See, for example, Gilbert Barnes, *The Anti Slavery Impulse, 1830–1844* (1933; rpr. New York, 1964).
7. See lists of agents printed in *Freedom's Journal* and the *Rights of All*. The James Cropper Papers contain repeated references to subscriptions for these newspapers.

ready established a colony for free blacks and recaptured slaves in Sierra Leone, and British humanitarians, particularly the Quaker William Allen and other members of the African Institution, had supported the earlier colonization efforts of the black American sea captain Paul Cuffee. At a time when the British antislavery movement was at its zenith, support from the abolitionists of that country would both guarantee a regular flow of funds to the society and enhance its image in the eyes of American abolitionists, who by 1830 had begun to seriously question its merits.[8] British and American advocates of immediate abolition were certain, for their part, that support for Cresson would both legitimize the ACS as a genuine humanitarian movement and impede progress toward full emancipation in America.

The significance of Cresson's visit cannot be overestimated, for it set the international stage on which the battle between colonizationists and abolitionists would be fought. Moreover, Cresson's promotion of colonization provided blacks and white American abolitionists with an issue around which they were able to unite with very little dissension. Not until the Free Church controversy in 1845–1847 were they again able to achieve such unity. Finally, the involvement of blacks in the movement to destroy Cresson's mission not only brought home to them the significance of international support in the fight against slavery and discrimination but also established them, in the eyes of British humanitarians, as leading proponents of American abolitionism.

To some extent Cresson's visit was unfortunately timed. Most British humanitarians were preoccupied with the campaign for West Indian emancipation. In addition, Cresson was forced to compete with the Reverend Nathaniel Paul for the attention of the British public. Paul, a Baptist minister from Albany, New York, had long been recognized as a leading black spokesman. He came to Britain soon after Cresson's arrival to raise money and other support for the

8. For early Anglo-American contacts, see Betty Fladeland, *Men and Brothers: Anglo-American Antislavery Cooperation* (Urbana, Ill., 1972); Floyd J. Miller, *The Search for a Black Nationality: Black Colonization and Emigration, 1787–1863* (Urbana, Ill., 1975); Sheldon H. Harris, *Paul Cuffee: Black America and African Return* (New York, 1972).

Wilberforce Settlement in Canada. The settlement had been founded in 1829 by blacks who fled Ohio when the state moved to enforce its black codes, which demanded, among other things, the posting of a five-hundred-dollar bond as a guarantee of good behavior. Throughout his four-year sojourn in Britain, Paul articulated free-black opposition to the ACS, and joining forces with Captain Charles Stuart and James Cropper, the wealthy Liverpudlian merchant, he worked to discredit colonizationist aims.

The combination of a respected black spokesman and two leading British abolitionists was a potent one. Here was a black American soliciting support for a colony that was not only a competitor of Liberia but also a refuge against racial laws enacted against free blacks. Moreover, Paul's ground had been prepared for him, and abolitionist circles in Britain were already aware of the extent of black opposition to the ACS. Cresson, however, was placed in the rather awkward position of having to discredit black opposition to colonization. Soon after his arrival, he set about this task, making what he called "a patient elucidation of our peculiar circumstances and the character of the blacks." He hoped, by using David Walker's *Appeal*, which called on slaves to employ violence to win their freedom, to convince British humanitarians that colonization was the only means of preventing a race war.[9] Given the popularity of abolitionism in Britain, Cresson felt sure that the success of his mission would also depend on the extent to which he could emphasize the antislavery dimensions of colonization. He pointed out that the society should not publish speeches and tracts containing proslavery sentiments, for such views were being used by opponents in Britain to expose the extent of the slaveholders' influence in the society.[10] In July, 1831, Cresson went so far as to suggest the removal from office of the society's slaveholding president, Bushrod Washington. "When I feel convinced," he argued, "that slavery will soon be destroyed in England, I tremble for the fate of those who act as we are doing, and who must pay a bloody recompense unless we are [not?] to repeat some of our atrocious acts—we should permit the introduction of

9. Elliott Cresson to R. R. Gurley, June 23, 1831, in ACS.
10. Cresson to My Dear Friend, July 22, 1831, in ACS.

religious instructions and enable them to read their bibles and to institute marriages among them instead of the intercourse now permitted and even encouraged."[11]

It is difficult to determine whether Cresson's antislavery posture was genuine or a mere ruse to win support for colonization. By the middle of 1831 Stuart had already launched his attack on the society, and Paul had arrived and begun advocating the merits of a competing colony in Canada that had the support of the free-black leadership. These factors must have influenced Cresson's stand. He seems to have believed, like American abolitionists, that the problems confronting free blacks resulted from white racism rather than innate black inferiority. But like his fellow colonizationists, he argued that circumstances in America had so hopelessly degraded the black population that only a change of country away from whites, who had refused any form of association with blacks, could possibly effect a change in their "character." Emancipation, in his view, could only be achieved by the very gradual process of persuading slaveholders to free their slaves on the condition that they would be transported to Liberia. In a circular addressed to the British public he said, "The great objects of that Society were the final and entire abolition of slavery, providing for the best interest of the blacks, by establishing them in independence upon the coast of Africa; thus constituting them the protectors of the unfortunate natives against the inhuman ravages of the slaver and seeking, through them, to spread the lights of civilization and Christianity among the 50 millions who inhabit these dark regions."[12]

If Cresson did see the society as a genuine antislavery organization and if he recognized the strength of immediatist sentiment among British abolitionists, it is hard to understand why he republished a speech by Henry Clay to the Colonization Society of Kentucky, a speech replete with ill-disguised proslavery views.[13] Such

11. Cresson to Gurley, September 6, June 23, 1831, both in ACS.

12. *Herald of Peace*, July–September, 1831; *Eclectic Review*, January, 1832; William Innes, *Liberia; or, The Early History and Signal Preservation of the American Colony of Free Negroes on the Coast of Africa* (Edinburgh, 1832), 230.

13. *Report of the Board of Managers of the Pennsylvania Colonization Society. With an Introduction and Appendix* (London, 1831), 34–36.

views were grist for the anticolonizationists' mill, as we shall see later on. Cresson may have genuinely seen the society and Liberia as the most practical means of bringing about emancipation, but it may have been the opposition from Stuart, Paul, and Cropper in the early months of his agency that forced him to give increasing emphasis to the society's antislavery role and to underplay its other aspects. This strategy, of course, would expose him to charges of duplicity and distortion.

Soon after his arrival in England, Cresson conducted a series of private meetings with the leading members of local communities, at which he emphasized the antislavery thrust of the society and the potential of Liberia to impede the slave trade and introduce Christianity to Africa. He consolidated these initial contacts through a series of letters to the local press, in which he extolled the merits of the society and Liberia. These letters were particularly important, for they emphasized Liberia's commercial progress and spoke of benevolent slaveholders freeing their slaves, of the society's commitment to black leadership in Liberia, and of the increasing demands of blacks to leave America under the auspices of the society. These visits and letters were intended to win the support of the local humanitarians, paving the way for a second round of visits to most of the same cities and towns, this time to hold public meetings aimed at achieving wider popular approval of Cresson's efforts.[14]

The approach met with some success in the early months of the mission. As George Thompson said, Cresson's efforts showed "a spirit of the purest friendship," and William Wilberforce wrote to Clarkson that he was particularly impressed by Cresson's arguments in favor of the society and Liberia.[15] But by far the most important supporter was Thomas Clarkson. After a number of meetings with Cresson, Clarkson wrote a commendation of the ACS and its work in Liberia. The society, it appeared to him, had two major objectives—first, to assist in the emancipation of American slaves,

14. Manchester *Courier*, April 14, 1832; Cheltenham *Chronicle*, January 25, 1832; *Scotsman*, January 25, 1832; Liverpool *Mercury*, April 13, 27, 1832.

15. William Wilberforce to Thomas Clarkson, October 11, 1831, in Thomas Clarkson Papers, British Library, London; George Thompson to Jenny Thompson, November 1, 1831, in RED.

and second, to send the newly freed to Africa as a means of stemming the slave trade and civilizing Africa. The latter would be accomplished by establishing a line of colonies on the coast in which land cultivation would be emphasized. The export of agricultural produce would provide an alternative source of income for local African rulers who had previously participated in the slave trade, and the schools and churches established by the colonists would result in the "improvement of the intellectual and moral character" of Africans. Clarkson, however, expressed some reservations. He was concerned that emigration should not be seen as the sole or most important agent of total emancipation. In addition, since it was crucial to the aims of the ACS that Liberia be supplied with skilled and educated colonists, the society should pressure slaveholders partial to the cause to provide their slaves with an education and Christian instruction.[16]

Although Clarkson's endorsement was not unconditional, the mere fact that the doyen of British abolitionism had publicly acknowledged the merits of the colonization scheme guaranteed Cresson a measure of increased support. At the same time, anticolonizationists were forced to intensify their public opposition to Cresson's efforts. Charles Stuart, in reply to Clarkson's letter, disagreed that the society aimed at the final extinction of slavery. On the contrary, the opinions of its advocates, as presented in the society's annual reports and its newspaper, the *African Repository*, suggested a strong proslavery influence. While Liberia might further civilization, introduce Christianity, and help to abolish the slave trade, Stuart argued, immediate emancipation would achieve the same ends in a shorter time. Nor was the society likely to promote the education of slaves, which was illegal in the South, for ACS supporters had led the opposition to the establishment of schools for free blacks in the North. Clarkson's hopes for the society would not be fulfilled, Stuart believed, until "the people of the United States see the criminal absurdity of the plan of removing upwards of one-sixth of their whole population, without even the pretence of a crime against them, to a foreign and barbarous land, . . . until they

16. *Patriot*, July 11, 1832.

see that emancipation, burthened with transportation, is a boon little worthy of an enlightened people; until, in short, they learn that coloured men have feelings as true and as tender as white men." If the British public wished to support any colonization scheme, the Wilberforce Settlement was a more practical and humanitarian effort since emigration was totally voluntary and the colony provided an accessible asylum from American slavery.[17]

Between January, 1832, and the arrival of William Lloyd Garrison in the summer of 1833, Charles Stuart published a series of pamphlets on the ACS. He argued that the society was conceived in a spirit of racism and nurtured by proslavery sentiments in violation of the precepts of Christianity and the teachings of Jesus Christ. The society, by pandering to white racism and openly accepting the slaveholder's right to his property, failed to recognize the equality of man in the eyes of God. Stuart called on all philanthropists to support that element of the society's work that aimed to civilize Africa, but only if colonization were made voluntary. He accused the society of an open hostility to free blacks that fostered racism and increased poverty. How, he exclaimed, can free blacks, "declared as a body, to be a little better than devils in the United States . . . be commuted, by mere transportation to Africa, into almost angels!"[18] By quoting extensively from the annual reports of the society, Stuart was able to show the strength of proslavery sentiment among colonizationists who supported the ACS. His pamphlets, cheaply produced and sold for a couple of pence, were widely circulated. Along with Garrison's *Thoughts on African Colonization*, they became the handbooks of British anticolonizationists in their attack on Cresson.

Despite all of Cresson's efforts, by the time Nathaniel Paul ar-

17. *Patriot*, August 1, July 18, 1832.

18. Charles Stuart, *Remarks on the Colony of Liberia and the American Colonization Society: With Some Account of the Settlement of Coloured People, at Wilberforce, Upper Canada* (London, 1832), 7. The other pamphlets were *A Letter to Thomas Clarkson*, by James Cropper and *Prejudice Vincible; or, The Practicability of Conquering Prejudice by Better Means Than by Slavery and Exile; in Relation to the American Colonization Society* (Liverpool, 1832), *Remarks on the Colony of Liberia: The American Colonization Further Unravelled* (Bath, 1833), and *Facts Designed to Exhibit the Real Character and Tendency of the American Colonization Society* (Liverpool, 1833).

rived in Britain, British philanthropists had begun associating the efforts of the ACS with other plans of compulsory expatriation. Cresson quickly realized that the success of the society depended on his ability to undermine the Canadian colony's credibility with British humanitarians. In April he wrote to the secretary of the ACS, the Reverend R. R. Gurley, "I think it deserves consideration whether the awful consequences which may spring from the Canadian colony if patronized to an extent, and which Paul . . . is now urging upon the Government ought not to be pointed out by you."[19] Meanwhile, with the endorsement of Stuart and other anticolonizationists, Paul undertook an extensive tour of the British Isles, advocating support for the Wilberforce colony and condemning the efforts of the ACS. As a minister, he had easy access to numerous pulpits from which he attacked colonization. Cresson lamented to Gurley that Paul was touring Baptist chapels throughout the country attacking Liberia and never failing "on all occasions to poison their minds against us." A circular issued by Paul and signed by a number of Baptist ministers condemned American slavery and racism and accused the ACS of being the handmaiden of American oppression.[20]

Although in later assessments of their victory over Cresson, both William Lloyd Garrison and George Thompson underestimated Paul's contribution, British abolitionists were conscious of his influence.[21] His color made him the "representative" of black Americans and gave him entry to abolitionist circles. Like other blacks, he was accorded a warm welcome wherever he went in Britain. His color made it impossible to doubt the authenticity and sincerity of his antislavery views. Cresson was not slow to recognize this and to suggest to Gurley the need to find a black man who could counteract Paul's impact. He suggested that the society train Robert McDowell, a mulatto of Scottish descent, as a doctor for work in Liberia. McDowell could detail the progress of Liberia in letters

19. Cresson to Gurley, April 16, 1832, in ACS.
20. *Ibid.*, May 22, September 2, 1832, both in ACS.
21. Compare Joseph Phillips' view that Paul was exposing the duplicity of colonization and the ACS during his lecture tours, with Thompson's rather self-aggrandizing assessment. *Liberator*, December 15, 1832, January 11, 1834, August 31, 1833.

home that would "overturn all the machinations of our enemies."
When this idea failed to elicit any response from Gurley, Cresson
suggested sending John Russwurm, editor of the *Liberian Herald*, on
a tour of Britain.[22] But by the summer of 1832, Paul, Stuart, and
other anticolonizationists had destroyed the likelihood that even that
would happen. Cresson was weekly losing the support of prominent British abolitionists. In February, William Wilberforce had refused to sign a memorial issued by Cresson's supporters in Ciren-
cester, and the following month both Zachary Macaulay and J. J.
Gurney publicly condemned the Colonization Society.[23]

The success of the anticolonizationists forced Cresson to the defensive. He avoided the challenges to public debate issued by Stuart
and the "lying mulatto preacher," as he called Paul, thus further undermining his credibility. But his opponents would not desist; they
disrupted his public meetings and flooded local newspapers with letters denouncing the ACS and Liberia. By late 1832 his lectures became less aggressive and more conciliatory toward what he thought
were British interests. In his lecture at Hull, for instance, he argued
that it was impossible to eliminate overnight an institution like
American slavery that had had such a long historical maturation.
Given that Britain had introduced slavery into America, concerned
British humanitarians should support the efforts of the ACS, which
aimed at the final elimination of slavery without the destruction of
American society. In addition, he said, Liberia was a potentially lu-
crative market for British goods. Cresson played on the consciences
and pockets of his British audiences and was not averse to stretching
the truth when necessary. He told his Hull listeners that the popularity of the society was growing daily and that, in the ten years of
its existence, the ACS had won the confidence of almost one-half of
the American population.[24] But all of this had little effect; Cresson
continued to lose supporters, and the ranks of the anticolonizationists continued to increase.

Cresson's main support in this period came from the noted Brit-

22. Cresson to Gurley, May 22, 1832, in ACS; *African Repository*, July, 1833.
23. Cresson to Gurley, February 20, March 17, 1832, both in ACS.
24. Hull *Advertiser*, October 26, 1832; Hull *Rockingham*, May 11, 1833; York
Herald, June 1, 1833; Innes, *Liberia*, 223.

ish physician, Dr. Thomas Hodgkin, who published three procolo-
nization pamphlets between 1832 and 1834. Although Hodgkin was
a strong supporter of the ACS, he differentiated between the benefits that colonization promised for the slave and for Africa and the
means by which the society proposed to achieve its goals. In his
view, the ACS had to categorically condemn slavery as a sin if it
ever hoped to win support. Hodgkin opposed the forced expulsion
of black Americans "as an entire class" but firmly believed that "the
opportunity of rising to importance on the coast of Africa, if proper
advantage were taken of it, might give to the persons of colour a
very commanding position in America and that the encouragement
to manumission which the Colonization Society holds out, might
under it [illegible] and so popular to do so that with the example of
our West Indies before their eyes many of your slaveholders would
be ashamed either to hold or to sell slaves."[25] Hodgkin epitomized
the dilemma or, more correctly, the ambivalence of antislavery colonizationists, who sought emancipation through a society that recognized the slaveholder's right to his property.

In his pamphlet *On Negro Emancipation and American Colonization*,
published in 1833, Hodgkin attempted to counter the arguments of
the anticolonizationists and win support for Cresson's mission. He
argued that colonization was a form of gradual emancipation that
replaced the heated and vitriolic denunciations of slaveholders with
reasoned discussion. In his view, not all slaveholders were callous or
evil men, and abolitionists should attempt to siphon off the more
humane among them and so split the ranks of slavery's supporters.
Immediate and unconditional abolition he saw as an act of cruelty
that would provide a "transient and partial advantage" at the price
of permanent reorganization and at the same time would foster "un-
christian feelings" among whites.[26] It would be better to convince

25. Thomas Hodgkin to James Fortune, November 17, 1840, in HP.
26. Thomas Hodgkin, *On Negro Emancipation and American Colonization* (London, 1833), 3–4. Hodgkin's other two pamphlets, *An Inquiry into the Merits of the
American Colonization Society: And a Reply to Charges Brought Against It. With an Account
of the British African Colonization Society* (London, 1833) and *On the British African
Colonization Society* (London, 1834), are to a large extent repetitions of the arguments found in his first work.

slaveowners that emancipation was necessary and inevitable and to prepare the slaves for a peaceful and orderly transition to freedom than to free them at once and in defiance of the slaveowners. "It seems due to the most orderly producing and saving slaves, who may have accumulated nearly enough to redeem themselves," he argued, "if a fair price were fixed, and the difficulty of manumission were obviated, that they should first receive the benefits of freedom. Their example would be a stimulus to their inferior brethren, and prepare the planter for the universal emancipation which should ultimately and speedily, but gradually, follow." This approach would not only punish the profligate slave and force him to reform but would also show him that consistent labor was advantageous to him. The planter would also see that his work was being properly performed and that he ran no risks of financial ruin. Such measures, Hodgkin predicted, would bring about "an immediate partial benefit, with the prospects of an ultimate general reformation."[27]

Such Smilesian notions were, as George M. Fredrickson has argued, the "conservative response" of antislavery colonizationists who were committed to peaceful and gradual emancipation. While they recognized the right of slaveholders to their property, they saw "the producing and saving slaves" as the wedge that would open the door to increased voluntary manumission. But it was precisely on these grounds that anticolonizationists attacked the supporters of the ACS. As Benjamin Lundy and free-black opponents of the society pointed out in the early twenties, very few slaveholding colonizationists had freed their slaves for emigration to Liberia. Moreover, in the eyes of immediate abolitionists, recognition of the slaveholder's right to his property was nothing short of support for the continuation of slavery.[28]

The arguments of antislavery colonizationists were predicated on one central "fact" of American society—the existence of an in-

27. Hodgkin, *On Negro Emancipation*, 4, 17.

28. *Genius of Universal Emancipation*, October, 1821, January, 1822; Stuart, *Remarks on the Colony of Liberia: The American Colonization Further Unravelled*, 4; Garrison, *Thoughts on African Colonization*, 20; George M. Fredrickson, *The Black Image in the White Mind: The Debate on Afro-American Character and Destiny* (New York, 1970), 6.

surmountable prejudice against blacks. Although Hodgkin condemned American prejudice, he argued that it would be removed
only when it no longer served the interests of white Americans.
Censure alone would not extinguish racial bias. Under these circumstances, blacks could choose among clear-cut alternatives. They
could remain in America under the current system, which was but
another form of exile, and run the risk of future expatriation by
force, or they could work for the success of Liberia. The establishment of Liberia was clear proof that colonizationists did not intend
to waste "their little strength against the fiend-like force of that
odious prejudice, which would have rendered their efforts abortive;
they have at least eluded the destructive attacks, if they have not actually engaged it in its own destruction." Hodgkin hoped that his
plan, by eliminating the fear that freedmen might foment slave re-
volts, would encourage slaveholders to free their slaves.[29] The plan
also offered hope to those blacks who remained in America that
slaveholders, no longer afraid of a rapidly rising free-black population, would be less inclined to impose and enforce laws limiting the
rights of blacks. Given the recognized intensity of white racism, this
"reflex reaction" argument did not predict full equality for those
blacks who remained in America; it merely suggested a benevolent
indifference.

Hodgkin hoped that his pamphlets would shift the issue of colonization to a more philosophical discussion of the merits of the ACS
and Liberia, but they met with immediate opposition. Stuart and
Paul continued to attack the society and Cresson's mission on the
old ground that their program violated the precepts of Christianity
by acquiescing in slavery and racial prejudice. Stuart condemned
Hodgkin's pamphlet as "a placid and specious defense of slavery
and prejudice; admitting as all sinners and all advocates of sinners
do, the *abstract* turpitude, but asserting the *practical necessity* of crime."
And an anonymously written pamphlet played on national jealousies by accusing Cresson of deluding the British public "into a belief, that the object and tendency of the Colonization scheme was

29. Hodgkin, *On Negro Emancipation*, 11–12.

the abolition of slavery." It was a ploy, the pamphlet said, that "nothing but American impudence could devise and prosecute."[30]

By the time William Lloyd Garrison arrived in Britain in the summer of 1833, the colonization drama being played out on the British stage was in its denouement. Even before Garrison's arrival, Cresson was expressing his deep sense of isolation from British abolitionists and from his own society in Washington. On the one hand, his inability to win substantial support in Britain significantly curtailed his remittances to Washington at a time when the finances of the society were being severely strained by an economic depression and by competition from state societies demanding greater freedom from Washington. On the other, the proslavery element in the society lost him a great deal of support in Britain. By the summer of 1832, Cresson's persistent criticism of the society's proslavery sentiments in his letters to Gurley and his failure to remit sufficient funds began to strain relations between Washington and its agent. In June, 1832, Cresson wrote Gurley, condemning the society for continuing to print proslavery materials and bemoaning the fact that Washington had isolated him by not providing recent information to counteract accusations in Britain. Garrison's *Thoughts on African Colonization*, which had been serialized in the *Eclectic Review* at the end of 1832, was harming the cause in Britain, and yet the society remained silent, offering little to refute its views. "If, in my zeal to serve the cause," he pleaded with Gurley, "I have written or spoken . . . ought amiss . . . why not frankly tell me so? Why not as a brother, set me right?" Cresson's plea continued to go unheeded, and in the following months he threatened on more than one occasion to return home.[31]

30. *Strictures on Dr. Hodgkin's Pamphlet on Negro Emancipation and American Colonization* (London, 1833), 7; Stuart, *Remarks on the Colony of Liberia: The American Colonization Further Unravelled*, 10. Cresson told an audience in York that a British abolitionist had made it clear to him that "John Bull does not like to have his cow milked by strangers; England is the preserve of the Anti-Slavery Society and you a poacher in it." York *Herald*, June 1, 1833. In *An Inquiry*, Hodgkin observed that the colonization argument was characterized by two types of prejudices: British national prejudice against Americans and white American prejudice against blacks.

31. Cresson to Gurley, July 6, June 9, 16, 1832, all in ACS.

Although he had been forced, mainly by the opposition generated by Stuart and Paul, to abandon the idea of winning general British acknowledgment of and financial support for the society, Cresson had managed in the early days of his mission to persuade a group of Edinburgh philanthropists to raise funds for the establishment of a new settlement called Edina in Liberia. He realized that it might be possible to obtain limited support for such specific projects, for British philanthropists differentiated between Liberia, as a missionary and "civilizing" enterprise, and the ACS. They were willing to support the colony while condemning the society.

Early in 1833 Cresson suggested to his small coterie of supporters that they form a British counterpart to the ACS. The new society, to avoid the stigma of association with the ACS, would be independent of Washington but supportive of the American society's efforts in Liberia. As he told Gurley, his intention was to avoid any open conflict with anticolonizationists and to attempt instead to win support from aristocratic Whigs and Tories in the hope that they could influence the British government to recognize Liberia. The new campaign aimed to raise two thousand pounds for the purchase of land at Cape Mount on which two settlements, Sussex and Wilberforce, "villages with at least 200 blacks of *high character*," would be established. Such settlements, according to Hodgkin, would not only provide Britain with an opportunity to repay Africa for past wrongs but would also establish markets on the west coast of Africa by encouraging a "taste for British productions, which British merchants may supply."[32]

This new approach was not likely to win Cresson support from Washington. The ACS was already concerned about possible encroachment from Sierra Leone on Liberia's sphere of influence. Moreover, Gurley and the society expected bigger things of Cresson's mission. Although Cresson gathered roughly £2,246 for the ACS during his two and a half years in Britain, Gurley claimed that his strategy also lost the society considerably more than that amount of support.[33] To some extent Gurley was correct, for Hodgkin re-

32. Hodgkin, *An Inquiry*, 56–57; Cresson to Gurley, June 28, 1833, in ACS.
33. Gurley informed a Mr. Tendall that Dr. F. A. Cox, the English clergyman, "does not think Mr. Cresson's Agency has been very efficient among the most en-

ported to Cresson in April, 1836, that there was money that had been raised for specific land purchases still unspent in the account of the defunct British African Colonization Society (BACS).[34] Cresson's attempt to win limited support for Liberia itself rather than for the ACS proved to be one more means of alienation from Gurley and the society.

The founding meeting of the BACS was held at Hanover Square, London, in early July, 1833, with the Duke of Sussex in the chair. The sparse attendance was an indication of anticolonization feeling. And as if that were not enough, the proposed society's opponents got wind of the meeting and attended in such large numbers that, one report suggested, if fifteen more abolitionists had been present, the BACS might never have been formed. Stuart, Thompson, and Garrison, newly arrived in Britain, disrupted the meeting by challenging the chair on every point at issue. Although the meeting agreed to form the BACS, few held out much hope for its success. Its list of prominent aristocratic supporters could do little to forestall its rapid demise.

Before Garrison arrived in England, Nathaniel Paul wrote to him: "Your 'Thoughts on Colonization' are the thoughts of the people here. I only regret that your book had not come sooner."[35] The book intensified the battle that Garrison hastened to continue in person. Soon after his arrival, he challenged Cresson to a public debate on the merits of the ACS. When Cresson demurred, Garrison organized, with the aid of Cropper, Paul, Stuart, and George Thompson, a series of lectures in which he accused Cresson of raising money from British abolitionists under false pretenses. At the first meeting Garrison reiterated arguments developed in *Thoughts*. Paul followed with a stirring exposition of free-black opposition to the society. America, he said, is the home of the black man, for he has fought to build and protect her. In the War of Independence "com-

---

lightened and cultivated of England. Mr. Cresson is full of zeal, has laboured hard and perhaps merits thanks, but I do not rely especially upon his wisdom." Gurley to Tendall, November 27, 1833, in ACS; *African Repository*, March, 1834.

34. Hodgkin to Cresson, April 5, 1836, in HP.

35. *Liberator*, June 22, 1833; *Eclectic Review*, November, 1832.

plexion was entirely out of the question (cheers); the black man was then considered as good as the white. We were all brethren—we were all kindred—we were bone of each other's bone, and flesh of each other's flesh. . . . I hold that I have as good a right to that country as any white man whatever may be said to the reverse. (Cheers)." He pointed out that free blacks in every major city in America had consistently opposed the society—which was welcoming European immigrants who had made no contribution to the country and at the same time was contriving to expel to Africa a group of its native sons. His statements had a decided impact on a group of men and women who were soon to witness the successful culmination of their work in the abolition of West Indian slavery.[36]

Following the third meeting at Exeter Hall, at which most of the leading British abolitionists endorsed the position of the anticolonizationists, Cresson took the only course left open to him: letters to newspapers. The alternative was to remain silent. By issuing a challenge to a public debate, as Stuart and Paul had previously done, Garrison again forced the issue of credibility. Cresson had either to accept the challenge to a debate that he had very little chance of winning, inasmuch as public sentiment was growing increasingly hostile to colonization, or to refuse and leave the stage completely free to anticolonizationists. As the London *Patriot* observed, "Mr. Elliot [*sic*] Cresson, notwithstanding the countenance he has been so fortunate as to obtain in high quarters, will do well to grapple with the charges brought against the Society he represents, or *take his passage for Philadelphia*."[37] Cresson turned to the same newspaper in another attempt to clarify the society's position. Colonizationists and abolitionists, he wrote rather imploringly, had different but perhaps not antithetical tasks to perform in order to accomplish the ultimate abolition of slavery and the elevation of blacks.[38] It was a vain attempt at reconciliation, however. The opposition had already destroyed his mission.

One month later James Cropper, Thomas Buxton, Zachary Ma-

36. *Liberator*, October 19, November 9, 16, 1833.
37. Quoted in *Liberator*, October 26, 1833.
38. *Patriot*, July 31, 1833.

caulay, William Smith, George Stephens, William Allen, and William Wilberforce, among others, issued their "Protest" against the ACS. Soon afterward, Wilberforce died, and as Fladeland observed, "the fact that signing it was one of Wilberforce's last public acts before his death made it a document worthy of veneration by abolitionists everywhere."[39] The "Protest," simply repeated, with an economy of words, all the points of opposition to the ACS. It said nothing new, but the fact that most of the leadership of British abolitionism had signed the document signaled the final rejection and defeat of Cresson's mission. As Garrison rather haughtily put it, the "Protest" became "a millstone around the neck of the American Colonization Society, sufficiently weighty to drown it in an ocean of public indignation."[40] But one name was conspicuously absent from the list of signatories to the "Protest"—Clarkson. Soon after the July meetings, Garrison and Paul journeyed to Norwich in the hope of persuading Clarkson to publicly condemn the society as he had once praised it. According to Garrison's account of the meeting, it was Paul's statement of free-black opposition to the society that persuaded Clarkson to question his previous support. Although Clarkson refused to issue a public statement, Garrison and Paul won an important concession. At the end of the meeting Clarkson told Garrison to "tell them [the Americans] that he refused to comply with the solicitation of Mr. Cresson to become an honorary member of it [the ACS]; and also refused to give his sanction to the British Colonization Society. . . . My letter to Mr. Cresson in favor of the American Colonization Society was extorted by his statement . . . that *one hundred thousand* slaves had been offered to the Society gratuitously, to be sent to Liberia."[41] Garrison could sail for America in the fall with the knowledge that one aim of his visit—the final defeat of Cresson's mission—had been accomplished.

When Cresson returned to America in the fall of 1833, however,

39. Fladeland, *Men and Brothers*, 217.
40. *Christian Advocate*, n.d., in *Liberator*, October 12, 1833.
41. Wendell Phillips Garrison and Francis Jackson Garrison, *William Lloyd Garrison, 1805–1879: The Story of His Life Told by His Children* (4 vols.; New York, 1885), I, 364.

he had very little to show for his efforts. The settlement of Edina was the only bright spot in an otherwise dismal situation. The series of branch societies formed in the first year of his mission had all disbanded under the systematic pressure of his opponents, and the BACS was a society in name only, notwithstanding its very prominent officers. The British society managed to stay afloat for a year, thanks to the tireless work of Thomas Hodgkin, but late in 1834, he wrote to inform Cresson that the BACS was defunct because of a lack of interest among its members.[42] Opponents of the ACS, led by Charles Stuart, Nathaniel Paul, and later William Lloyd Garrison, had mounted a well-planned and well-organized public campaign against Cresson and the society he represented. They wrote pamphlets that were widely disseminated, flooded local newspapers with letters condemning the ACS, challenged Cresson to public debates that he could not hope to win, and followed him about the country, challenging him every step of the way. It was no wonder that Cresson lamented to the editor of the New York *Commercial Advertiser* that he had "very often felt, when thus surrounded by enemies of the fiercest stamp, that unless I had been supported by the consciousness of performing an imperative and holy duty for the good of man, and the extension of the Redeemer's kingdom, that I must have been utterly overwhelmed."[43] One could forgive Cresson's rather pious claim, for the struggle for British approval had been long, exhausting, and acerbic. His supporters had had a difficult time persuading him to reject the many challenges issued by Stuart, Paul, and Garrison, for he was never one to shun a fight. As Stuart said, in a backhanded compliment, Cresson was "a staunch idolater, and display[ed] an energy, a tact and a perseverance, worthy of a totally different cause."[44]

The defeat of Cresson's mission destroyed the possibility of future British support for the ACS, although it did not undermine the image of Liberia as a missionary and civilizing agent in Africa; a differentiation that Paul and Stuart consistently emphasized. The

42. Hodgkin to Cresson, November 4, 1834, in HP.
43. Quoted in *Liberator*, September 21, 1833.
44. *Liberator*, August 31, 1833.

victory of anticolonizationists was significant precisely because it laid the foundations for future Anglo-American abolitionist contacts. Paul's contribution to this success set the stage for future black involvement and leadership in the transatlantic movement. As we shall see, blacks would continue to lead the fight against subsequent attempts to interest British humanitarians in colonization. The dispute also brought home to British abolitionists the complexity of the American problem and opened a new era of Anglo-American abolitionist cooperation that lasted, with varying degrees of intensity, well into the 1870s. More immediately, success against Cresson persuaded Garrison to use the British abolition movement to promote abolitionism in America. As a first step George Thompson was invited to tour America the following year, but his mission proved to be a liability. As Rice has argued, it gave proslavery elements an opportunity "to whip up patriotic distrust of their opponents" by claiming foreign interference in America's domestic affairs.[45] It is quite possible, however, that Cresson's failure was sufficient justification for those Americans—among them colonizationists—who were anxious to destroy the fledgling abolitionist movement. In October, 1833, the claim of foreign interference helped to justify a mob attack instigated and led by New York colonizationists determined, once and for all, to put paid to immediate abolitionism.[46] The specter of British interference would continue to haunt Anglo-American abolitionist cooperation throughout the antebellum period.

The international debate over colonization did not disappear with Cresson's failure; the fortunes of the ACS fluctuated dramatically following a series of financial crises in the thirties, while abolitionist opposition grew. Cresson, whose inability to win British support may have hastened the society's problems, never forgave his abandonment by Gurley. On his return to Philadelphia, he assumed a prominent role in the efforts of the Pennsylvania State Society to

45. C. Duncan Rice, "The Antislavery Mission of George Thompson to the United States, 1834–1835," *Journal of American Studies*, II (1968), 26.

46. Leonard L. Richards, *Gentlemen of Property and Standing: Anti-Abolition Mobs in Jacksonian America* (London, 1970), 26–30.

establish settlements in Liberia independent of Washington's jurisdiction. Gurley was demoted in the reorganization that followed on
the heels of growing internal differences, and another economic depression in 1839 and 1840 threatened to permanently disable the society. In the midst of this gloom came a ray of hope—the publication of Sir Thomas Fowell Buxton's *The African Slave Trade* in 1839
and *The Remedy* in 1840. The first described the barbarity of the
continuing trade; the second proposed a string of agricultural settlements in West Africa, led by a select group of skilled West Indians
capable of educating the Africans in cultivation techniques and Christianity. These settlements, by providing income to local kings, would
eliminate their need to participate in the slave trade. With the formation of Buxton's African Civilization Society (AFCS) and the possibility of British government support for its proposed expedition
to Africa, American colonizationists once again turned their attention to Britain in the hope of regaining some of the ground lost by
Cresson.

Speaking before the annual meeting of the Pennsylvania State
Colonization Society in 1840, Gurley observed that Buxton's views
were an adoption of "the original principles and policy of the American Colonization Society," and his plans, a mere "republication of
ours."[47] Throughout the latter half of 1839 and during the early
months of 1840, Gurley toured the major state societies recommending a mission to Britain to establish contacts with the AFCS.
In May, 1840, the New York society adopted a series of resolutions
praising the British government's support of the AFCS and calling
on the ACS to undertake a similar expedition.[48] Support for Gurley's
recommendations, however, was more a reflection of growing internal differences in the movement than a genuine belief in the merits
of expanding African colonization. Some of Gurley's opponents even
reasoned that his absence on a mission to Britain would provide them
with an opportunity to destroy forever his influence in the society.
The new leaders of the society, however, fearful that a successful

47. *Pennsylvania Freeman*, March 12, 1840.
48. Ralph R. Gurley, *Mission to England in Behalf of the American Colonization Society* (Washington, D.C., 1841), 3–4.

mission to Britain would only enhance Gurley's power, initially demurred but were finally forced, under threat of possible secession by the New York society, to accept Gurley's recommendations.[49]

Having been forced to accept the mission, the society retaliated by restricting the terms of Gurley's commission. At a time when an English society was about to implement plans similar to and possibly in competition with the efforts of the society in Liberia, Washington, showing little foresight, gave Gurley's mission almost no authority. He was merely mandated to "promote the interest of the . . . Society; to explain and enforce its objects, to remove prejudice against it," to collect information on the proposed expedition, and "to cement the friendship and secure harmony and co-operation between the friends of Africa in England and the United States in the great work of introducing civilization and Christianity into that quarter of the globe." Gurley, for his part, was convinced that the success of his mission depended on a clear statement of particular goals and the power necessary to achieve them. He was particularly anxious to be empowered to negotiate agreements with the British, for he knew that the British government's participation in Buxton's expedition posed a direct threat to Liberian interests in west Africa. Liberia, not fully in control of all its territory, hoping to expand its borders, and under open pressure from Sierra Leone merchants who continually violated its trading laws, was in danger of being stifled by expanding British interests in the area. But headquarters refused to grant Gurley the plenipotentiary powers necessary to negotiate agreements with the British.[50]

To compound Gurley's problems his agency faced formidable opposition from American abolitionists attending the first World Anti-Slavery Convention in London in the summer of 1840. The American contingent consisted of some of the leading lights of American abolitionism: James Birney, Henry B. Stanton, Charles Lenox Remond, William Lloyd Garrison, and Lucretia Mott, among others. Although the American Anti-Slavery Society had recently

49. Judge Reese to Samuel Wilkeson, June 3, 1840, Benjamin Coates to Wilkeson, June 8, 1840, both in ACS.
50. Gurley, *Mission to England*, 9–12.

split between supporters of the New York and Garrisonian wings of the society, they were united in opposition to the ACS. The unanimous rejection by the convention of Hodgkin's address on African colonization brought home to colonizationists the strength of continuing Anglo-American abolitionist opposition to their efforts.[51]

On his arrival in Britain at the end of July, Gurley decided to approach his task from a number of angles: to persuade Buxton that the aims of the AFCS were similar to those of the ACS, to attempt to win the support of British abolitionists and the British public for the society and so regain some of the ground lost by Cresson, and finally to reactivate the BACS. But Buxton had his own troubles with many British abolitionists who saw his scheme as nothing more than a badly disguised colonization plan. One correspondent to the *Irish Friend* wrote of Buxton's plan, "notwithstanding the high opinion I entertain of the purity of Sir T. F. Buxton's motives, I cannot but look upon it as a most dangerous inroad on the straightforward course of seeking the entire, unconditional emancipation of the slave, as well as from its tendency to tempt friends to compromise the peace principle, which it is extremely important should be held inviolate."[52] Gurley was wary of being seen as a petitioner to the AFCS, but he and Buxton held a series of meetings late in the summer. Like Cresson before him, Gurley stressed the antislavery potential of his society and attempted to win from Buxton an agreement on spheres of influence among all nations "engaged in introducing among the barbarous tribes of that distracted country [Africa] the knowledge of liberty, civilization and Christianity."[53] Meanwhile, American abolitionists were pressuring Buxton to publicly renounce the ACS as he had done in 1833. "It is due, we think, to all parties—especially will the Abolitionists of the United States consider it due to them," Birney and Stanton informed him, "that

51. For Hodgkin's address, see *African Repository*, October 5, 1840; British and Foreign Anti-Slavery Society, *Minutes of the Proceedings of the General Anti-Slavery Convention, Called by the Committee of the British and Foreign Anti Slavery Society, Held in London, 12th of June, 1840, and Continued by Adjournments to the 23rd of the Same Month* (London, 1840).

52. *Irish Friend*, May 1, 1841.

53. Gurley to Executive Committee, August 17, 1840, in ACS.

your position and that of the Society for the Civilization of Africa
. . . in relation to the American Colonization scheme, should be
clearly defined."[54] But Buxton was not to be rushed. He remained
silent after his meetings with Gurley, and one can only assume that
Gurley had persuaded him to reexamine his previous position.

Abolitionists, however, kept up their pressure on Buxton and finally won from him the public disassociation they sought. Buxton,
like other British abolitionists, differentiated between Liberia's civilizing potential and the ACS. He took the position that the AFCS,
unlike the ACS, did not aim to colonize but to civilize Africa. It did
not aim, he said, to make itself master "of the resources of that continent, but to teach its natives their use and value, not to procure an
outlet for any portion of our surplus population, but to show to Africa the folly as well as the crime of exporting her own children."
The proposed settlements under the jurisdiction of the AFCS were
meant to provide security for the introduction of schools, agriculture, commerce, etc. Once these traditions had been established, the
society would withdraw. The society had no intention of expatriat-
ing a large number of people to Africa—only a well-chosen few
who would act as "a leaven amongst her people." As an immediate
abolitionist, Buxton could not condone the ACS's refusal to condemn American slaveholders, nor its aim to remove the free-black
population against their will, a policy which, in his view, would
isolate the slaves from potential leadership and support. In rejecting
the notions of the natural antipathy of the races, Buxton concluded
that "the arguments for your scheme are, in themselves . . . repul-
sive to me."[55]

There was nothing startlingly new in Buxton's letter, but it
forced Gurley and his supporters onto the defensive. In his defense
of the society's position, Gurley argued that Christian action was
based not only on "reciprocal and equal benevolence" universally
applied but also on careful reasoning that recognized particular circumstances and constraints. In the case of America, where immedi-

---

54. Dwight L. Dumond (ed.), *Letters of James Gillespie Birney, 1831–1857* (2 vols.;
New York, 1938), II, 599; *Pennsylvania Freeman*, March 12, 1840.
55. *Irish Friend*, April 1, 1841.

ate abolition was impossible, concerned people must perform "such acts of mutual justice and kindness as are compatible with the necessities of their condition and the public welfare," acts that must be "governed by their own judgement, deliberately and conscientiously formed under responsibilities to the Author of all wisdom."[56] In his judgment, there were two dimensions to American slavery, one the institutional and the other a "relation between the individual masters and slaves." Whenever violations of Christian precepts occurred, under either of these two situations, they should be "immediately remedied." By failing to say exactly what sort of "violations" did evil to Christian precepts, Gurley left himself open to refutation by abolitionists, who argued that the whole system of slavery was sinful and, therefore, had to be immediately abolished. He went on to argue, however, that while reciprocal and equal benevolence were "the sole foundation of human rights," there were, nonetheless, specific situations where its practice would be detrimental to the slave. As an example, he argued that a humane master may have inherited slaves who had lived for a considerable length of time in one area and had married slaves on adjoining plantations. To free these slaves, especially in states that required the removal of manumitted slaves out of the state, would be to destroy families. Under these circumstances a master might refuse to free his slaves. Such a restraint upon the slave, Gurley argued, "is among his rights and blessings."[57] The strength of Gurley's argument, as his opponents pointed out, rested upon his presupposition that there were two dimensions of slavery. This view, they positively rejected. Their condemnation of slavery was directed at the institution, and while they recognized the existence of benevolent masters, they argued that the only remedy possible, once the sinfulness of slavery was accepted, was immediate and total abolition. Gurley's arguments were no more successful than Cresson's had been.

Soon after his arrival in London, Gurley, with the aid of Hodg-

56. Ralph R. Gurley, *Letter to the Hon. Henry Clay, President of the American Colonization Society, and Sir Thomas Fowell Buxton on the Colonization and Civilization of Africa* (London, 1841), 4–5.

57. *Irish Friend*, April 1, May 1, July 1, 1841.

kin, requested a meeting with the BFASS. He hoped to persuade the British abolitionists that their previous rejection of the American Colonization Society had been based on false and inaccurate information. The BFASS appointed a subcommittee to meet Gurley and invited Stanton and Birney to attend. According to Birney's report, the meeting totally rejected the ACS and accused it of trying to forcefully expatriate the free-black population.[58] But more significant for Gurley's mission was his failure to gain the endorsement of Thomas Clarkson. Under increasing pressure from anticolonizationists, Clarkson had moved from his position of neutrality following Garrison and Paul's visit in 1833 to open disavowal of the society. According to Hodgkin, even Clarkson thought that the Colonization Society had failed "to perform its promises and . . . he is moreover much annoyed at some alterations that were made in a letter written by himself and published in America."[59]

During their tour of the British Isles throughout the summer and fall of 1840, Birney, Stanton, Remond, and John Scoble, secretary of the BFASS, actively campaigned against the ACS. Remond, described by many as one of the most articulate American abolitionists, led the attack on the society. Following where Paul had left off and representing the views of his fellow black Americans, he reconfirmed free-black opposition to colonization. The society, he told a Glasgow audience, was founded with the express purpose of removing the free-black population from America. Even if, as colonizationists claimed, free blacks were all vicious, low, and irreligious, it appeared to him that not Africa, but "America was the land of all others fitted to elevate and civilize and educate them." As he later told an Ipswich audience, "America was a land lined with institutions of education; the steeples towered to the clouds, and the meeting houses and churches were as thick—I had almost said, as frogs of Egypt—and yet the coloured man, if he would procure education, or enjoy the solacements of religion, must go to Africa." Free blacks, he thundered, in a land boasting of democracy and freedom, had never been allowed the liberty of choosing. They were continu-

58. Dumond (ed.), *Letters of Birney*, II, 597–98.
59. Hodgkin to Dear Friend, September 26, 1840, in HP.

ally told that Africa was their home, and all efforts were being marshaled to force them to leave. The ACS was designed and organized to protect the interests of slaveholders. It professed antislavery in the North and proslavery in the South, a duplicity that abolitionists had consistently opposed. Abolitionists, he observed, had advocated "either slavery or liberty, and no middle ground. The ACS only afforded a place for those who were ashamed to say, on the one hand, they were in favour of slavery, and who were equally ashamed to say they were abolitionists; these people were glad to call themselves colonization men, and thus they cut both ways."[60]

Remond spoke to overflowing houses wherever he went and, in some of the most moving scenes, reconfirmed British opposition to the ACS. Following his meetings in Scotland, he informed Garrison that Scotland had pledged itself against colonization and that Gurley had failed to attract more than twenty people to any of his meetings. As Hodgkin lamented to Governor Thomas Buchanan of Liberia, "the statements of Raymond [sic], in addition to those of Birney, Stanton and others, have produced a very prejudicial influence" against the ACS. And like Cresson in 1832, he suggested that only a colonist from Liberia could possibly turn the tide in favor of colonization.[61]

In his efforts to win public support, Gurley also attempted to reactivate the BACS. At a meeting in early August, it was decided to press for the possible unification of the BACS and AFCS. The new society, to be called the British African Colonization Society for the Civilization of Africa, would implement the aims of the AFCS by establishing colonies of free blacks from the United States and the West Indies along the coast of Africa. In these settlements, schools and "institutions for moral, religious, intellectual, agricultural and commercial improvement" would be established as agents of civilization. Even before Gurley could meet with the AFCS, the Executive Committee of the ACS informed him that they thought it "inex-

60. *Anti Slavery Reporter*, October 21, November 4, 1840; *Liberator*, November 27, 1840; Ipswich *Express*, January 5, 1841.

61. Hodgkin to Thomas Buchanan, March 20, 1841, Hodgkin to Dr. Lovell, March 28, 1841, both in HP; *Liberator*, November 13, 1840. Gurley confirms this. He had invited two hundred clergymen to attend his Glasgow meeting but only a handful showed up. Gurley, *Mission to England*, 45–46.

pedient to enter into any . . . arrangements with the British African Colonization Society for the Civilization of Africa or other British authorities."[62] That was not all; by year's end, Gurley was informed that his salary had been stopped and that he could either return to America to raise money for the society or continue his mission in Britain without pay. Elliott Cresson, who continued to blame Gurley for the failure of his mission to Britain seven years earlier, fueled the suspicion of Gurley's intentions. Rumors were rife in Washington that Gurley had intended to join forces with the AFCS to destroy the society's interests in Liberia. Cresson called Gurley's mission "rank treachery" and suggested to Washington that it could rid itself of Gurley's "annoyance for a year or two" by terminating his agency and persuading Hodgkin to find him a job with the AFCS.[63]

Although Gurley remained in Britain until the fall of 1841, his agency had lost authority by December, 1840. Like Cresson before him, he had little to show for his efforts. British abolitionists had done no more than reconfirm their opposition to the society. The failure of Cresson and Gurley can be attributed to both abolitionist opposition and differences within the ACS. Both found themselves abandoned by Washington at a time when anticolonization pressure was at its strongest. The success of Anglo-American abolitionist opposition to Cresson's mission formed the basis for the success against Gurley. The anticolonization tradition had been so firmly established during Cresson's visit that Gurley could raise only one £5 contribution in five months.[64]

Paul and Remond were instrumental in this victory over colonization. Black Americans took great pride in their contributions to the international effort against colonization. "The *voice* of the free colored people," one observer (possibly Pennington) wrote, "has done more to kill the influence of colonization in Great Britain, than any thing else."[65] Not only did the arguments of free blacks provide

62. Gurley, *Mission to England*, 48, 38.

63. Cresson to Executive Committee, August 15, 1840, Cresson to Wilkeson, October 1, 1840, John B. Pinney to Wilkeson, October 23, 1840, Reese to Wilkeson, December 4, 1840, all in ACS.

64. Gurley to Board of Directors, February 5, 1842, in ACS.

65. *Colored American*, August 4, 1838.

the foundations on which the international movement built its opposition to colonization, but the activities of Paul and Remond in Britain lent legitimacy to that opposition. It would be a callous man indeed who could attempt to justify a plan that was so vigorously condemned by the group it was intended to benefit. And although colonizationists like Hodgkin attempted to discredit and dismiss free-black opposition as being of "very light weight" and influenced by white abolitionists, the average British audience, hearing the moving denunciations made by Paul and Remond, thought otherwise.[66]

This success confirmed in the minds of both blacks and white abolitionists the importance of a united international alliance against American slavery and discrimination. The kind of unity achieved in the fight against colonization, however, would rarely be achieved again in the years leading up to the Civil War. This is precisely why the issue of colonization was so important to the transatlantic abolitionist movement. As we shall see, throughout the antebellum period, blacks, who bore the brunt of American slavery and prejudice and were even more aware of their significance than their white colleagues, continued to keep a careful vigil against subsequent attempts by the ACS to win support in Britain.

66. *Irish Friend*, April 1, 1841.

Chapter 3

Frederick Douglass and the International Movement

The successes of Nathaniel Paul and Charles Lenox Remond laid the foundations for the emergence of blacks as the principal spokesmen for the American slave on the international scene in the 1840s, a decade of controversy and schisms in Anglo-American abolitionism. Remond's diligence, eloquence, determination, and independence were in large measure responsible for keeping the cause alive and the movement at least partially unified at a time of growing sectarian squabbles. The American abolitionist Abby Kimber attributed his success to his "cloak of Humility" and pleasant disposition, and his Irish co-worker, Richard D. Webb, never reluctant to give his assessment of others, to Remond's consideration and personality, which, he believed, won over many who were initially reluctant to publicly endorse the cause. "The colored race," Webb told his American friends, "have a most creditable representative in Remond. His eloquence, his demeanor, and the discretion with which he moves, are all calculated to make a most favorable impression— and they have done so effectually." Remond's attempt to bridge the divisions in the movement by openly communicating with "new" organizationists was the kind of independence, however, that rankled with Webb. When it was rumored that Remond might accompany Douglass on his visit, Webb quickly wrote Maria Chapman to protest: "I don't know an individual who would be really glad to see Remond again. He begged too much and too undisguisedly, and behaved very often like a spoiled child." This was

sheer nonsense; Webb was well aware that Remond was directly responsible for establishing contacts between American and British
abolitionists where they had not previously existed and rekindling
interest among those who had withdrawn because of the 1840
schism. His views are even more startling given the fact that Remond's major successes were in Ireland, where he did more than
any other visiting American to consolidate the Irish-American anti-
slavery connection. His popularity and success in Ireland paved the
way for Douglass, who arrived in the summer of 1845.[1]

Although Remond directed most of his efforts elsewhere, the
major thrust of visiting American abolitionists in the forties centered around attempts to win British approval for the isolation of
those American churches that refused to condemn slavery and expel
slaveholders. In the 1830s many British churches—the Board of
Baptist Ministers in 1833, for example—had called on their American brethren to protest against slavery and work for its abolition.
The reply from the Baptist Board of Foreign Missions in America
set the tone of future responses to these addresses. The board
argued that the suggestion was impractical, given the nature of
American slavery, and that its implementation would disrupt the
"pleasing degree of union among the multiplying thousands of Baptists throughout the land." But not all Baptists adhered to this position; a convention in Boston opposed the American board's position
and pledged to work for abolition.[2] Numbers meant more to the
Baptist board and to most other evangelical churches than did the
emancipation of the slaves.

British delegations often attended the annual meetings of American churches to plead the cause of antislavery. In 1834 two ministers, Andrew Reed and James Matheson, represented the Con-

1. Douglas C. Riach, "Ireland and the Campaign Against American Slavery"
(Ph.D. dissertation, University of Edinburgh, 1975), 293; Gilbert Osofsky, "Aboli-
tionists, Irish Immigrants, and the Dilemmas of Romantic Nationalism," *American
Historical Review*, LXXX (1975), 896; Richard Webb to Maria Chapman, n.d., Abby
Kimber to Elizabeth Pease, May 18, 1840, both in ASB; *Liberator*, September 24,
1841.
2. Thomas Franklin Harwood, "Great Britain and American Anti Slavery"
(Ph.D. dissertation, University of Texas, 1959), 285–87.

gregational Union of England and Wales at the annual meeting of American Congregationalists. Although they also criticized the extremism of the American Anti-Slavery Society, their condemnation of slavery created a furor in America. The following year the Baptist Union heightened the controversy by sending a deputation to the convention of American Baptists. The deputation, led by Dr. F. A. Cox, a known abolitionist, was committed to raising the issue of abolition at the convention but abandoned the idea after coming under heavy pressure from their hosts. Such silence, American abolitionists argued, was a refutation of the principles of abolitionism and a concession to slavery. American abolitionists, aware of the importance of international support, their recent victory over the American Colonization Society being a case in point, saw such silence as a serious challenge to future efforts. Protests from Britain placed American slavery under the "moral embargo of the civilized world;" silence broke it. Cox, responding to abolitionist protest, argued that his deputation was concerned to build bridges of trust, not to throw "the apple of discord" at Americans who were too prone to interpret British advice as interference in their domestic affairs. Having already declined an invitation from the AASS, the deputation found itself in a further quandary when colonizationists, still smarting from their defeat in Britain and hoping to regain some lost ground, invited Cox to attend their annual meeting. Cox thought it best to decline both invitations in the hope of defusing the situation. But for abolitionists the damage was already done and refusing to attend the AASS meeting only exacerbated the situation.[3]

When protest and remonstrance failed to move American churches toward an antislavery position, abolitionists shifted their tactics. On the international level the new approach called on British churches to refuse communion and fellowship with proslavery American churches. The adoption of such a policy would isolate American churches from the international community of Christians and force a reassessment of their position on slavery. By pandering to slavery, abolitionists contended, American churches, more concerned with maintaining their numbers in an increasingly competi-

3. *Ibid.*, 290; *Patriot*, May 9, 1836; *Slavery in America*, XII, June, 1837.

tive situation and wary about challenging an economic system on which they were dependent, had abdicated their responsibility to work for the elimination of oppression. This attitude condoned slavery and even allowed churches in the South to openly participate in it. To hold fellowship with such churches, therefore, both sanctioned and gave respectability to their actions abroad and, in so doing, undermined the efforts of evangelicals working for a change in church policy at home.

The World Anti-Slavery Convention of 1840 provided an opportunity for the development and articulation of an international approach to the problem. Protracted discussion followed the Reverend C. Stovel's motion calling on British churches to reject all communion with slaveholders and with churches that condoned slavery. Supporters of the motion argued that isolation of American churches, the main props of slavery, would force them to reevaluate their stand. The committee assigned to consider the issue approved the resolution, and it was adopted and circulated to British religious unions for implementation. Impressed by the unanimity of the decision, James G. Birney decided to compile evidence to support abolitionists' claims against American churches. His *The American Churches, the Bulwarks of American Slavery*, published in 1840, became one of the major handbooks of Anglo-American abolitionism.[4]

It was to this issue that Frederick Douglass directed most of his attention during his nineteen months in Britain. Like most other black American visitors, Douglass began his work in Ireland. From the beginning, his simple and unrelenting approach was guaranteed to attract widespread interest and to create some consternation. Few listeners were left untouched by the stirring eloquence of his lectures, in which he described American slavery and racial discrimination, recounted his own experiences as a slave and the story of his escape, and explained how American churches were protecting and encouraging slavery by their silence. In the first few weeks of his visit, British chapels provided him with a forum for attacking their

4. *Anti Slavery Reporter*, June 17, 1840; Douglas H. Maynard, "The World's Anti-Slavery Convention of 1840," *Mississippi Valley Historical Review*, XLVII (1960–61), 470.

American counterparts, and when one denomination refused him the use of their hall because of his views, another offered theirs. For example, when he condemned American Methodists in one of his Dublin lectures, as Douglas Riach points out, Webb "spent most of the meeting dashing through the audience trying to silence those Roman Catholics who were delighted at the Methodists' discomfort, to pacify those Methodists who threatened a noisy demonstration unless Douglass present a similar indictment of the Catholic Church in America and give a more balanced view of their endeavours in antislavery, and to reassure the Quakers present that the customary peace of their Meeting House was not about to be shattered."[5] Methodists in Cork did not take this kind of criticism lightly and attempted to discredit Douglass in their communications with Methodists in Belfast. Turning criticism to advantage, Douglass responded by pointing out the depths to which his opponents had sunk in their attempts to discredit him and in so doing protect "Christians" who tie up "men and women and even girls not more than 17 years of age—who lash them until the blood streams down their backs—who brand them with red-hot irons hissing into their flesh—who cut off their ears—who put iron collars around their necks, and heavy chains upon their bodies—who hunt them with bloodhounds trained for the purpose, and who shoot them mercilessly when they refuse to surrender."[6]

Soon after his arrival in Belfast in December, 1845, Douglass found himself the center of another controversy involving British and American churches. Following the Scottish Disruption in 1843, the newly established Free Church of Scotland had sent a high-level commission to America to open contacts with American churches and raise money for its Sustentation Fund. The commission's decision to visit the South and accept money from southern churches, in spite of warnings and protests from American abolitionists, won for it their ire. If the visit was impolitic, the acceptance of southern

5. Riach, "Ireland and the Campaign Against American Slavery," 287, 292; Limerick *Reporter*, November 11, 1845; *Banner of Ulster*, December 12, 1845.

6. *Evening Packet*, September 16, 1845; Frederick Douglass to Richard Webb, December 5, 1845, in ASB; Belfast *News Letter*, n.d., in *Liberator*, March 20, 1846.

money, was a direct challenge to abolitionists' attempts to isolate proslavery churches both at home and abroad. On the return of the commissioners, abolitionists in Britain, led in Scotland by the Glasgow Emancipation Society and Henry C. Wright, the American abolitionist, and in Belfast by the Belfast Anti-Slavery Society, launched a public campaign aimed at pressuring the Free Church into returning the money it had collected in the South. The campaign used public meetings, petitions, and appeals to the general assemblies of the Free Church and other Presbyterian churches.

Belfast abolitionists initiated their campaign against the Free Church in 1844 with Wright's aid. His visit polarized opinion among Presbyterians, for it equated antislavery in Belfast with, in the words of Riach, "condemnation of the Free Church and those who chose not to attack it." The campaign did win support, especially among independent clergymen and Reformed Presbyterians, who called for a return of the money and declared a commitment to abolitionism. But because of close fellowship with the Free Church and sister churches in America, the Irish Presbyterian church refused to demand a return of the money or to sever denominational ties, recommending only that American Presbyterians "take active steps to abolish slavery wherever it existed."

Local abolitionists supplied Douglass with information, and soon after his arrival in Belfast, he took up the battle against the Free Church. How, he asked a Belfast audience, could he unmask the hypocrisy and "tear from the wrinkled brow of the beldame the pontifical tiara, and expose" the "deformity" of American proslavery churches if British churches continued to hold fellowship and receive money from "cradle plunderers"?[7] Douglass' criticism increased public interest in the issue of American slavery and in the relationship of British churches to those who sustained it, but it also led to divisions in the Belfast Anti-Slavery Society and bitter debate in the local press. The *Banner of Ulster*, which had at first supported Douglass, now turned against him for his condemnation of the Free Church. In reply, the Reverend Isaac Nelson, a Belfast abolitionist,

7. *Banner of Ulster*, December 12, 1845; Riach, "Ireland and the Campaign Against American Slavery," 278–82.

charged the editors not only with misrepresenting and garbling "the eloquent lectures of Frederick Douglass but with having contributed to swell the torrent of abuse with which a stranger and a fugitive was met on his arrival among *Christians*."[8]

Part of the abuse was directly attributable to a rumor circulating in Belfast that Douglass had been seen coming out of a house of ill repute in Manchester. Douglass' supporters claimed that the Reverend Thomas Smyth had started the rumor in an attempt to discredit Douglass and the "send back the money" campaign against the Free Church. Smyth, born in Belfast at the turn of the century, had emigrated to Charleston, South Carolina, where he became a pillar of the local Presbyterian Synod and a strong defender of the church's policy on slavery. He had also been the main promoter of the Free Church's efforts in the South, and as a concession to him, the Reverend Thomas Chalmers had agreed to soften his criticism of American churches and slavery. The start of the rumor coincided with the appearance of posters on the streets of Belfast calling on the population to "send back the nigger." Douglass threatened to sue for defamation of character and only withdrew the suit when Smyth, through his lawyers, issued an apology.[9]

This rather transparent and tasteless attempt to discredit Douglass only enhanced his popularity in Belfast. Public opinion, he and other abolitionists hoped, would pressure the General Assembly of the Irish Presbyterian Church to reevaluate its position on communion with proslavery American churches and disavow the policy of the Free Church. Even before the convening of the General Assembly, Belfast Presbyterian leaders were well aware of the dilemma they faced: they could either bow to abolitionist pressure and abandon the Free Church or encourage further criticism by refusing to take a strong antislavery position. Neither alternative was palatable, and Smyth's presence at the assembly's meeting only heightened

8. *Banner of Ulster*, January 2, 1846; Belfast *Commercial Chronicle*, January 21, March 30, 1846; Belfast *News Letter*, January 6, 1846.

9. George Howe, *History of the Presbyterian Church in South Carolina* (2 vols.; Columbia, S.C., 1883), II, 761–62; Louisa Cheves Stoney (ed.), *Thomas Smyth: Autobiographical Notes, Letters, and Reflections* (Charleston, S.C., 1914), 362–75; Richard Webb to Chapman, July 16, 1846, in ASB.

tensions. In an attempt to prevent further criticism, the church leaders rather undiplomatically suggested to Smyth that he should not participate in the proceedings. When the reply to a previous appeal to American Presbyterians was read, the Reverend Isaac Nelson called on the General Assembly to issue a strong condemnation of and sever all ties with their American brethren. The issue was submitted to committee for consideration.

At a public meeting on the same day, Douglass attempted to add some weight to the proabolitionist position in the assembly by calling on the Irish church to adopt Nelson's motion, arguing that, like sheep stealers, manstealers should not be admitted as members. The committee's report, while calling for open and unequivocal condemnation of slavery and the banning of slaveholding clergy and supporters of slavery from church meetings, stopped short of breaking off contacts on the ground that keeping open channels of communication could influence American churches to adopt an antislavery position in the future. The assembly's address rejected the arguments employed in the American reply, arguing that "no Christians ought to hold in forcible servitude any one of whom he has obtained possession, directly or indirectly, by the crime of man-stealing," that withholding religious instruction and separating families violated the principles of Christianity, and that "no Church should hold communion with those who are guilty of such violation, alike of the law of nature and revelation." Defense of slavery and criticism of abolitionists, it observed, only impeded speedy abolition.[10]

Such ambivalence pleased no one but the leaders of the Irish church, who could now claim, albeit somewhat illogically, that their stand improved the likelihood of abolition. In addition, this approach put little or no pressure on the Free Church to alter its policy. But the debate in Belfast set the stage for the larger battle with the Free Church in Scotland, a battle that would consume the energies of Douglass, Wright, James Buffum, Garrison, and George Thompson for the next year and would leave the Glasgow Emanci-

10. Belfast *Commercial Chronicle*, July 13, 11, 1846; Belfast *News Letter*, July 17, 10, 1846; *Banner of Ulster*, July 14, 1846; Riach, "Ireland and the Campaign Against American Slavery," 302–303.

pation Society almost bankrupt. All the arguments used in Belfast were further developed and employed in an attempt to bring public pressure on the Free Church. Although Douglass undoubtedly created some enemies in Ireland, he also heightened Irish interest in antislavery, especially among groups that had previously remained aloof, and won important allies in his efforts to isolate American proslavery churches.

Prior to Douglass' arrival in Scotland, the protest against the Free Church had been led by the Glasgow Emancipation Society (GES) and Henry Wright. This outside pressure, coupled with growing internal dissent, had already forced the leadership of the church to explain its stand on slavery in light of its acceptance of money from churches that openly endorsed or offered explanations in extenuation of slavery. When in 1845 Dr. John Duncan, a member of the commission to America, recommended to a meeting of the Free Presbytery of Edinburgh that the church issue a strong condemnation of slavery and hold "any moneys which may have been received from churches in which slave holders were admissible to membership . . . separate, and . . . unemployed, till such time as these churches shall have professed repentence, and proved it by reformation," Dr. William Cunningham, his fellow commissioner, rejected the suggestion out of hand as "distracting the attention, and occupying the time of ministers that might be much better employed."[11] The church, having already backed itself into a corner by the public pronouncements of its leaders and being determined not to bow to public pressure, found it impossible to take an unequivocal position on the issue.

Pressured by Smyth, who had complained of too much antislavery in the Free Church and had warned that southerners might discontinue contributions to the Sustentation Fund, Dr. Thomas Chalmers, the undisputed leader and intellectual giant of the church, issued two letters that explained his and the church's position on slavery and the excommunication of slaveholders. Although war, like slavery, he wrote Smyth, was inimical to Christianity, there were, nonetheless, Christian soldiers. Similarly, a distinction had to

11. *Presbyterian*, May 3, 1845.

be made between slavery as a system and "the persons whom circumstances have implicated therewith." Under these circumstances,
excommunication did nothing to improve the system. Admitting
that slavery vitiated the moral character, he argued that the Scriptures, while dictating no fellowship with fornicators and idolaters,
was silent on slavery. Fornicators and idolaters must be excommuni-
cated because the Scriptures specifically mandated it and because
Christianity was concerned with moral issues, not "civil and political institutions" like slavery. The onus, he concluded, was on abolitionists to prove their charges that certain churches encouraged
through their fellowship men who violated these Christian precepts.
Chalmers' letters were the basis of the position that the church assumed throughout the ensuing controversy and were warmly received by American Presbyterians as endorsements from very high
quarter. His letters quickly appeared in the American press and
were reprinted and widely circulated, much to the discomfort of
abolitionists.[12]

The 1845 report of the church's committee on slavery reflected
both Chalmers' influence and the church's committed refusal to return the money. While condemning slavery in theory, the report totally ignored the position taken by its American brethren and offered no practical suggestions for ameliorating the situation. Further,
the report in effect pleaded ignorance of all the information available
on southern laws and customs. The Free Church might have plausi-
bly claimed ignorance of American slavery in 1843, but by 1845 the
efforts of Wright and the GES must surely have provided it with an
abundance of pertinent information. The church, intent on justify-
ing its actions, simply ignored the available facts. Continued communication, the report insisted, would improve the chances of influ-
encing American churches to work for abolition.[13]

12. Annie H. Abel and Frank J. Klingberg (eds.), *A Side-Light on Anglo-
American Relations, 1839–1858: Furnished by the Correspondence of Lewis Tappan and
Others with the British and Foreign Anti-Slavery Society* (Lancaster, Pa., 1927), 196–
97; William Hanna, *Memoirs of the Life of Thomas Chalmers* (4 vols.; Edinburgh,
1849–52), IV, 582–91; George Shepperson, "The Free Church and American Slavery," *Scottish Historical Review*, XXX (1951), 132.
13. *Anti Slavery Reporter*, June 11, 1845.

From his arrival in Glasgow in early 1846, Douglass led the effort to pressure the Free Church to "send back the money." Along with James Buffum, the New England abolitionist, Douglass embarked on a lecture tour that took them to almost every important city and town in Scotland. Crowds flocked to see and hear the famous fugitive slave. By the end of April, John Murray and William Smeal, leaders of the GES, wrote Garrison optimistically that the church's position on American slavery was now understood by more Scots "in consequence of the sympathies of the people having been excited by the powerful appeal of Frederick Douglass."[14] He was the main attraction at a meeting organized by the GES a few days later. Wright paved the way for Douglass by wondering whether the church would have met with the same reception in the South had its commissioners called for abolition. Douglass in his turn criticized the church for ignoring the pleas of American abolitionists who for fifteen years had been attempting to change the position of American churches towards slavery. The visit by the commissioners, he argued, undercut all their previous efforts by lending legitimacy to southern churches. Mustering all the power of his famed eloquence and playing on the conscience of the Free Church, he told the audience, "I verily believe, that, had I been at the South, and had I been a slave—and I am a slave still by the laws of the United States—had I been there, and that deputation had come into my neighbourhood, and my master had sold me on the auction block, and given the produce of my body and soul to them, they would have pocketed it, and brought it to Scotland to build their churches and pay their ministers." The meeting called on the Free Church to sever its ties with slaveholding churches and send back the money.[15]

In all of this the abolitionists employed a simple approach; they hoped that memorials and petitions, backed up by widespread popular agitation, would force the Free Church, already in an untenable position, to return the money. In Paisley, addressing a crowd large enough to fill two churches, George Thompson called upon his lis-

14. John Murray and William Smeal to William Lloyd Garrison, in *Liberator*, April 24, 1846.
15. *Liberator*, May 29, 1846.

teners to teach their children "to lisp . . . in the streets when they
see a black coat and a white cravat—SEND BACK THE MONEY" and to
paint the slogan on every available wall. Douglass accused the Free
Church of lining its pockets with the money that should have been
used for his education; it was an approach guaranteed to win favor
from the large number of workingmen in the audience. And indeed,
popular opinion did seem to be on the side of the abolitionists. "In
Arbroath," Douglass informed his audience, "there was painted in
blood red capitals SEND BACK THE MONEY. A woman was sent to
wash it, but the letters still remained visible SEND BACK THE MONEY.
A mason was afterwards got to chisel it out, but there still was left
in indelible characters SEND BACK THE MONEY. I want men, women,
and children," he concluded, "to send forth this cry wherever they
go. Let it be the talk around the fireside, in the street, and at the
market-place." Such popular opposition, he argued, would help sur-
round America with an antislavery wall of opposition. Other ob-
servers confirmed the success of this approach. The editors of a local Dundee newspaper reported that they saw two lads outside the
Gaelic Chapel and thought they were up to some mischief but as it
turned out they were only trying to read an inscription on the wall:
"Send back the money—Louis is wors nor Tom Pain." Evidently
there were similar slogans in many other parts of the city. Poems
and songs set to popular airs were published praising Douglass and
condemning the Free Church. George Shepperson points out that
the police were very concerned about safety during a proposed pro-
cession of the Free Church in Edinburgh. For abolitionists there
were promising signs from other directions. There were rumors of
widening dissent in and the withdrawal of members from the Free
Church, and in May both the Secession Synod and Relief Synod
passed resolutions at their general assemblies advocating no fellowship with slaveholders.[16]

Even though the battle lines appeared firmly drawn on the eve of
the Free Church's general meeting in June, 1846, there were still

16. *British Friend*, May 30, 1846; *Liberator*, June 12, 1846; Dundee, Perth, and
Cuper *Advertiser*, February 17, 1846; Shepperson, "The Free Church and American
Slavery," 129; *Renfrewshire Advertiser*, May 2, 1846.

grounds for hope among abolitionists that the church would bend to popular pressure. As it turned out, such optimism proved totally unfounded. The leadership of the Free Church, besieged by criticism from abolitionists, opponents in other denominations, and large audiences throughout Scotland, pulled up their drawbridges and retreated behind thick walls of convoluted theological argument. The Reverend William Candlish led the defense at the 1846 General Assembly. To him the main issue revolved around the question of whether the Free Church should maintain friendly relations with American Presbyterians. On this score, he argued, the standards of the church were clear; they were bound to keep up friendly relations with other churches. Severence could only be accepted as a last resort when all else had failed and only when the other church, ignoring all possible remonstrances, had shown that it "ceased to be a church of the living God." Candlish, of course, offered no suggestions as to when remonstrances ceased being effective and other policies became necessary.[17]

Candlish's arguments assume even greater significance in light of the position of American churches on slavery. As early as 1837 the convention of the Old School Presbyterians, in an attempt to avoid conflict and division in the church, had agreed not to discuss slavery in future general assemblies. American evangelicals were becoming increasingly dependent on and powerless to influence the economic forces that ruled their culture and had taken the road of expediency rather than morality. In particular, southern evangelicals explained their withdrawal from antislavery activity by arguing that improvement came not by attacking and destroying the system, but "by providing those who were demeaned and degraded with an inner faith in themselves and their destinies quite apart from their social condition."[18] The logic of Candlish's argument, which led him

17. Free Church of Scotland, *Report of the Proceedings of the General Assembly on Saturday, May 30, and Monday, June 1, 1846, Regarding the Relations of the Free Church of Scotland and the Presbyterian Churches of America* (Edinburgh, 1846), 9–17.

18. Donald G. Mathews, *Religion in the Old South* (Chicago, 1977), 78–79; Ann Douglas, *The Feminization of American Culture* (New York, 1977), 33–34; Victor Howard, "The Anti-Slavery Movement in the Presbyterian Church, 1835–1861" (Ph.D. dissertation, Ohio State University, 1961), 44–46.

to conclude that American churches that did not apply his eligibility test were committing a sin, seemed to demand a different stand by the Free Church, for it was widely known that American churches had abrogated their responsibility to agitate for the removal of social inequalities.

Ostensibly a hypothetical and philosophical discussion, Candlish's defense of the Free Church's position is riddled with non sequiturs. For example, in defending continuing communication with American churches, he argued rather surprisingly that American churches contained a "large amount of piety and godliness" among their ministers and congregations. It was a point no abolitionist would have disputed, and it neatly skirted the abolitionist argument that the evil of slavery must be treated like other evils, for anything else would be hypocrisy. Douglass captured the essence of this contradiction when he told an Arbroath audience that "the Free Church, in vindicating their fellowship of slave holders, have acted upon the damning heresy that a man may be a Christian, whatever may be his practice, so his creed be right."[19] As if to further confound the church's critics, Dr. Cunningham argued for a distinction between *slaveholding* and *slave having*. If it became law in Britain to hold slaves, he explained, then he under law was a slaveholder, but if he did not implement these new powers by treating his slaves "harshly or oppressively," then he was only a slave haver. Furthermore, a slave haver may conclude after careful examination that he was obliged "on the grounds of necessity and mercy, to retain that position, and of course might retain it without being guilty of sin."[20] Such sophistry only made the church's opponents more resolute.

Henry C. Wright had earlier exposed the fallacy of this argument. Individuals, he wrote, must be held responsible for their actions. Slaveholders could not escape censure by claiming that the system prevented them from freeing their slaves, for it was these very slaveholders and their supporters, not "the *Slave Laws*—nor the *system* or the *institution* of Slavery," he observed, that kept men

---

19. Arbroath *Guide*, n.d., in *Liberator*, April 3, 1846; Free Church, *Report of the Proceedings of the General Assembly*, 18, 22–23.

20. Free Church, *Report of the Proceedings of the General Assembly*, 37–39.

slaves.[21] At a meeting in Dundee, Douglass poked fun at Cunningham's argument, asking whether the divine would obey a fiat from Parliament that ordered everyone to "become worshippers of Juggernaut." If he did not, Douglass mocked, "his reasoning about the powers of Parliament would be the most fallacious that could be imagined." With the orator's skill for quickly feeling the pulse of his audience, Douglass appealed to his listeners to understand the logic of Cunningham's argument on the sanctity of law. It meant, he told them, that if Parliament decreed the enslavement of whites, Cunningham "would have no more scruples in ordering any of them—their wives, their sons and daughters—to mount the auction block than he would have in commanding any of the African race to do so." Returning to the same theme one month later, Douglass, played on nineteenth-century sensibilities, wondering aloud to the ladies in his audience whether Cunningham would accept a law that called on all female servants to become concubines of their employers.[22] The obvious flaws of Cunningham's logic easily lent themselves to the ridicule and censure of Douglass and other abolitionists. Furthermore, the arguments of Cunningham and others were refuted by a fact that they all seemed to overlook or chose to forget, namely, that slaveholders and their supporters wrote the very laws under which they lived.

All of the arguments employed by Cunningham, Candlish, and other leaders of the Free Church and repeated almost verbatim at the church's 1847 convention were *ex post facto* attempts to explain a policy that had seriously embarrassed the church's leaders, who previously had had pretty solid antislavery credentials. Having received money from "churches tainted with the guilt of slavery . . . and finding it difficult to retrace its steps," the Free Church, the *Anti Slavery Reporter* believed, became "encumbered with 'difficult questions and scruples, on scriptural and moral grounds.'" Douglass told a meet-

21. Henry C. Wright, *American Slavery Proved to Be a Theft and Robbery: With a Letter to Dr. Cunningham* (Edinburgh, 1845), 20–24; Henry C. Wright, *The Dissolution of the American Union: . . . With a Letter to the Rev. Drs. Chalmers, Cunningham, and Candlish . . . and a Letter to the Members of the Free Church* (Glasgow, 1845), 44–45.

22. *Perthshire Constitutional*, October 23, 1846; Dundee, Perth, and Cuper *Advertiser*, September 29, 1846.

ing of the BFASS that they had "worked themselves up to believe that it would be wrong for them to send it back, or at least that it would be humiliating to do it." An antislavery song published during the controversy bitingly captured the church's dilemma: "The Free Church is like the toad in the fable / It blows itself up as big as it's able."[23] Retreat that would have been difficult for the Free Church once Chalmers' letters to Smyth were made public was now next to impossible, given the publicity of the "Send Back the Money" campaign. The leadership, playing on long-established fears of "mob rule," were determined to resist popular pressure, while abolitionists were equally determined to garner as much popular support as possible to force a change in policy. Their successful public campaign may have defeated their purpose by cutting off all possible retreat and thereby stiffening Free Church resistance. To have sent back the money under these circumstances would have been to concede to "mob rule." As we have seen, thousands attended abolitionists' meetings, and the slogan "send back the money" became the rallying cry against the Free Church. Wright reported that the issue was discussed by nearly every newspaper in Scotland and that "the discussion and excitement have gone into parlors, kitchens, bedrooms, and nurseries—in the shops, and by the wayside." In early 1845 Cunningham warned in reply to a Wright pamphlet that the "folly and extravagance" of American abolitionists did as much harm to the cause "as the infidelity and excess of the French Revolution did to the cause of good government."[24] The Jacobin scare was still a potent reality in mid-nineteenth-century Britain. Middle-class abolitionists, having raised the specter of popular protest, may themselves have retreated from further agitation for fear of its consequences.

The Free Church and its supporters stoutly defended themselves by attacking the "extremism" of American abolitionists who called for the excommunication of American churches and by dismissing their opponents in other Scottish churches as hypocrites. Support for Douglass and his cohorts, the Aberdeen *Banner* claimed, "pro-

23. *Anti-Slavery Songs* (Edinburgh, n.d.), 7; *Anti Slavery Reporter*, June 1, July 1, 1846.

24. *Presbyterian*, May 31, 1845; *Liberator*, June 12, 1846.

ceeded less from a desire to liberate the slaves in America, than to
gratify their dislike of the Free Church of Scotland." To the *Free
Church Magazine*, the opposition to the church was a "bad cause,
prosecuted by bad men, in a bad spirit, and for a bad end." This
motley crew consisted of a "hypocritical portion of the ministers
and members of the Establishment—a sprinkling of the more secu-
lar and malignant members of other Dissenting Churches, and a
mass of Heathens, who, having broken loose from all the restraints
of religion, are delighted to have an opportunity of pouring out
their venom against the Free Church."[25]

The *Banner* and other supporters of the Free Church were not
above reverting to *ad hominem* attacks and racial slurs in their attempt to discredit Douglass and his "renegade Scots" allies. The
Banner flew into a rage against "the 'talented' Frederick Douglass,"
who had called Dr. Chalmers an artful dodger with, the paper said,
"an elegance of language that might have been expected, and the
mimicry for which his race is proverbial." The *Scottish Guardian*, responding to the same issue concluded that "Mr. Douglass (the
black) was (as he himself tells us) a 'chimney-sweeper,' when the
abolitionists promoted him to the questionable honour of being one
of the orators, and sent him forth to try his hand in throwing dirt at
Dr. Chalmers." Throughout the whole controversy there was a
sense almost of disbelief on the part of church supporters that foreigners—and American parvenues at that, people of little repute or
standing—could be so bold as to attack and ridicule some of the
great intellects of Scotland. When Cunningham and Chalmers declined to publicly debate Free Church policy, the *Scottish Guardian* in
mock disbelief commented that abolitionists "have yet to learn that
they are not persons entitled to any such consideration, and that it
would be improper in ministers of the gospel to discuss matters of
Christian duty with those whose mouths are full of Billingsgate."[26]

Interestingly enough, while Wright was criticized for extremism
and radicalism, Douglass seems to have been relatively immune
from such criticism. Audiences came to hear him and went away dis-

25. *Free Church Magazine* (1846), 145–51; Aberdeen *Banner*, May 8, 1846.
26. *Scottish Guardian*, May 5, 1, 1846; Aberdeen *Banner*, May 8, 1846.

appointed if he did not deliver one of his marathon speeches. "A Free Churchman" in a letter to his local newspaper captured the significance of Douglass' effect on the controversy. "Discontent has been deep," he observed, "although not loud, and strange as it may appear, the deliverance of a runaway slave has completely unsettled the 'dollar question' and produced a greater effect on the public mind than the united wisdom of the Free Assembly."[27] But Douglass' success and popularity may have worked to the advantage of the Free Church, for he unwittingly did more than any other abolitionist to foster the Jacobin scare among middle-class Scots.

In spite of all their efforts, abolitionists failed to persuade the Free Church to return the money. Some members formed the Free Church Anti-Slavery Society in September, 1846, in an attempt to persuade the church to aid those fighting for immediate emancipation and to ban fellowship with slaveholding churches. However, efforts to distance themselves from the radicalism of Garrisonian abolitionism were unavailing and they were consistently denounced as traitors bent on destroying the church.[28] There were other casualties of this controversy. The Reverend James MacBeth, one suspects, was driven out of the church for his opposition to its position. He was accused of "lewd approaches" and "immodest demeanour towards women," but George Shepperson points out that the conducting of the hearing by the General Assembly *in camera* in 1849 raised serious suspicions that the Free Church was punishing MacBeth for his opposition to its stand on sending back the money. Although the verdict of "not proven" was returned, MacBeth's reputation was damaged sufficiently to make him leave for Canada in 1850.[29] Although the campaign to persuade the Free Church to send back the money and sever ties with American churches failed, as Douglass wrote later, "it provided an occasion for making the peo-

27. Montrose *Standard*, March 13, 1846.

28. Anne Murdoch to John Scoble, May 25, 1847, in BFASS; Free Church Anti Slavery Society, *An Address to the Office-Bearers and Members of the Free Church of Scotland on Her Present Connexion with the Slave-Holding Churches of America* (Edinburgh, 1847).

29. Shepperson, "The Free Church and American Slavery," 140–41.

ple thoroughly acquainted with the character of slavery and array-
ing against it the moral and religious sentiment of that country."[30]

While the dispute over the Free Church continued in Scotland,
Douglass and others attempted to broaden the debate on communion with American churches at the founding meeting of the Evangelical Alliance. For some years evangelicals on both sides of the
Atlantic had been working to form an international association.
From the outset their efforts were plagued by disputes over the ex-
act nature, function, and composition of the alliance. Domestic jealousies and disputes among evangelical churches in both America
and Britain only complicated the issue. How could churches with
apparently irreconcilable sectarian differences, many of which held
no communion with one another at home, work together in a united
international alliance? As was the case with all other attempts at
early international cooperation, supporters of the proposed alliance
also had to confront the issue of jurisdiction. There was a long but
inconclusive debate over the merits of independent national alliances compared to an international assembly with jurisdictional authority. Preparing for the first meeting in London in August, 1846,
supporters of the alliance decided on a broad, catholic approach in
the hope that the meeting would be able to solve the many problems
and create its own rules of association.

The Free Church debate only added to the problems of the alliance by raising the issue of communion with American churches.
The British organizers of the convention had initially left the selec-
tion of delegates to the individual synods despite pressure from abolitionists to exclude slaveholders. The leaders of the Free Church,
anxious to deflect some of the criticism against it, also called on the
preliminary conference of the alliance in Birmingham not to "invite" slaveholders. Arguing that it was inexpedient to discuss slavery and slaveholding or the difficulties facing Christians in slaveholding states, they moved that "individuals who, whether by their

30. Frederick Douglass, *Life and Times of Frederick Douglass* (1892; rpr. New
York, 1962), 254.

own fault or otherwise, may be in the unhappy position of holding their fellowmen as slaves" not be invited. The motion was accepted, and Candlish hurried back to Scotland to continue his defense of the Free Church, secure in the knowledge that, at least in the eyes of some evangelicals, the church had reaffirmed its antislavery credentials.[31] The new rule arrived too late to affect the composition of the American delegation, but it did raise the ire of Americans, who saw this as a direct attempt by supporters of abolitionism to isolate those who had not openly endorsed the work of abolitionists. It also extended the debate already raging in Scotland.

The Birmingham resolution and the decision to form a general organization—which had, interestingly enough, been suggested by American evangelicals—rather than independent national associations forced the alliance to confront the thorny problem of whether members from proslavery churches would be accepted. Even if the Birmingham resolution had not existed, however, the Free Church controversy would have made it next to impossible for the alliance to avoid a discussion of the issue of slavery in any meeting with British evangelicals. The alliance was soon thrown into an uproar when the Reverend J. Howard Hinton, citing the Birmingham resolution, called for the exclusion of slaveholders. Accepting that some slaveholders could be Christians, Hinton called for their rejection on the grounds that they were manstealers and that the rules of the alliance gave them the authority to exclude some Christians, as they had already done by refusing to invite Unitarians, Quakers, and Plymouth Brethren to participate in the movement. Pointing out that he was a supporter of the American and Foreign Anti-Slavery Society and not a Garrisonian abolitionist, Hinton criticized the antiabolitionist position of the American delegates. In an attempt to avoid open debate and possible division, the Reverend J. Angell James moved that the issue be submitted to a special committee of Americans and Europeans. The Reverend S. H. Cox demurred, calling for open debate, and the Reverend S. L. Pomeroy of Maine counseled patience, calling on both the American and the British

31. Garrison and Garrison, *William Lloyd Garrison*, III, 164–66; Abel and Klingberg (eds.), *A Side-Light*, 125; *Liberator*, June 26, 1846.

branches of the alliance to adopt measures they thought proper and "in three, or four, or seven years, if the discussion of the subject came up again, it could be looked at."[32]

Thomas Smyth, smarting under the whole Free Church controversy and his treatment in his native Belfast, would have none of it. Calling Hinton's motion unnecessary and irrelevant to the object of harmonizing "in Christian Union and Christian love," he warned that the issue would only politicize the alliance. To Smyth it was solely an issue of expediency. Everyone at the meeting, he argued, agreed that slavery was an evil which should be removed "as soon as God in His providence should open the way." He warned that the discussion would do irreparable damage to their efforts by rousing national jealousies. This could only be avoided and abolition ultimately achieved if the alliance placed its faith in the spread of Christian principles. A fellow American, Dr. William Patton, rose in defense of Smyth, arguing that neither the Birmingham resolution nor the rules of general assembly necessitated a discussion of this kind. Given the relationship of state to church and the widespread use of alcohol in Britain, Patton observed, "a great many of us in America feel, that England is not free herself and the Englishmen are not free men." Adding national insult to injury, Patton pointed out that the bulwark of slavery was not the American church but the price paid for cotton in Liverpool. Finally, he warned that discussions of this kind would only be viewed by Americans as another attempt at foreign intervention in their domestic affairs. The Reverend Ralph Wardlaw, attempting to reduce tension, suggested that exclusion of slaveholders should not be interpreted as a criticism against American Christianity. He proposed a compromise that would condemn "all Slavery" and would express the alliance members' determination "in their respective spheres, to use all means, which may by them be deemed legitimate, to effect its universal abolition." The alternative, Wardlaw suggested, would be either the formation of two alliances or the loss of a large portion of British and Irish members.

32. Evangelical Alliance, *Report of the Proceedings of the Conference Held at Freemasons' Hall, London, from August 19th to September 2nd Inclusive, 1846* (London, 1847), 290–303.

The majority of Americans, supported by some British members, would have none of Wardlaw's compromise. Dr. F. A. Cox's suggestion that the issue be sent to a committee of forty-seven, made up of delegates from America, Britain, and the continent, finally broke the deadlock.[33]

The dispute raged on for days without any sign of abating. There was little hope that the committee, given its size and the stand of the American delegation, would achieve very much. The committee had three possible choices: it could accept the American demand for further concessions and save the alliance, oppose them and destroy it, or agree to postpone any decision. The meeting adopted the third alternative, deferring complete organization of a general alliance on the grounds that constituent delegations did not have sufficient time to consult adequately with their countrymen. In the interim, national organizations were to be formed "in accordance with their peculiar circumstances, without involving the responsibility of one part of the Alliance for another." Hinton and others confronted by an almost totally united American delegation had little chance of overriding the committee's recommendation. Nevertheless, he argued that the foundations of the alliance had been laid by those present, among whom there were no slaveholders. But Hinton and his supporters were well aware that the decision sounded the death knell of the alliance.[34]

The failure of the alliance was due in part to its catholic approach and the amorphousness of its organization. It is quite clear that some British and most American evangelicals were so eager to promote the alliance that they ignored the burning issue of the relationship of American evangelical churches to slavery. Five years before or even five years after the meeting, the alliance might have succeeded in ignoring the issue; but in 1846 in the midst of the Free Church controversy, this was not possible. Abolitionists had succeeded in making the issue central to any attempts to promote Anglo-American evangelical cooperation. Hinton was right; no British evangelical (especially in 1846) could fly in the face of his

33. *Ibid.*, 304–40.
34. *Ibid.*, 436–58.

country's antislavery traditions and concede totally to American demands. American evangelicals, already sceptical about the potential
of the alliance because of its amorphousness, came to London determined to resist the abolitionist pressure that had already split many
of their churches at home. Hiding behind a wall of national jealousies they successfully argued that British pressure would be interpreted at home as foreign interference.

But abolitionists continued to agitate against British communion
with American churches that had refused to condemn American
slavery. To have done otherwise would have been to concede that
their opponents had breached the moral cordon. Following the arrival of Garrison at the end of July and the formation of the Anti
Slavery League—a Garrisonian society—in August, Douglass, Garrison, Thompson, and Wright toured Britain, condemning the Free
Church and the Evangelical Alliance and promoting the league. Understandably, they were highly critical of the reluctance of British
evangelicals to ban slaveholders from the alliance and viewed the
compromise as both a denial of Britain's antislavery traditions and a
dangerous precedent.[35] Their meetings kept the issue alive and,
judging from the audiences that came to hear them, reached a large
section of the British public. As in the Free Church controversy,
Douglass, especially after Garrison's return to America in early au-
tumn, took the lead in the league's attempt to win public endorsement of its position.

Criticizing the refusal to ban slaveholders from the Evangelical
Alliance, Douglass told a Sunderland audience that in American
churches "the blood-stained gold of the slave goes to support the
pulpit,—while the pulpit covers the infernal business with the garb
of Christianity. Here are religion and robbery," he thundered, "devils dressed in angels' robes and hell presenting the semblance of
paradise." These were not the kind of churches with which British
Christians could associate without themselves violating the principles of Christianity. Many British delegates having agreed to the
compromise found themselves in the uncomfortable position of

35. *Patriot*, September 17, 1846, in *Liberator*, October 16, 1846; *Scotsman*, n.d.,
in *Liberator*, November 20, 1846.

having to defend the alliance's stand, a position made even more untenable by the decision to exclude Quakers, Unitarians, and Plymouth Brethren from the ranks of the organization. How then, Douglass and others asked, could the alliance refuse to categorically ban slaveholders. The response of the Reverend William Horton, superintendent of the Sunderland Wesleyan Circuit, to Douglass' criticism was typical; he argued that British Wesleyans should not be condemned, for they had no contact with southern churches. But Douglass countered that this argument was irrelevant to the issue of the alliance's compromise. Always informed and never reluctant to take on an opponent, Douglass accused local Wesleyans of welcoming the Reverend James Caughey, an American Methodist who was not noted for his abolitionism. The debate became so heated that even the mayor gave up his chair to defend the absent Caughey. The following December, a Reverend Caughey was refused admission as a local preacher by the Sheffield Wesleyan Conference. Douglass' attacks on the alliance prompted similar defenses in other cities, many leading as in a meeting at Darlington to "great confusion and a scene of tumult and uproar."[36]

The alliance's decision simply shifted the locus of the debate to national associations and provided British evangelicals with a loophole that they readily employed. They could now condemn slavery without directly raising the issue of communion with the American churches. But in America the problem could not be dismissed that easily; when American evangelicals met in New York the following year to form a national organization, they committed themselves to admit as members only respectable persons from evangelical churches and recognized that their aims would be only furthered by a frank statement on slavery. Their objective was the "promotion of Christian Union and brotherly love," but they declared "deep unalterable opposition to this stupendous evil" and called on all Christians to fight for its destruction. Many participants opposed this approach, argued that the issue of slavery was irrelevant to the aims of the

36. Durham *Chronicle*, January 15, 1847; Wakefield *Journal*, January 21, 1847; *Western Times*, September 26, 1846; Doncaster, Nottingham, and Lincoln *Gazette*, January 1, 1847; Sunderland *Herald*, September 25, 1846.

association, while others insisted that the adoption of antislavery principles was necessary for any future alliance with British evangelicals. The Reverend E. N. Kirk, who had led the resistance to the antislavery resolution in London, warned that the association was degenerating into an antislavery society and threatened to withdraw his support. In an attempt at compromise, the association's antislavery resolution differentiated between those who held slaves for gain and those who held them out of a sense of duty. The *Presbyterian*, railing against this "utopian" scheme, lamented that an alliance "to promote Christian fellowship, and a union of Christian effort," had instead produced an "*abolition* society, not in name, but in fact."[37]

This was more than any abolitionist could have expected given the results of the London meeting. But it is clear that the excitement over the Free Church and the debate surrounding the alliance did influence some American evangelicals to move closer to an antislavery position. For the rest of the decade abolitionists continued to follow the debate. Individual American evangelicals kept up contacts with British brethren and attended some of their annual meetings. But if it appeared that these informal contacts and the passage of time would improve the chances of reactivating the general organization, developments in America, particularly the passage of the Fugitive Slave Act in 1850, destroyed these hopes. The new law forced previously uncommitted British churches and organizations to pass resolutions banning slaveholders and their supporters from attending their annual meetings as visitors. These new developments reopened old wounds, and at the 1851 annual meeting of the British Evangelical Alliance, Dr. Baird, an American, again raised the issue of British interference in America's domestic affairs. He called on his audience to leave American slavery to Americans, who knew best how to deal with it, and urged the British to concentrate on their own problems, such as the alliance between church and state, which had done more "to subvert the rights of conscience, and of religious worship, and, in a word, to prevent men from entering heaven than all the slavery that ever existed." The continuing

37. *Presbyterian*, May 22, 15, 1847; New York *Observer*, May 15, 1847.

debate, Baird suggested, was responsible for keeping British and American evangelicals apart as it had subverted the intent of the 1846 conference. Although the British Evangelical Alliance continued to refuse to sever all ties with American proslavery clergy, Baird's frustrated plea suggests that abolitionists could claim a measure of success in their efforts to isolate American proslavery churches.[38]

Many of the American evangelicals who went to London in 1846 to attend the alliance meeting stayed to participate in the first World Temperance Convention. Their presence and the abolitionists' policy of using other organizations to raise the issue of American slavery made for a potentially explosive situation. Garrison, eager to continue the debate recently concluded at the alliance meeting, launched an attack on the Reverend Kirk's views on slave masters and Christianity, only to be summarily silenced by the chair. Douglass, attending as an accredited delegate from Newcastle, bided his time until the public meeting at Covent Garden. He had already established his credentials as an advocate of temperance, and the soirée held in his honor by Father Theobald Mathew, the leading figure in British temperance, enhanced his image as a universal reformer. Douglass spoke to the meeting, he told his listeners, as a British not an American delegate, for American temperance societies discriminated against blacks. This opening salvo was met with shouts of opposition from some Americans in the audience, but Douglass was undeterred; his concern, he continued, was not to insult Americans but to prod them to adopt an abolitionist position on their return home. He devoted the rest of his speech to an account of the many ways in which discrimination undermined the attempts of free blacks to elevate themselves. When Kirk, stung by this condemnation, protested that Douglass' speech left the impression that temperance men supported slavery and racial discrimination, he was silenced by shouts of "no, no" from the audience.[39]

38. The Bristol and Clifton Ladies Anti Slavery Society failed to persuade the Bristol meeting of the alliance to ban all American clergymen who were apologists for slavery. *Nonconformist*, November 26, August 27, 1851; *Anti Slavery Reporter*, June 2, 1851.

39. *National Temperance and Temperance Recorder*, September, 1846; *Liberator*, September 11, 1846, December 12, 1845; *Patriot*, December 20, 1845.

If they had previously only suspected it, now many visiting American evangelicals were firmly convinced that there existed a conspiracy between American abolitionists and their British supporters, which, according to S. H. Cox, aimed at fanning the flames of "national exasperation and war." That, of course, was sheer nonsense, but the Americans seemed genuinely mystified by the success of Douglass and other abolitionists, and Cox certainly took the conspiracy theory seriously. In a letter to the New York *Evangelist*, he complained against the kind of "abuse" and "iniquity against the law of reciprocal righteousness" that "call thousands together to get them, some certain ones, to seem conspicuous and devoted for one sole and grand object, and then all at once, with obliquity, open an avalanche on them for some imputed evil or monstrosity, for which, whatever be the wound or injury inflicted, they were both too fatigued and too hurried with surprise, and too straitened for time to be properly prepared." Cox went even further; the crowd, he said, "taken with the spirit of the Ephesian uproar," were "furious and boisterous in the extreme," so much so that they prevented any response to Douglass' condemnation. Douglass, "the colored abolitionist and ultraist . . . petted, and flattered and used, and paid by certain abolitionists not unknown to us of the *ne plus ultra* strain," knowing that they had all gathered to discuss temperance, deliberately, Cox told the editor, "lugged in antislavery or abolitionism" in an attempt to discredit Americans. Douglass, chortling at Cox's discomfort and confusion, later responded with a point-by-point refutation.[40]

Douglass' open letter was not necessary; Cox had exposed the depth of frustration and concern suffered by many American evangelicals. They were convinced beyond all doubt that the Free Church controversy, the failure of the Evangelical Alliance, and Douglass' speech at the World Temperance Convention were all part of a carefully orchestrated conspiracy by American abolitionists and their British allies to interfere in America's domestic problems. Faced with continuous abolitionist criticism, they chose to retreat behind

40. Philip Foner (ed.), *The Life and Writings of Frederick Douglass* (6 vols.; New York, 1950–78), I, 189–99; *Liberator*, November 20, 1846.

national fears and jingoism. The fact that abolitionists consistently refuted these claims mattered little to men like Cox, whose reactions by themselves provide sufficient testimony to the effectiveness of the abolitionist's moral cordon.

Following the World Temperance Convention, Douglass joined Garrison, Thompson, and Wright on an extensive lecture tour. When Garrison returned to America in early fall, Douglass continued to lecture on slavery, the Free Church, and the Evangelical Alliance, under the auspices of the Anti Slavery League. The initial successes of the league were directly attributable to Douglass' almost legendary popularity. Even when he lectured with other famous abolitionists like Garrison and Thompson, his views were given the place of prominence in local newspaper reports. At their second Glasgow meeting, for instance, Buffum spoke first so that by the time he was finished the continually arriving crowd would have settled in to hear Douglass. The Hutchinsons, a famous family of antislavery singers from New England, attributed their initial successes in Ireland to having joined Douglass at his antislavery meeting. Thousands from all walks of life came to hear his lectures, and his narrative sold as fast as it could be printed. Following one of his Glasgow meetings Catherine Paton wrote Henry Wright that "there was not so much broad cloth as we have sometimes seen, there was the fustian and true and honest hearts beating . . . under fustian jackets." He was equally popular among the working classes in Ireland, where, according to Ralph Varian of Cork, the "poorer trades' people" showed an increased interest in antislavery following the visit of Douglass. Forgetting his previous praise of Remond, Webb, in assessing Douglass' contributions, told Garrison, "we have never had one among us better qualified to proclaim the wrongs of the bondmen, or to excite sympathy in his behalf." Mary Carpenter of Bristol concurred, informing Maria Chapman that Douglass was "perhaps more generally appreciated than Garrison, though the few who have enjoyed Mr. Garrison's friendship in England feel that he has a place in their hearts that no other can take."[41]

41. Mary Carpenter to Chapman, March 31, 1847, in ASB; *Liberator*, December 12, 26, 1845; Catherine Paton to Henry C. Wright, January 7, 1846, in HCW;

Like other blacks, Douglass seems to have been temporarily bemused by the reception he received, notwithstanding the opposition of a few. He wistfully wrote Francis Jackson from Dundee that it was quite "an advantage to be a nigger here. I find I am hardly black enough for British taste, but by keeping my hair as woolly as possible I make out to pass for at least half a Negro at any rate."[42] In a series of letters published in the *Liberator*, Douglass played upon American jealousies by comparing this reception to the experiences of free blacks in the northern states. Soon after his arrival in Dublin he wrote Garrison, "one of the most pleasing features of my visit thus far has been a total absence of all manifestations of prejudice against me, on account of my color. The change of circumstances, in this, is particularly striking. I go on stage coaches, omnibuses, steamboats, into the first cabins, and in the first public houses, without seeing the slightest manifestation of that hateful and vulgar feeling against me. I find myself not treated as a *color*, but as a *man*— not as a thing, but as a child of the common Father of us all." He sardonically quipped that the differences in treatment may have had something to do with the fact that "white people in America are whiter, purer, and better than the people here." Giving his acerbic wit full rein he wrote that on his visit to Eaton Hall "the statuary did not fall down, the pictures did not leap from their places, the door did not refuse to open, and the servants did not say 'We don't allow niggers in here.'"[43]

Douglass' popularity and acceptance in Britain, however, may have created jealousy among some British abolitionists. Always willing to consider the advice of his friends but never reluctant to make decisions for himself, Douglass soon found himself at odds with some British Garrisonians. Like Remond, he saw no reason to raise unnecessary sectarian issues that would alienate other British abolitionists. When it was suggested that he join Wright on the lecture

John W. Hutchinson, *Story of the Hutchinsons (Tribe of Jesse)* (2 vols.; Boston, 1896), I, 157–58; Glasgow *Argus*, January 22, 26, 1846; Liverpool *Mercury*, October 23, 1846.

42. Foner (ed.), *Life and Writings of Frederick Douglass*, II, 136–37.

43. *Liberator*, January 30, 1846, October 24, November 28, 1845.

circuit, Douglass demurred, arguing that he did not agree with Wright on "the importance of discussing in this country the disunion question." Besides, he told Webb, "Friend Wright has created against himself the prejudices which I as an abolitionist do not feel myself called upon to withstand. My mission to this land is purely an antislavery one, and although there are other good causes which need to be advocated I think that my duty calls me strictly to the question of slavery."[44] Like Remond, he never shied away from defending Garrison when he thought it necessary. For example, he told a Leeds audience, "I like Joseph Sturge, of Birmingham, I revere the Anti-Slavery Committee, I love the abolitionists of England; but they ask of me too much when they desire me to step down from the side of Garrison. Sacrifice the man from whom I have received more than from any man breathing—my first, my last, my most steadfast friend—the friend of liberty, the great parent of freedom! Impossible!"[45] Following the approach of other black visitors, Douglass' principal concern was to harness, not weaken through unnecessary sectarian squabbles, international opposition against American slavery.

Reaching out to other British abolitionists, Douglass soon found himself in conflict with British Garrisonians, particularly Webb, who coordinated and arranged most of his early lectures in Ireland. Throughout the period, Webb consistently alienated black Garrisonians, who found him overweening and demanding. Dismissing others as incompetent or beggarly, he was particularly ambivalent about Douglass—one minute praising him to the skies; the next, condemning his arrogance and aloofness. Their first conflict arose over Douglass' refusal to use a portrait prepared for the second edition of his narrative and his insistence that letters of commendation

44. Douglass to Richard Webb, November 10, 1845, in ASB. Some American abolitionists agreed with Douglass' assessment of Wright. When Lydia Child heard he was going to Britain she wrote Ellis Gray Loring that Wright was as "little calculated to do good, as almost any person they could select." Child to Loring, April 6, 1842, in Lydia Maria Child Papers, Personal Miscellaneous, Rare Books and Manuscripts Division, the New York Public Library, Astor, Lenox, and Tilden Foundations.

45. Leeds *Times*, n.d., in *Liberator*, February 5, 1847.

from Belfast clergymen be included in its preface. Such "trifling," Douglass warned him, was unacceptable; the decision about what to include in the narrative was his, not Webb's. Stung, Webb naïvely attributed Douglass' independence to the flattery and attention of British abolitionists. "I don't at all feel confident," he wrote Wright, "that his head will be strong enough for the attention he receives. I have not found him as agreeable as I would wish."[46] Their differences increased when Webb undiplomatically read Douglass a portion of a letter from Maria Chapman in which she suggested that Webb "warn Douglass of the ill effects it has on a man's respectability to aim at anything for himself in the prosecution of a philanthropic enterprise" and wondered whether he would be strong enough to endure temptation "when the endurance shall seem to threaten him with loss." The suggestion that he needed supervision so that pampering and money would not influence him was more than Douglass could take. Enraged, he wrote Chapman demanding to know her reasons for suspecting him and warning that if she wished to drive him from the American Anti-Slavery Society putting him under "overseership" was guaranteed to succeed. "Set someone to watch over me for evil," he warned Chapman, "and let them be so simple minded as to inform me of their office, and the last blow is struck."[47]

If Webb, as I suspect, was aiming to put Douglass in his place by reading portions of Chapman's letter to him, then his plan sadly misfired. He not only angered Douglass but drew the ire of Chapman for his insensitivity. His fingers burnt, Webb wrote Chapman in extenuation that Douglass, in spite of his great talents, tended to magnify the smallest cause of "discomfort or wounded self esteem into insurmountable hills of offense and dissatisfaction." Douglass, wrote Webb, was the "least lovable and least easy of all the abolitionists," and he was prone to overreact when he was "in the slightest degree hurt." Webb's explanation of his faux pas and his assessment of Douglass' character may have influenced Garrisonians in

46. Richard Webb to Wright, February 22, 1846, in HCW; Douglass to Richard Webb, April 16, 1846, in ASB.
47. Foner (ed.), *Life and Writings of Frederick Douglass*, I, 143–44.

their later disputes with Douglass, but in Britain others totally disagreed with Webb's views. Isabel Jennings, one of his avid supporters, contended that Douglass "could bear to have fault found with him if it was not taken for granted he *must* be wrong" and, in an obvious reference to Webb, pointed out that there were some who "*dictated* to him more than he liked." The experiences of other black visitors, particularly Charles Remond, the Crafts, and William Wells Brown, suggest that Jennings' assessment of the situation was nearer the truth. Douglass, recognizing that he may have overreacted, later wrote to Webb in an attempt at reconciliation that the tone and insinuations of Chapman's letter had "stuck in his crop."[48] Subsequent developments in Britain confirm that Garrisonian concerns about the implications of Douglass' growing independence were well founded. In fact Douglass' later letter to Webb may have been a rather transparent attempt to win the support of the leading British Garrisonian in disputes with his former allies.

Matters were made worse when Douglass accepted a number of invitations to attend meetings sponsored by the BFASS and its auxiliaries. After rejecting the first invitation from the BFASS to attend one of its meetings on the grounds that the Free Church controversy demanded his full attention, Douglass, persuaded by Thompson, accepted a second invitation to speak at its meeting in Finsbury Chapel. The following month he was also the main speaker at a meeting of the Birmingham auxiliary of the BFASS.[49] Many Garrisonians, with the notable exceptions of Lucretia Mott of Philadelphia and the Reverend S. May, Jr., viewed Douglass' apparent apostasy with some dismay. Douglass, Webb wrote, was being bamboozled by Joseph Sturge, that "intensely bigotted quaker of the Gurneyite school" and was not helping matters by refusing to understand or examine the concerns of his friends in the "old organization." But Douglass, aware of the implications of his actions and the history of sectarian disputes, dismissed these concerns, arguing that abolitionists of "every antislavery creed" would be encouraged by this show

48. Douglass to Richard Webb, September 12, 1850, Isabel Jennings to Chapman, July 2, 1847, Richard Webb to Chapman, May 16, 1846, all in ASB.
49. *Midland Counties Herald*, July 2, 1846.

of unity. Mott and May supported Douglass' action. The invitation, Mott suggested, showed that the members of the BFASS may have repented "their past misdoings" and were now more interested in genuine abolitionist work. May openly praised the BFASS for inviting Douglass, knowing that he was a member of the AASS. When criticism from Boston continued, Douglass, still smarting from the earlier attempts to control his actions, wrote Chapman another stinging rebuke in which he made it plain not only that he had no intention of apologizing for his actions but that he would speak at any meeting "where freedom of speech is allowed and where I may do any thing toward exposing the bloody system of slavery."[50]

While Douglass was determined to maintain his independence, he may not have realized that the BFASS' reasons for courting his favor were not entirely altruistic. An endorsement from Douglass would certainly have enhanced the image of the BFASS, and his mere presence at their meetings attracted thousands who, one suspects, would not have attended otherwise. But Douglass, while enjoying the attention and the opportunity it gave him to promote the cause, never forgot his friends in America. He insisted that his actions were dictated by the best interests of abolitionism. Garrison's visit in July raised the hopes of some British Garrisonians that he would be able to bring Douglass back from his dangerous wanderings. Once Garrison arrived, Douglass, for a while at least, seems to have deliberately adopted a secondary role. Where previously he had been the main attraction at antislavery meetings, during the tour organized by the Anti Slavery League, he initially confined his brief remarks to accounts of slavery. But public demand soon changed that, and even before Garrison's return, Douglass' efforts were again being given place of prominence in local newspaper reports. Rather than reprimanding Douglass, Garrison may have warned Webb and others about the dangers of alienating Douglass by their continuous criticism. In early September, Webb wrote Chapman, "I take back nothing I have said of his defects in the minor points I

50. Foner (ed.), *Life and Writings of Frederick Douglass,* I, 184–86, 165–73; Richard Webb to Chapman, July 16, 1846, Lucretia Mott to Chapman, July 23, 1846, Samuel May, Jr., to John Estlin, September 26, 1846, all in ASB.

complained of, but I admire and value him so much for the cause's sake that I would bitterly regret if any thing occurred to end his usefulness." This was generous praise from Webb, who was always ambivalent in his feelings toward Douglass and always quick to criticize him. The following month he reported that people of the "highest rank" in Edinburgh were competing for Douglass' favors and making him "quite a lion." If Douglass survived such flattery unimpaired, he thought that it would be to the benefit of the cause; but it was quite obvious that Webb had grave doubts about Douglass' ability to remain true to his friends in the face of this attention. Webb left no doubt that many of the "highest rank" were women who in many instances exceeded the bounds of nineteenth-century propriety in their behavior towards Douglass. "I wonder," Webb wrote Chapman, "how he will be able to bear the sight of his wife after all the patting he gets from beautiful, elegant and accomplished women."[51] It was the same accusation that Smyth had used unsuccessfully to discredit Douglass, and it would be made again.

By the end of 1846 it must have appeared to many Garrisonians that Douglass had been finally beguiled from the cause by the women who were actively raising money to purchase his freedom. The originator of the scheme, Anna Richardson of Newcastle, was a critic of Garrisonian abolitionism, and the scheme itself violated the strongly held belief of Garrisonians that fugitives should not be purchased. Garrison himself defended the purchase of Douglass as morally acceptable, but some of his followers, including Wright and Webb, publicly condemned it.[52] Wright, calling on Douglass to reject the transaction, argued that he would wield greater moral power against slavery if he returned as he had left. "It was worth running some risk," he continued, "for the sake of the conflict, and the certain result" of ultimate freedom, for only as "a self-emancipated captive" could Douglass arraign "that piratical Republic before the world." Webb concurred, thinking it foolish to pay "so much money" to a master who had no right to it. Besides, Douglass "was a grand slave and to make him a freeman by the Southern plan, of cash in

51. Richard Webb to Chapman, October 31, September 1, 1846, both in ASB.
52. *Liberator*, January 15, March 5, 1847.

hand and the possession of free papers, make[s] too little of such a glorious Numibian as he is." Unlike Wright, Webb did admit, however, that his "scruples might melt away before the terrible realities of his position" if he were a fugitive liable to recapture.[53] The plan may have embarrassed Douglass and forced him to explain acceptance of it to his Garrisonian friends. His work and popularity abroad, he argued, would make him a prime target for slave catchers on his return home. Moreover, the purchase was not made to recompense the owner; the £150 paid Hugh Auld "to induce him to give up legal claim to something which my friends deemed of more value than money" was like giving up one's purse to a pirate holding a knife at one's throat. More important, his free papers would have a most beneficial effect on attempts to discredit American slavery and isolate those who supported it. "Those papers," he wrote, "will be their condemnation in their own handwriting; and may be held up to the world not only as an evidence of brazen hypocrisy, but as a means of humbling that haughty republic into repentence."[54]

In spite of attempts by both sides to play down the significance of the disagreement by the use of gentle language, public debate of the issue must have further strained relationships between Douglass and his friends, already suspicious of his intentions. The debate and his continuing success also established Douglass in the eyes of many British abolitionists as an able, independent figure, capable of working with all those who wished to see the abolition of slavery. Less concerned about ideological purity, Douglass, like all other black visitors, deliberately and with the full knowledge of his friends, refused to discuss issues that he believed worked against the spread of antislavery sentiments in Britain. Abolitionists, he firmly believed, had to overlook sectarian differences whenever possible if they hoped to achieve their objectives. Many British abolitionists, angered by the radicalism of Collins, Wright, and Garrison, were also anxious to find more "practical" ways to aid antislavery efforts in America. Anna Richardson and her Free Produce movement, which

53. *National Anti Slavery Standard*, May 6, 1847; *Liberator*, Janaury 29, 1847.
54. *Patriot*, February 22, 1847; Foner (ed.), *Life and Writings of Frederick Douglass*, I, 199–206.

was rekindled in 1846, saw Douglass as just such an acceptable alternative. These abolitionists were willing to purchase his freedom, and they were also the main contributors to Douglass' testimonial, which raised $2,175.[55]

Douglass returned home in many ways a new man. In the freedom of Britain he had had time to reflect on his previous life in America. His acceptance by all classes of British society and the knowledge that he had carried the battle to the Free Church, Evangelical Alliance, and the World Temperance Convention and had been primarily responsible for the heightened opposition to American slavery must have enhanced his self-esteem. In turn his popularity must also have strengthened his independent spirit, which even before his departure for Britain had led him to question the restricted role that his co-workers had assigned him in the movement. No one who had experienced such success or felt the warmth of popular acclaim could have been expected to return unaffected and unchanged; and Douglass did not.

But his success also heightened suspicion among his co-workers. When he decided to establish his own newspaper—financed mainly with the proceeds of his testimonial—in spite of opposition from Garrison and others, his British friends rallied to his side. His efforts at Rochester were supported by donations from a wide cross-section of British abolitionists, some of whom still considered themselves Garrisonians. Webb woefully reported to Boston that donations traditionally earmarked for the Boston antislavery bazaar were in 1848 to be shared with Rochester. The Edinburgh Ladies Emancipation Society, he pointed out, was leaving it up "to the option of contributors to send their gifts to Boston or Rochester." The Belfast society was sending nearly all of its money to Rochester, and the Cork and Manchester societies had decided to divide theirs between the two American societies. The following year Elizabeth Pease reported that Carlisle's donations were going to Rochester, and in 1850 Mary Estlin wrote from Bristol that Bridgewater had agreed to contribute to Douglass' efforts. Webb attributed the change to the abolitionists' "strong romantic personal interest" in Douglass and lamented that

55. *British Friend*, December, 1847.

it was not to "Douglass' credit that he should have used his influence in this way for his own benefit and to the damage of the main instrumentality of a cause which has done so much for him."[56] When the break between Rochester and Boston finally came it was Douglass who received the majority of British contributions. Calling the split "unwise on both sides," Jane Wigham reported that it was "exciting great sympathy for Frederick Douglass" in Britain because many believed that he had been "very ill used" by his former friends.[57]

Douglass' popularity can be measured to some extent by the reaction to Julia Griffiths' tour of Britain. In 1855 Griffiths, Douglass' co-worker in Rochester, returned home to England to raise funds to pay off debts on the newspaper. Building on the existing support for Douglass, she quickly increased contributions to Rochester and formed or rekindled a number of female antislavery societies. By the end of the decade, Griffiths claimed that she had formed twenty new societies and reorganized many old ones. The Sheffield Ladies Anti Slavery Association announced that they were organized to aid Douglass' paper and to send aid to fugitives escaping through Rochester. By May, 1857, they already had contributed four hundred pounds to Douglass' paper. In 1856 there were thirty-nine people, of whom only one was a man, collecting contributions for the Rochester bazaar in Britain.[58]

Although Garrisonians had initially decided against any open attack on Griffiths' mission for fear that it would redound to Douglass' benefit, they were obviously responsible for the rumor that Douglass, heavily indebted to Griffiths for the mortgage on his home, had sent her on the mission to raise money to meet this debt. Parker Pillsbury, driven almost to distraction by "Douglass disci-

56. Richard Webb to Chapman, September 26, 1848, Richard Webb to Anne Weston, November 11, 1848, Pease to Chapman, November 19, 1849, Mary Estlin to Weston, September 17, 1850, all in ASB.

57. Eliza Wigham to My Dear Friend, November 9, 1853, in ASB.

58. *Frederick Douglass Paper*, July 4, 1856; Sheffield Ladies Anti Slavery Association, *To the Women of Sheffield* (n.p., n.d.); *Anti Slavery Reporter*, May 1, June 1, 1857; Edinburgh Ladies' New Anti Slavery Association, *Annual Report of the Edinburgh Ladies' New Anti Slavery Association for the Years 1856 and 1857* (Edinburgh, 1858).

ples" as he called them, and vitriolic at the best of times, thought that the mortgage "might be a figurative rather than a legal one. We all know," he wrote May, "that in such a sense they have long been mortgaged to each other and both to the devil, *dropping* the figure." The *Anti Slavery Advocate*, edited by Webb, did its best to publicize the rumor, only to be embarrassed when it was discovered that the mortgage had already been paid off.[59] Douglass' supporters, many of whom were convinced that Boston had dealt with Douglass unfairly, now had ample confirmation of their views.

By the time of his second visit to Britain in 1859, Douglass was by far the most renowned American abolitionist. To a large extent his popularity stemmed from his successes in 1846 and 1847. As Douglas Riach has argued, the enthusiasm his efforts generated increased interest in abolition where it already existed and created it where it did not. The purchase of his freedom and the contributions at his testimonial speak of his popularity. To many he was the epitome of Smilesian success. "In him," one editor observed, "is combined our admiration of a man, whose mind exhibits one of the noblest specimens of self-culture and of his successful pursuit of knowledge under difficulties which the world has ever seen."[60] Because of his determination to underplay differences in the interest of the cause, he was able to partly bridge the gap dividing abolitionists in 1846. Many obviously supported him purely as a statement of opposition to the radicalism of men like Garrison and Wright. When the break with Boston occurred, Maria Webb, a relative of Richard Webb, attributed her support for Douglass to the infidel views of Garrisonianism and to her desire to promote free-black self-reliance and improvement.[61] When in 1857 Douglass wrote the secretary of the Edinburgh New Anti-Slavery Association that Garrison and his friends in America were carrying on a war against him because he had broken with Garrisonianism, "an 'ism' which comprehends op-

59. *Anti Slavery Advocate*, July, 1857; Samuel May, Jr., to Richard Webb, March 9, 1858, Parker Pillsbury to Samuel May, Jr., February 14, 1856, May 4, 1855, all in ASB.

60. Stockport *Advertiser*, n.d., in *National Anti Slavery Standard*, December 24, 1846; Riach, "Ireland and the Campaign Against American Slavery," 385.

61. Maria Webb to Louis Chamerovzow, June 20, 1855, in BFASS.

position to the Church, the ministry, the sabbath, and the Government as Institutions in themselves considered and viewed apart from the question of Slavery," many took heart that "true" and "Christian" abolitionism had finally found a leader of international reputation.[62] Equally, Garrisonians, remembering the views expressed by Douglass during his visit to Britain, could claim with some justification that this was indeed a strange reversal in views.

62. Douglass to the Secretary, Edinburgh New Anti-Slavery Association, September 7, 1857, in FDP.

Chapter 4

A Third
Alternative

The Free Church and Evangelical Alliance controversies significantly contributed to the growing rift between "old" and "new" organizationist supporters in Britain. In spite of Douglass' efforts to bridge the division, the visits of Wright and Garrison made rapprochement between the contending groups almost impossible. Those who drifted away from the radicalism of Garrisonian societies did not automatically join forces with the BFASS. Many provincial abolitionists in Dublin, Belfast, Glasgow, Edinburgh, and Newcastle, jealously guarding their independence from London, found little to attract them in the BFASS. A number of local auxiliaries of the BFASS had already established a tradition of independence, strengthened, one would suspect, by their contacts with Remond, Douglass, and others, who recorded their greatest successes in the provinces. Many others who might have been partial to the BFASS were put off by John Scoble, the cantankerous and vitriolic secretary of the society. Left with a choice between Garrisonian societies and the BFASS, many provincial abolitionists opted for nonaffiliation. As the rift widened in the late 1840s, both "old" and "new" organizationists increasingly retreated into exclusivity from which they fired salvos at one another. When such Garrisonians as Maria Chapman, Anne Weston, Sarah Pugh, J. Miller McKim, and S. J. May visited Britain in the 1850s, they confined their efforts to areas where support was assured. Gone were the days when visitors like Collins, Wright, and Garrison attempted to appeal to the widest possible cross section of British opinion. The one exception was

Parker Pillsbury, whose 1854 visit coincided with an·attempt by Louis Chamerovzow, the new secretary of the BFASS, to bring about a reconciliation between the contending groups. Initially successful, Chamerovzow's efforts soon fell prey to old jealousies.

The tradition established by Remond and followed so successfully by Douglass of appealing to all sections of British abolitionism provided unaffiliated British abolitionists with an alternative. Their catholic appeals may have influenced many British abolitionists to aid the cause of American abolitionism and at the same time to avoid disputes over the merits of either wing of the American movement. British support for vigilance committees and schools and churches for fugitives in Canada, while reaffirming a Christian commitment to the elimination of slavery, avoided the odium of association with radical movements. As sectarian divisions hardened in the late 1840s, black visitors became a third force, an alternative to American abolitionists who advocated increased participation in the American political system and Garrisonians who condemned the Constitution as "an agreement with Hell and a covenant with death." The fact that black visitors were affiliated with one or the other wing of the movement was of little significance; what mattered was that their independent approach provided many British abolitionists with a "practical" alternative.

This is not to suggest that blacks were passive onlookers in this new development; on the contrary, they actively contributed to it. One of the contributors was Henry Highland Garnet, who in 1850 joined the Free Produce movement (FPM) as its agent. The movement was central to British abolitionism before West Indian emancipation and remained important, if peripheral, in subsequent years. Following the 1843 World Anti-Slavery Convention, Joseph Sturge tried unsuccessfully to reactivate the movement with pledges of support from the American Free Produce Association. The failure of British abolitionists to stop the rising importation of slave-grown sugar following the reduction of import duties in 1846 prompted Sturge, J. J. Gurney, G. W. Alexander, and others to advocate the boycott of slave-grown products as one means of bringing about American emancipation. They argued that British purchases of American cotton were partly responsible for the continuation of American slavery and announced that there were a number of British manufacturers willing to produce fabrics from cotton grown by free laborers. Although motivated by moral principles, Gurney and others were convinced that their objectives could be achieved by economic means. Their optimism proved unfounded. British manufacturers cared little about the source of their supplies. The effort sputtered on ineffectively until Henry and Anna Richardson and their daughter Ellen, Quakers from Newcastle, assumed leadership of the movement in 1848. In the summer of 1849 they announced that supplies of free-grown cotton goods were available from Josiah Browne, a Manchester Quaker cotton manufacturer.[1]

It was the Richardsons who invited Garnet to join their efforts in Britain. Soon after his arrival, Garnet undertook an extensive tour of Britain to promote the movement and lecture against slavery. As a fugitive slave, he was able to capitalize on the heightened opposition to American slavery as well as give legitimacy to the work of the FPM. His lectures combined analyses of the nature of American slavery and discrimination and the plight of fugitives and appeals for support of the movement. These moral appeals were reinforced by economic arguments that British dependence on American cotton increased the profits of slaveholders, thereby enhancing their political power. There was an integral relationship, Garnet told his audiences, between the price of cotton in Britain and the value of slaves in America. An increase of one cent per pound of cotton in Britain raised the price of slaves in America by a hundred dollars; when cotton fetched fifteen cents per pound on the British market, the asking price for a slave was a thousand dollars. Britain was participating, therefore, in an international system that promoted American slavery. While America built the "fleetest vessels" and Spain and Portugal provided the crews, "England wove the fabrics that were exchanged for the captive African and forged his chains." The solution, Garnet argued, was the boycott of American cotton and

1. Louis Billington, "British Humanitarians and American Cotton, 1840–1860," *Journal of American Studies*, XI (1977), 316–21; *Anti Slavery Reporter*, May 1, 1845, January 1, 1846; Howard Temperley, *British Antislavery, 1833–1870* (Columbia, S.C., 1972), 165.

the development of alternative sources in India, South Africa, and the West Indies.[2]

Garnet was an immediate success. Thousands attended his meetings and local societies were formed wherever he lectured. In four weeks he claimed that eight associations had been formed, a figure that rose to twenty-six by the end of January, 1851. A Belfast newspaper, ignoring earlier work in order to praise Garnet, observed that he had "excited an interest on the subject of American slavery more intense than that which has previously existed in the history of this town."[3] Garnet was not alone in promoting the movement; J. W. C. Pennington, Alexander Crummell, William Wells Brown, and others joined the effort in other parts of the country. Pennington, for instance, lectured extensively on free produce in Edinburgh and Leeds. He was also one of the supporters of a short-lived project that aimed to settle fugitives from Canada in Jamaica. Crummell was actively involved in the activities of the Birmingham Ladies Negroes' Friend Society (BLNFS), which submitted a memorial to the Queen signed by 59,686 calling for a boycott of slave-labor produce. Displaying their general disregard for sectarian differences, Brown, the leading American Garrisonian in Britain at the time, joined Garnet on a number of occasions in his call for the boycott of American cotton. At an Edinburgh meeting he called for the adoption of "every means" to promote the overthrow of slavery: circulating information in Britain so as to bring pressure on America, refusing communion to slaveholders, boycotting slave-grown produce, and "continuing to assist the true-hearted labourers in the antislavery field, wherever they are to be found."[4]

Brown's Garrisonian allies did not take too kindly to this kind of

2. Gateshead *Observer*, September 21, 1850; Carlisle *Journal*, November 22, 1850; *Banner of Ulster*, January 24, 1851.

3. *Banner of Ulster*, January 3, 1851; *Non-Slaveholder*, November 1, 1850.

4. *Scottish Press*, January 1, 1851, in *Liberator*, January 24, 1851; Birmingham Ladies Negroes' Friend Society, *Twenty Fourth Report* (Birmingham, 1849); Birmingham Ladies Negroes' Friend Society Minute Book, 1837–59 (MS in Public Library, Birmingham, England, reproduced by permission of the Reference Library, Local Studies Department, Birmingham, England); *Non-Slaveholder*, July 1, 1849; *Anti Slavery Reporter*, June 1, 1849, April 1, 1850.

apostasy. Not only were they opposed to the movement, which, they argued, distracted attention away from the true instrumentalities of abolitionism, but they viewed Garnet as one of their major opponents. Mary Estlin informed a coadjutor in Boston that her father had promised to keep a sharp eye on Garnet if he visited Bristol, and John Estlin, in a letter to Weston, castigated Garnet for his "nonsense about freeing the slaves by the quaker Ladies giving up the use of dresses made with American cotton." The whole scheme, the *Anti Slavery Advocate* later argued, was as fruitless as spending time "keeping out the tide with a pitchfork." According to some Garrisonians, Garnet was cutting into traditional support for the Boston bazaar, and Mary Estlin predicted that he and Pennington would "stop our supplies in many quarters for one year at least and sometimes irrevocably."[5] Already smarting from increased British support for Douglass in Rochester, British Garrisonians saw the efforts of Garnet and other "coloured ministers" as a further attempt to erode their support. Andrew Paton and other members of the Glasgow Emancipation Society were worried that Brown's appearance with Garnet would be interpreted as a Garrisonian endorsement of the FPM and would lead to a further diminution of support for their position.

These concerns were legitimate, for the FPM claimed wide support and boasted dozens of local auxiliaries and seven warehouses in London and Manchester. However, the availability and distribution of its goods remained problematic. It never imported more than a few hundred bales of free-grown cotton at a time when Britain was importing almost 2 million bales from the South. There were also complaints of inferior goods, and it proved impossible to ensure that free cotton was not tainted by slavery. In addition, the movement suffered an irreversible setback with the death of Henry Richardson in 1854 and the retirement of Anna Richardson from the antislavery field.[6] What mattered to Garrisonians was not so much that the Free Produce movement was attracting support, but that

5. Mary Estlin to Anne Weston, August 21, 1852, February 13, 1851, John Estlin to Weston, March 1, 1851, all in ASB; *Anti Slavery Advocate*, June, 1858.
6. Billington, "British Humanitarians," 328–30.

many black visitors in Britain were encouraging and exploiting the divisions in British abolitionism. As we shall see, however, Garrisonians were in many cases their own worst enemies. Fitting black visitors into the same rigid and simple categories of the abolitionist schism, they failed to capitalize on their traditional broad appeal. In turn, blacks, particularly the "coloured ministers," confronted by this organized opposition, took their support where they could and joined the broad opposition, splitting the international movement further.

In spite of these conflicts, blacks continued to display a startling degree of unanimity. There were some potentially explosive tensions between them but these were usually papered over in a show of united effort. They continued to work together across party lines, their actions in large measure predicated on the belief that sustaining international support for activities at home was more important than "ideological" purity. William Wells Brown joined forces with Henry Highland Garnet for a series of lectures on American slavery. Ignoring Garrisonian opposition to the FPM, Brown called on his Darlington listeners to boycott American slave-grown cotton and promote free-grown cotton from India. One year later they were together again in Edinburgh at a meeting called to protest the tarring and feathering of Robert Edmonds, a Scotsman who had attempted to teach slaves in South Carolina to read, and to condemn the newly enacted Fugitive Slave Law. Garnet condemned the law and called for the boycott of American cotton, while Brown explained the clauses of the new law and what effect they would have on efforts to support destitute fugitives. The audience requested a second meeting the following night so that Pennington, viewed by many British Garrisonians as their main opponent, could attend. Earlier Pennington and Garnet had worked as an effective team in northeast England and had drawn large crowds to meetings at which they condemned the Fugitive Slave Law and promoted the FPM.[7]

7. Sunderland *Herald*, October 4, 1850; Newcastle *Guardian*, n.d., in *Non-Slaveholder*, November 1, 1850; *Scottish Press*, November 16, 1850; Edinburgh *News*, November 16, 1850, in *Liberator*, December 20, 1850; Darlington and Stockton *Times*, December 22, 1849.

The team of Brown and William and Ellen Craft was by far the most popular in this period. Soon after the Crafts' escape to Britain at the end of 1850, William Craft, leaving his ailing wife with Francis Bishop in Liverpool, hastened to Newcastle to join Brown and continue a partnership that had won much acclaim in America. Ellen joined them later in Scotland. For the next six months the Crafts and Brown toured Scotland and northern and western England, strongholds of British Garrisonianism, lecturing on slavery and temperance. From Newcastle, Brown and Craft traveled to Edinburgh to attend the annual meeting of the Edinburgh Ladies' Emancipation Society in December. Their presentation there followed a simple but most effective plan. Brown spoke first, giving an analysis of the development of American slavery in the South and prejudice in the North that had culminated in the Fugitive Slave Law. He called on his audience to sever all contacts with Americans who supported slavery and to refuse their pulpits to American clergymen who did not openly condemn slavery. Brown was followed by William Craft who narrated the escape from Georgia. William had had limited experience as a public speaker, but he told a captivating tale with suspense and wit. Although British audiences had heard and read of the daring escapes from slavery of men like Douglass and Roper, never before had they heard a tale that involved such boldness and romance. Brown and Craft held three more meetings in Edinburgh before going on to Glasgow to attend the annual meeting of the Glasgow Emancipation Society (GES). The GES, which had been relatively inactive since 1847, used the presence of Brown and the Crafts (Ellen had joined them by then) to call its second meeting in four years. Three thousand people came to hear the fugitives' attack on American slavery.[8] For the next four days they lectured at the Glasgow Trades' Hall where Brown's panorama on American slavery was on display.

From Glasgow they moved on to Aberdeen. By then their reputation was so widespread that large crowds flocked to all of their meetings and to the display of Brown's panorama. Each day was completely taken up with lectures. In the morning school children

8. *North British Mail,* January 7, 1851; *Scottish Press,* January 1, 1851.

came to see the panorama and listen to the fugitives; in the after-noon and evening large crowds came to hear them speak. In these lectures Brown and the Crafts followed the pattern used in Edin-burgh and further developed in Glasgow. Brown spoke against American slavery; William told of their escape; and at the end of his narrative, Ellen was invited onto the stage, adding the last touch of pathos to the carefully orchestrated evening. The approach was guaranteed to excite the strongest protest against American slavery. No country that deliberately destroyed such talent, one local news-paper observed, could seriously claim the mantle of freedom. The appearance of Ellen, who was almost white, crowned their dismay, for it was one thing to enslave a black person but enslaving a white woman was totally reprehensible. Her enslavement became the symbol of southern slavery's barbarity (particularly of the defile-ment of women) for British abolitionists. After their visit to Melrose a local newspaper observed, "no antislavery address by the most eloquent advocate of the cause could more effectively stir up the in-dignation of a Christian audience than did their unvarnished story."[9]

After three months of successful campaigning in Scotland and the north of England, Brown and the Crafts traveled south in April to attend a meeting of the Bristol and Clifton Ladies Anti-Slavery Society (BCLASS). They followed the same pattern in their presen-tation, but by this time, William's lectures showed a marked im-provement and sophistication. The narrative was now placed in the context of an analysis of American slavery. He ridiculed the concept of the happy slave. "God forbid," he thundered, "that there should exist any man in man's form so base, so low, so wretchedly de-graded as to be content to drag out a miserable life in bondage for any tyrant on the face of the earth." He showed that black men in the South, free and slave, had no legal rights against whites and that the laws of the South prohibited the teaching of slaves. Using the experiences of his own family, he demonstrated the ease with which families were broken up and sold separately. A local newspaper commented on William's speech, "the recital of this narrative, which

9. *United Presbyterian Magazine*, February, 1851; Aberdeen *Journal*, February 12, 1851; Kelso *Chronicle*, February 22, 1851.

was told with simplicity but without any attempt at display, produced quite a thrilling effect on the audience." Throughout April and May the Crafts and Brown continued their efforts in the west country, lecturing in such cities as Devonport, Exeter, Bridgewater, Gloucester, and Bath.[10]

As in the case of the GES, the visit of the Crafts and Brown to Bristol helped to reactivate the BCLASS. Formed as an auxiliary of the BFASS in 1840, this society had had a checkered career. For the first six years of its existence it was little more than a paper organization. The visit of Garrison and Douglass to Bristol in 1846 had brought about a brief revival and, more important, had established contacts with Garrisonian abolitionists. Although the BCLASS continued to maintain a delicate neutrality between "old" and "new" organizationists after the visit, it was becoming increasingly dismayed by what it saw as the inactivity of the BFASS. Contacts between Boston and Bristol continued to expand between 1846 and 1850, and these were reinforced by Brown's visit in March, 1850. When the Crafts arrived in Britain they made Bristol their base and held extensive discussions with the BCLASS on the relative merits of the antislavery organizations in America. As late as February 1851, the society was still maintaining a neutral position. However, a perceptible shift towards Garrisonianism appeared after the visit of the Crafts and Brown. The later visit of the Boston abolitionists Maria Chapman and Anne Weston and the lecture tour of George Thompson in September firmly established Bristol as a Garrisonian stronghold.[11]

In a special report published by the BCLASS in 1852, an attempt was made to explain its new posture: "The Crafts described with much emotion the constant, self-denying labours of the Boston abolitionists; the great personal kindness they had received on first settling in that city." But if the Crafts were instrumental in altering the society's stance, they were also being used in the sectarian controversies between "old" and "new" organizationists. The report, for

10. Bristol *Mercury*, April 12, 1851; Gloucester *Journal*, May 25, 1851; Plymouth and Devonshire *Weekly Journal*, May 1, 1851.

11. Bristol and Clifton Ladies Anti-Slavery Society Minute Book (Estlin Papers, Dr. Williams Library, London).

instance, made the rather fantastic claim that the Crafts had never heard of the American and Foreign Anti-Slavery Society (AFASS) prior to their arrival in Bristol, which seems highly improbable. As evidence, the report claimed that the Crafts were not told about the AFASS when they arrived in New York on their escape north. In fact, however, the Crafts did not pass through New York on their escape, and their story was so well known that it seems unlikely that they would have claimed otherwise.[12] However, this was only a minor point in the large concerns of Bristol Garrisonians. More than anything else, they feared that Brown and the Crafts might be lured away by the opposition.

The concern stemmed from their participation in an Edinburgh soirée at which J. W. C. Pennington was present. In a letter to Eliza Wigham, secretary of the Edinburgh Ladies Emancipation Society, John Estlin, the Bristol abolitionist warned against working with Pennington, the "special protege" of the BFASS. Wigham and others were satisfied with Pennington, but Estlin warned that he was not a man to be trusted. He laid down a rule by which black advocates should be judged: "Be always suspicious of coloured men, Ministers especially, who come before the public under the patronage" of the BFASS and be more partial to those who do not. Estlin's daughter Mary found it necessary to defend Brown and the Crafts to Weston in Boston. They had clearly stated their allegiances to Eliza Wigham, she wrote, "but considered her judgement superior to their own from her intimate acquaintance with the parties with whom she had to deal." Wigham had evidently made it clear that "Pennington adorers," who were a majority in the audience, would have protested his exclusion, and to decline participation would have been to present Pennington with a convenient stick with which to beat his opponents. Pennington, Mary Estlin reported, had already exposed his duplicity by questionable "pecuniary transaction," and time would soon work against his popularity. This left only Garnet their

---

12. Bristol and Clifton Ladies Anti-Slavery Society, *Special Report of the Bristol and Clifton Ladies Anti-Slavery Society: During Eighteen Months, from January, 1851, to June, 1853; with a Statement of the Reasons of Its Separation from the British and Foreign Anti-Slavery Society* (London, 1852), 14, 23, 61; Temperley, *British Anti Slavery*, 239–42.

"chief remaining antagonist among the *coloured* ministers (to all of whom *we* have the strongest aversion) and he has had already sundry intimidations, and hints to take care how he plays with edged tools."[13] That kind of bravado was for private consumption; it reaffirmed Estlin's credentials with Garrisonians in America, but did little to undermine the growing popularity of Pennington, Garnet, and the other "coloured ministers."

Garrisonian suspicions of Pennington may have originated with the honorary doctorate in divinity that he received from the University of Heidelberg in December, 1849. The evidence suggests that the movers behind the award were members or supporters of the BFASS. Why Pennington was chosen above the host of other visiting black Americans remains a mystery. The fact that he was a leading member of the AFASS and had worked closely with the BFASS during his first visit to Britain in 1843 may have influenced the decision. Although understandably flattered by the award, Pennington recognized its symbolic value. In a letter to the *British Banner* he observed that although the degree was awarded ostensibly for "his writing, personal character and merits," he recognized that he received it "in trust" for his "people, and as an encouragement to the Sons of Ham to rise with others in the acquisition of learning."[14]

Pennington's stock rose with this recognition of his contributions to the antislavery, peace, and temperance movements. Openly endorsed by supporters of the BFASS and FPM and working through the extensive network of contacts he had established during his first visit, Pennington undertook a tour of Britain on his return from Germany. At one of his meetings in Edinburgh, he argued, as had many other abolitionists, that Paul's epistle to Philemon did not condone slavery, contrary to the views of some advocates of slavery. Onesimus, called a "brother in flesh" and "brother beloved" to Philemon, was a debtor, Pennington said, but this was not the case with American slaves. There was no evidence in the New Testament to suggest that the apostles received slaveholders in the Church. More-

13. Mary Estlin to Weston, May 12, 1851, John Estlin to Eliza Wigham, May 3, 1851, both in ASB.
14. *British Banner*, January 9, 1850; *Patriot*, January 21, 1850.

over, if one claimed that the principle of slaveholding was endorsed by the New Testament, then one should be aware that it was not confined to blacks.[15] This speech was clearly in line with the views of many Garrisonians during the Free Church controversy in 1846; but it was 1849, and most Garrisonians had already accepted the fact that American churches had no intention of expelling slavery supporters from their ranks. Their solution called on Christians to "come out" from churches that refused to adopt an antislavery stance. Pennington, as a leading member of the Third Presbytery of New York, epitomized the abolitionist who condemned slavery while continuing to hold office and communion in proslavery churches.

But it appears that Pennington's opponents, especially the leaders of the GES, were more concerned with the growing strength of Scottish "new" organizations and black support of them. Both Garnet and Pennington were agents of the Glasgow New Association for the Abolition of Slavery and of the women's society formed after one of Garnet's meetings in Dundee to work with the men's society.[16] Pennington also promoted the New York Vigilance Committee (NYVC) throughout Scotland, and he was seen as the major threat by Garrisonians. Initially the GES welcomed him to their meeting where they discussed, among other topics, his position on "fellowshipping slaveholders and slaveholding Ministers." The minutes recorded that the meeting was satisfied with Pennington's position, but because he was in fellowship with the General Assembly of the American Presbyterian church, the committee "as a Committee" did not think it could publicly recognize his position, "ecclesiastically considered," especially in light of its stance on the Free Church and Evangelical Alliance. The meeting agreed that it would be "most expedient" if during his lecture tour he acted "independently of any Society" with the clear understanding that individual members could cooperate with him.[17] The wording seems to sug-

15. *Scottish Press*, December 26, 1849.

16. Dundee, Perth, and Cuper *Advertiser*, December 2, 1851; *North British Mail*, November 5, 1851; Kilmarnock *Journal*, February 19, 1852; Glasgow New Association for the Abolition of Slavery, *Eighth Annual Report* (Glasgow, 1859), 9.

17. Glasgow Emancipation Society Minute Book 4, 1845–1876 (Glasgow Emancipation Society Papers, Smeal Collection, Mitchell Library, Glasgow).

gest that there were differences of opinion among members of the GES and that the decision may have been arrived at in an attempt to forestall possible splits. There matters rested for the remainder of the year while Pennington continued to work with Scottish "new" organizationists and to promote the efforts of the NYVC.

By the end of the year William Smeal, secretary of the GES, was clearly worried that competitors, particularly the newly formed Glasgow New Association for the Abolition of Slavery, were making considerable inroads into traditional areas of GES support. Smeal wrote William Wells Brown in December that he wanted to organize a "vigorous" antislavery meeting at which Brown would be the main speaker. His aim was to reactivate the GES (which had held only one public meeting since the Free Church controversy) as a counter to the anti-Garrisonian "new" society. Smeal was concerned that "new" organizationists also intended to form another men's society and hoped that the Brown meeting would take the wind out of their sails. He informed Brown that "prudence" had prevented the GES from refuting its opponents. The society had not wanted to publicly reveal the split in abolitionists ranks. He hoped that the proposed meeting would answer the society's opponents and clear the society's debts. Smeal made it clear that in his view the "division in our Anti-Slavery camp" was "not a little aided, as we apprehend, by Dr. Pennington."[18]

At one of the meetings organized by the GES for Brown and the Crafts, Smeal and other members of the society launched an attack on the recently formed ladies' "new" society. In response R. Wright, a Glaswegian with no known abolitionist credentials, countered with a series of letters to the *Daily Mail* accusing the GES of supporting radical abolitionists who advocated "un-Christian" views.[19] The debate reopened old disputes between "old" and "new" organizationists but achieved nothing of substance except to confirm the irreconcilability of the division. The GES leadership, however, were not

18. William Smeal to William Wells Brown, December 12, 1850, in ASB.

19. Later published as a pamphlet: Glasgow Female Association for the Abolition of Slavery, *A Defence of the Glasgow Female Association for the Abolition of Slavery from the Misrepresentations of Revs. Messrs. Jeffrey and Scott and Mr. W. Smeal* (Glasgow, 1851).

to be denied; they were convinced that Pennington was the originator of these new problems and that he had to be exposed. They suggested that he had been collecting money under false pretenses and wrote to their American friends for evidence to substantiate these claims. In the meanwhile, Pennington agreed to meet with the society to discuss their concerns. At the January, 1851, meeting he was asked to explain his attempts to raise money for the purchase of his freedom, which according to his narrative had already been collected during a visit to Jamaica in 1846. In a prepared statement Pennington informed the committee that the money raised in Jamaica had been insufficient to pay for his free papers. The meeting also discussed "some points connected with his proceedings in different parts of the Country" and, following his explanations, "resolved itself into a *confidential conversation* no vote being taken regarding the merits of the case each member of Committee being left at full liberty in the meantime to form his own conclusion." A subsequent informal meeting also failed to arrive at any unanimous decision on how to deal with Pennington.[20]

The inconclusiveness suggests either that Pennington persuaded some members of the committee that his actions were legitimate or that his opponents were unable to find sufficient evidence to substantiate their claims. Andrew Paton, a leader of the society, was convinced that Pennington had hidden his true intentions behind a façade of abolitionist activities. Pennington, he told Sydney Howard Gay, did "not exactly ask contributions directly, tho' there can be little doubt this is also one object in view. I strongly suspect there is something decidedly wrong in this ransom business, could we only have it brought out, but unless clear evidence of wrong doing can be obtained, we can do nothing in it."[21] Paton was here prodding Gay to respond to an earlier request for incriminating evidence that he had sent after the January meeting. Paton had told his American co-worker that Pennington was present at a public meeting at which the new female society was formed. He was also the main speaker at a subsequent meeting at which he called for support for the

20. Glasgow Emancipation Society Minute Book 4.
21. William Paton to Sydney Howard Gay, March 21, 1851, in Sydney Howard Gay Papers, Rare Book and Manuscript Library, Columbia University, New York.

NYVC, a request he repeated during a meeting in Kilmarnock where a committee was formed to raise funds. Paton suggested that Gay collect information on the religious affiliations of the leaders of the NYVC to see if they were as unorthodox as those of the AASS. It was rumored, moreover, that Pennington had already collected the six hundred pounds needed to meet the debts of his church, and Paton wondered if any of this had been remitted to New York. "*If not,*" he wrote, "get some of them stirred up to insist on having what money he has collected remitted to them without delay. Ascertain what he writes them as to this money and generally inform me." Praising Brown and condemning the "coloured ministers," Paton found "the *phenomenon* of the coloured D.D.," totally unpalatable.[22]

There is no evidence to suggest that Pennington withheld money collected in Britain from his church; he was able to return without immediate problem to his pastorate in 1852. After Pennington's return to the United States, however, it became abundantly clear that he had not been totally honest when raising money for his purchase. What Paton had only suspected, later events confirmed, but Paton needed irrefutable evidence, and this he lacked. Unable to find it, and unwilling to publicly condemn Pennington on a mere suspicion for fear of further alienating British abolitionists, Garrisonians retreated and bided their time in the hope that his supporters "the quakers and others" would soon realize that "Pennington has been taking them in."[23] Nothing of the kind occurred, and Pennington continued to promote the NYVC, which throughout the 1850s received substantial support from British abolitionists.[24] In the very month of his final meeting with the GES, Pennington's supporters in Dunse started their own drive to raise money for his ransom. Contributions came in from Dunse, Kelso, and Berwick, and within six months, they had raised £98. They paid £54.18.7d to his former owner, and the balance was used to defray the cost of Pennington's

22. Paton to Gay, January 30, 1851, *ibid.*
23. Mary Estlin to Weston, May 8, 1851, in ASB.
24. The NYVC reported that between January 1, 1851, and March 31, 1853, it received $3,166.11 from Britain. *Report of the New York Vigilance Committee* (New York, 1853).

return ticket to America.[25] The conclusion of this transaction seems to confirm the suspicions of Smeal and Paton. It is not at all clear what Pennington had done with the money collected in Jamaica and Britain before 1851; in addition, £54.18.7d seems a rather trifling sum to pay for a fugitive D.D.

Interestingly, the controversy seems to have affected Pennington after his return to America. In January, 1853, the Third Presbytery of New York elected him moderator. It is surprising that Pennington accepted the post, for he must have known that his opponents would make capital out of his decision to accept an office in a church that had repeatedly refused to take an abolitionist stand. The effects of the controversy in Scotland were reflected in his address to his presbytery later in the year. He praised a resolution passed earlier calling on southern presbyteries to provide statistics on the number of slaves in their churches as "a *manly vindication* of the principles of *Christian discipline.*" "Some of *us,*" he told his listeners, "who have travelled abroad have been made to smart under the odium of this common-fame report," of Presbyterians holding slaves. Regretting that some Presbyterian theologians had "undertaken to justify slavery from the Bible," he called for a "*fair and open discussion*" of the issue. In conclusion, he observed that he felt "the uncomfortableness of this position" but still trusted "in the workings of our system to bring us unanimously to the ground now occupied by our United Presbyterian brethren in Scotland, and other bodies of Christians in that country and this." Despite his disclaimers, however, American Garrisonians and some blacks gave him no quarter, and Pennington was reduced to *ad hominem* attacks on his opponents. In one letter to *Frederick Douglass Paper* he defended his position: "I have yet to learn that a mere profession of abolitionism gives any white man a right to take me by the coat button and lead me whithersoever he will."[26]

Although the opposition of the GES had little effect on Penning-

25. *Kelso Chronicle,* January 24, 1851; *Scottish Press,* June 28, 1851.

26. *Frederick Douglass Paper,* May 4, 1855, June 9, 1854, February 23, April 6, May 11, 1855; *Pennsylvania Freeman,* February 24, 1853; J. W. C. Pennington, *Christian Zeal: A Sermon Preached Before the Third Presbytery of New York in Thirteenth Street Presbyterian Church, July 3, 1853* (New York, 1854), 13–14.

ton's activities in Britain, it did cause dissension among British Garrisonians and may have lent further justification to the Edinburgh Ladies Society's decision to withhold contributions to the Boston bazaar. Paton was convinced that Pennington and his supporters had deliberately contrived to undermine support for Garrison by inviting Brown and the Crafts to attend the Edinburgh meeting. When Brown and the Crafts ignored his advice, participated in the meeting, and failed to openly endorse Garrison, he "scolded them." Brown responded with a scathing letter castigating Paton for his presumptuousness.[27] Since his arrival in Britain, Brown had displayed an independence that did not always meet with the approval of his Garrisonian allies. But they had learned from experience that they stood to gain nothing from attempts to control the activities of black supporters. Brown, however, must have been more diplomatic in his dealings with British Garrisonians to have won the admiration of Webb, who found him "excellent company, full of anecdotes, has graphic and dramatic powers of no mean order, and a keen appreciation of character. . . . He and I get on so pleasantly together, and he is so much beloved by my friends that I naturally look on him as a perfect rock of sense." Although he was "not so great as Douglass," Webb found him less "haughty and impatient." Mary Estlin agreed, adding that, unlike Douglass, Brown was not likely to be accused of womanizing, for he was not a "lady's man."[28] These views never changed even when Brown endorsed the Reverend Edward Hoare and Ellen Richardson's plan to raise money for his ransom. It appears that Hoare of Tunbridge Wells had initiated the plan in 1852 with a letter to Brown's former master offering to pay fifty pounds for his ransom, but his master demanded a hundred pounds. There the matter rested until early 1854 when Ellen Richardson reopened the drive after Brown's master lowered his demand to sixty pounds. The drive aimed to raise more than the required amount for the ran-

27. Mary Estlin to Weston, August 5, 1851, in ASB; Clare Taylor (ed.), *British and American Abolitionists* (Edinburgh, 1974), 362–63.
28. William E. Farrison, *William Wells Brown: Author and Reformer* (Chicago, 1969), 167; Taylor (ed.), *British and American Abolitionists*, 339; *National Anti Slavery Standard*, September 13, 1849.

som, any extras going towards the cost of return tickets for Brown and his daughter, who had recently completed her education in London and Paris.[29]

Although in America the *Pennsylvania Freeman* condemned the purchase of Brown's freedom, in Britain Garrisonians acquiesced.[30] This was in part because of their past experiences with Douglass and in part because of Brown's contributions to their efforts. He worked closely with John Estlin, George Thompson, Robert Smith, and others in the formation of the Anglo-American Anti-Slavery Association, and the publication of the *Anti Slavery Advocate*. But their attitude towards him may also have been influenced by the fact that Brown was having his share of troubles with John Scoble. Scoble considered Brown an intractable Garrisonian, openly opposed him, and refused to include reports of his meetings in the *Anti Slavery Reporter*. Joseph Sturge of Birmingham agreed with Scoble's position although others, like William Tanner of Bristol, argued quite convincingly that Brown, in spite of his Garrisonian association, was "free from party influence."[31] But Brown had other problems to deal with: in early 1850 a letter from his estranged wife appeared in the New York *Tribune* accusing him of deserting his family, being unfaithful, and being so popular with "Abolition ladies" that he no longer wanted "his sable wife." It appeared that Mary Estlin's earlier observation was incorrect! The accusation caused a stir in Britain and "new" organizationists wrote Tappan for confirmation. After extensive inquiries Tappan reported that opinion was split, some supporting Brown; others his wife. Given the inconclusiveness of the inquiries, Joseph Sturge suggested that the matter be dropped in the interest of the cause. But the accusations not only persisted, they were embellished; Brown was further accused of touring Britain in the company of another woman. Brown, who had pre-

29. See broadside issued by Ellen Richardson, Ellen Richardson to Louis Chamerovzow, February 23, 1854, both in BFASS; *Kentish Mercury and Home Counties Advertiser*, September 3, 1853.

30. *Pennsylvania Freeman*, April 20, 1854.

31. William Tanner to John Scoble, April 20, 1850, Joseph Sturge to Scoble, December 5, 1849, both in BFASS.

viously maintained that his domestic affairs were no concern of others, was forced to issue a public disclaimer refuting the accusations.[32] There the matter rested until Brown's condemnation of Josiah Henson's activities in Britain infuriated Scoble. Henson arrived in Britain in early 1851 to raise money to pay off debts incurred by the Dawn Institute in Canada. As early as 1838, British abolitionists had contributed to the establishment of schools for fugitives in Canada. The visit of Hiram Wilson and James Fuller in 1843 netted a thousand pounds for building schools and employing teachers.[33] But from its inception the Dawn Institute was plagued with problems and remained financially insolvent. As if this were not enough, political disputes threatened the existence of the institute and the settlement to which it was attached. Henson was at the center of these controversies. Not noted for organizational and financial acumen, Henson was accused by his opponents of misappropriation of funds and faulty administration. He owed Amos Lawrence, Samuel Elliot, and J. J. Bowditch of Boston between $2,700 and $2,800 on a loan that was to be repaid from the proceeds of lumber shipped from Dawn to Boston.[34]

Soon after his arrival the *Liberator* reprinted a statement signed by two trustees of the Dawn Institute warning supporters in Britain that Henson had no credentials "worthy of credit" and was not a man to be trusted. The Reverend Edward Matthews, an emissary of the American Free Baptist Mission Society, arrived in Britain in early 1851 with the express purpose of undermining Henson's efforts. Matthews, encouraged by Bristol Garrisonians, circulated the trustees' statement to a number of leading British abolitionists. In April, George Sturge, a supporter of the BFASS, attempted to mediate the dispute by suggesting the formation of a committee to investigate the claims of Matthews. The committee, which met in July, exonerated Henson of any wrongdoing following Matthews' admission that the resolutions he had circulated from a Chatham, Ontario, meeting had not actually been passed. Soon after, Scoble and Hen-

32. Farrison, *William Wells Brown*, 168–70, 201; Joseph Sturge to Scoble, July 18, 1850, in BFASS; *Liberator*, July 12, 1850.

33. *Anti Slavery Reporter*, September 20, 1843.

34. Amos Lawrence to Scoble, March 30, 1851, in BFASS.

son left for Canada ostensibly to investigate the conditions of fugitives there; Scoble's real purpose, however, was to carry out an on-the-spot investigation of the accusations. Satisfied that the accusations were unfounded, they returned to Britain where Henson successfully raised $7,500.[35]

In 1851 Brown wrote Garrison warning that Henson was the agent of a secret plan to persuade blacks in Canada to emigrate to the West Indies. It was part of Brown's wider attack on Henson, whom he accused of raising money by deliberately belittling the improvements made by fugitives and of planning to take English teachers out to Canada despite an adequate supply of competent black teachers who could minister to the needs of the fugitives.[36] It is impossible to determine whether Henson was actually involved in such a scheme. He later denied any support for West Indian emigration, but proposals for West Indian emigration were circulating in 1851. Interestingly enough, the idea had Pennington's support. At a meeting in Kelso he approved the suggestion of sending fugitives to Jamaica where, he said, they could cultivate cotton, rice, and other staples. These men and women of "strong muscle and sinew," who "had learned the first lessons of civilization" were more skilled than the indentured laborers sent to the island. Such a scheme would not only benefit the West Indies but also prove that free labor was more profitable than slavery. Some Scots from Berwick had already asked Earl Grey, the colonial secretary, for the government's reactions to their proposal and were told that the American government's views would have to be canvassed before the plan could be entertained. In a letter to Grey, Pennington supported the scheme and argued that, given southern influence in American government and the government's partiality to African colonization, there was little chance that the United States would give the proposal its blessing. Grey agreed

---

35. *National Anti Slavery Standard*, May 5, 1853; John Lobb (ed.), *The Autobiography of the Rev. Josiah Henson* (London, 1890), 128–32. For a full discussion of the dispute, see Alexander Lowell Murray, "Canada and the Anglo-American Anti Slavery Movement: A Study in International Philanthropy" (Ph.D. dissertation, University of Pennsylvania, 1960), 459–65; *Patriot*, July 15, 1852; George Sturge to Scoble, April 1, 1852, in BFASS; *American Baptist*, n.d., in *Liberator*, April 11, 1851.

36. *Frederick Douglass Paper*, June 24, 1853; *Liberator*, October 24, 1851.

but suggested that the decision ultimately rested with blacks themselves and not with the efforts of the British government.[37]

It is difficult to understand why Brown should so oppose the
scheme. He himself had suggested in a letter to the *Times* that British philanthropists should look into the feasibility of sending destitute fugitives in England to the West Indies.[38] Granted Brown's suggestion dealt only with the rising number of fugitives fleeing the
Fugitive Slave Law and was specifically voluntary, but Pennington
and others could also claim that their plan was voluntary and that it
was intended to deal with a difficult situation in Canada. From these
facts, it seems clear Brown's target was not the plan but Henson
and, through him, Scoble who apparently was still repeating the
rumor that Brown had abandoned his wife. By the summer of 1852,
Brown was threatening to sue Scoble for "untrue and slanderous
statements." George Sturge, who seems to have been the arbiter in
all disputes involving Scoble, suggested that Brown and Scoble submit their cases to an impartial committee. Brown agreed to the suggestion, but the dispute evidently died with the second departure of
Scoble for Canada.[39]

In spite of their serious differences, Brown attended public meetings of the BFASS, particularly their annual meetings. The period of
rapprochement between British abolitionists following the departure of Scoble increased these contacts. But they were short-lived,
and once again Brown found himself the center of a dispute between
"old" and "new" organizationists. The reconciliation engineered by
Louis Chamerovzow had almost collapsed during the early months
of Parker Pillsbury's visit to Britain. Chamerovzow's attempts to
hold it together were threatened by Pillsbury's insistence that "new"
organizationists openly recognize the work of the AASS. Pillsbury
was right in his contention that, if the BFASS was sincere in its
efforts to reunite the movement, it had to recognize the contribution
of a society it had long vilified. But by making recognition the price
of cooperation, Pillsbury effectively destroyed Chamerovzow's ef-

37. *Scottish Press*, March 1, 1851; *Kelso Chronicle*, January 3, 1851; *Anti Slavery
Reporter*, August 1, 1850.
38. London *Times*, July 3, 1851, in *Liberator*, July 27, 1851.
39. George Sturge to Scoble, May 26, 1853, June 10, 7, 12, 1852, all in BFASS.

forts; only time and extensive cooperation could have healed the wounds caused by the rift of 1840. In summer, 1854, Chamerovzow accused Brown of deliberately delaying a letter from Pillsbury sent to him through Brown. The letter, sent from Paris, contained Pillsbury's refusal to attend a meeting organized by the BFASS. Garrisonians, already sceptical about Chamerovzow's intentions instituted an investigation into the charges and agreed, not surprisingly, that Brown was blameless. Thompson admonished Chamerovzow for his actions and Webb wrote Boston that "this Brown letter affair is a very sad one, and shows an amount of duplicity, meanness and unscrupulousness that leaves one no room to hope for a continuance of the *entente cordiale* with Mr. Chamerovzow or with New Broad St."[40] This affair contributed to the final breakdown of cooperation between the two factions of the movement.

Of all the black supporters of Garrison who visited Britain, Brown seems to have adhered most closely to the "party line." This may account for the absence of any conflict with Webb, who at one time or another alienated every other black Garrisonian he met. As we have seen, Brown's affiliations did not hinder him from working with blacks like Pennington and Garnet who were considered "new" organizationists. But he was never reluctant to criticize the "coloured ministers" who almost drove British Garrisonians to distraction. Following an Exeter Hall meeting for Calvin and Harriet Beecher Stowe, Brown wrote Garrison that the Reverend Samuel Ringgold Ward had effectively exposed the hypocrisy of American churches "in a way that caused Professor Stowe to turn more than once upon his seat. I have but little faith," he went on, "in the American clergy—either colored or white; but I believe Ward to be not only one of the most honest, but an uncompromising and faithful advocate of his countrymen. He is certainly the best colored minister that has yet visited this country."[41] Ward had just arrived, and one suspects that Brown would have changed his mind when Ward became an active ally of "new" organizationists. But even Brown

40. Richard Webb to Samuel May, Jr., August 16, 1854, in ASB; Taylor (ed.), *British and American Abolitionists*, 408; F. W. Chesson Diary, July, 1854–October, 1855, in RED.

41. *Liberator*, June 3, 1853.

showed his independence when he thought it necessary. His letter to Paton and his agreement to have himself ransomed show that he maintained some flexibility in dealing with other abolitionists.

By now it must have been clear to British Garrisonians that blacks would rebel at attempts to control their activities. Yet, in the case of the Crafts, Garrisonians reverted to the old approach that had so alienated Douglass. Always patronizing towards them, some British Garrisonians seemed genuinely amazed when the Crafts rejected any of their suggestions, especially since they had been instrumental in organizing their successful lecture tours and raising money for their education at Ockham School in Surrey. The Crafts never allowed their support for Garrison to get in the way of a broad appeal to British abolitionists. Not only did they work with the BFASS, but in 1853 William publicly supported the purchase of a slave family in violation of Garrisonian principles. He argued that the family, whom Garnet was trying to redeem, was not the usual case. He was strongly "opposed to giving slaveholders money for refugees after they had fought their way through many perilous difficulties, and reached a land of liberty. However, the Weimms family does not come under this head, and therefore, I deeply sympathise with them: in fact were my dear wife and babe, or myself again in slavery, I should most heartily concur in any plan that might be devised for our restoration in liberty."[42] Matters were made worse when William ignored the advice of his Bristol supporters and decided to open a boardinghouse in London. He was determined to show that fugitives should not depend solely on the benevolence of British supporters—a position to which most British Garrisonians subscribed. Therefore, he was understandably dismayed when Webb attributed his decision to pride and secretiveness and John Estlin wrote the Reverend Samuel May, Jr., rather condescendingly that William was "suspicious and self-willed, but . . . really a good fellow."[43]

These internal differences appear insignificant in the face of larger Garrisonian fears that the growing popularity of black oppo-

42. *Slave*, March, 1853.
43. John Estlin to Samuel May, Jr., November 3, 1853, Richard Webb to Maria Chapman, May 29, 1853, both in ASB.

nents not only hindered their efforts but also seriously threatened their survival. As we have seen, the GES, the strongest Garrisonian society in the 1840s, was in 1850 anxiously awaiting the arrival of Brown and the Crafts, hoping that the famous fugitives would increase its stock in the eyes of the public. They did attract three thousand people to the meeting, but those who attended were more anxious to see and hear the fugitives than to promote the cause of the society. The GES continued to languish, and by 1852 the locus of British Garrisonian abolitionism had shifted to the small cadre of abolitionists in Bristol.

Throughout this period, the popularity of black visitors continued unabated. Wherever they lectured thousands attended. It would have been surprising indeed if they had not harnessed this popularity for their cause, which by 1850 had grown increasingly independent of both factions of the movement in America. The growing independence of blacks at home was due not only to the failure of abolitionists to effect changes in the system of slavery in the South and discrimination in the North but also to successes abroad that must have enhanced their self-worth and convinced many of their own abilities. While black Americans continued to work with the BFASS, the organization's support in the 1850s came mainly from the many provincial societies that emerged in the years after 1846. Although many of these were harshly anti-Garrisonian and partial to the BFASS, support for the fugitive in America and Canada was their primary goal. Societies were formed with the express purpose of sending support to the NYVC and other organizations aiding fugitive slaves and to aid other black causes like Douglass' newspapers. By the early 1850s blacks had become a third force in the Anglo-American antislavery movement, one that attracted an increasing share of British support in the years before the Civil War. While support for the Boston bazaar diminished during the decade, black causes continued to attract increasing support. In spite of the controversy, Henson managed to raise $7,500; Ward collected $7,000 for the Canadian Anti-Slavery Society; and contributions continued to pour into the coffers of the NYVC and to support the construction of churches and schools in Canada.

Smeal was right when he observed that Pennington had "succeeded in organizing a *New* Female Association for the Abolition of Slavery" connected with the NYVC, but it was not, as Robert Bingham has suggested, solely because "he had been rebuffed by the GES due to his church's affiliation with the slaveholding churches and his anti-Garrisonian attitudes."[44] There appears to have been sufficient dissension among members of the society to give Pennington hope that he could win their endorsement. When this failed, he turned to other means. Pennington had other options; the GES had none. Confronted by growing isolation and a dry treasury, they tried in vain to hold the line against their opponents. Operating from a position of strength, blacks remained aloof from sectarian squabbles. Pennington never publicly reacted to his critics while in Britain; he had no need to. Only Ward of all the "coloured ministers" defended the actions of the "three Maryland lads"—himself, Pennington, and Garnet—from the attacks of American Garrisonians, whom he called patronizing and racist. In many instances they were able to bring together British abolitionists of differing persuasions. For example, Garnet's Belfast meetings in July, 1851, won the endorsements of many who stood on opposing sides during Douglass' campaign against the Free Church. This pattern continued throughout the decade and when Sarah Parker Remond, an abolitionist with unimpeachable Garrisonian credentials, held meetings with Chamerovzow and lectured with Douglass during his second tour of Britain, her colleagues offered no resistance.[45]

This third alternative produced a proliferation of causes, all competing for British support. By the end of the decade Julia Griffiths Crofts reported:

> The subject of slavery is certainly being brought considerably before our people at this time, and subscriptions towards some branch of the cause are being levied in all directions. In one town we have Mr. Mitchell begging for a chapel and school in To-

44. Robert LeBaron Bingham, "The Glasgow Emancipation Society, 1833–1876" (M.Litt. thesis, University of Glasgow, 1973), 197; Smeal to Chamerovzow, April 16, 1853, in BFASS.

45. *Anti Slavery Reporter*, July 1, 1859, January 1, February 1, 1860; *Banner of Ulster*, August 12, 1851; *Frederick Douglass Paper*, April 13, 1855.

ronto. In another, Mr. Troy, collecting for a similar object in Canada West. *Here*, there is Rev. William King [white], asking contributions for Buxton settlement; and *there* is Mr. Day, raising funds towards starting a newspaper. Then we have a host of colored friends going up and down the country east, west, north and south, collecting money to buy their various relatives out of slavery.[46]

Many contributors to these individual causes, aware of the social cachet gained from their support, no longer seemed overly concerned about abolitionism and the large issues raised by early abolitionists. "Money-raising for individual 'causes'" Brian Harrison observed in his discussion of Victorian philanthropy, "often led philanthropists to ignore the interrelation of social ills, and promoted competition where co-operation was most desperately needed."[47]

The emergence of blacks as a third force in Anglo-American abolitionism seriously threatened their traditionally united front in Britain. Once Douglass became an alternative to the "old" and "new" societies, it became necessary for him to defend his domain. As in the case of the American abolitionist split in 1840, differences between Douglass and other blacks had international consequences. The Douglass-Garnet conflict, which first emerged in 1843 over Garnet's advocacy of violence, came to a head when Garnet accepted Henry Richardson's invitation to tour Britain as an agent of the Free Produce movement. Douglass had initially supported Richardson's invitation to Henry Bibb, the fugitive slave, but when Bibb declined and was replaced by Garnet, Douglass found it impossible to conceal his anger. Not only had Garnet never supported the FPM in America, but his advocacy of violence, according to Douglass, expressly contradicted abolitionist principles of nonviolence. How could such a person, Douglass asked, "appeal to the moral sense of England, and ask the moral aid of England?" Douglass was also concerned that Garnet would attack his *North Star* and would at-

46. *Douglass Monthly*, November, 1860, June, 1861.

47. Brian Harrison, "Philanthropy and the Victorians," *Victorian Studies*, IX (1966), 367.

tempt to undermine the support in Britain on which the paper heavily depended. Interestingly, the Garrisonian *Anti Slavery Bugle* agreed
that Douglass' fears were well founded: "That he will misrepresent
and malign Douglass in Great Britain we have no doubt, and therefore we anticipate that he will do more harm than good."[48]

Recognizing the popularity of his antagonist, Garnet thought it
expedient to explain to some friends the reasons for his visit to Britain. He was going, he wrote Lewis Tappan, to promote not only the
FPM but, more important, "the cause of freedom generally." A year
later on the eve of his departure he seemed to have lowered his
sights, however, for he wrote George Whipple of the American
Missionary Association that he had agreed to work for the FPM, a
cause that "deeply interests me, and I believe with others, that it is
the only medium through which we can bring the English people to
work efficiently to destroy the African Slave trade and promote the
cause of freedom throughout the world." Garnet was obviously
concerned about the impact of Douglass' criticism on his visit to
Britain. Before leaving he toured northern cities lecturing on the
FPM to mainly black audiences.[49]

Although it appears that Douglass also wrote letters to his British supporters warning against Garnet, these seem to have had little
impact on Garnet's activities. Garrisonians opposed to the FPM and
the activities of the "coloured ministers" were disappointed that
Douglass' attacks proved totally ineffective. Observing that Pennington was running into trouble "getting money . . . under false
pretenses," Elizabeth Pease, for instance, asked her American friends
to supply her with incriminating evidence on Garnet. She reported
that in spite of Douglass' views she found Garnet "pleasing"; he not
only won friends wherever he went but was "intelligent as well as

48. *Anti Slavery Bugle*, August 18, 1849; *North Star*, n.d., in *Liberator*, August 10,
1849; Philip Foner (ed.), *The Life and Writings of Frederick Douglass* (6 vols.; New
York, 1950–78), IV, 142–44; *Anti Slavery Reporter*, May 1, 1848; Joel Schor, *Henry
Highland Garnet: A Voice of Black Radicalism in the Nineteenth Century* (Westport,
Conn., 1977), 103–107.

49. *Non-Slaveholder*, June 1, 1850; *Impartial Citizen*, n.d., in *Non-Slaveholder*,
March 1, 1850; Henry Highland Garnet to George Whipple, July 10, 1850, Garnet
to Lewis Tappan, August 25, 1849, both in AMA.

agreeable."[50] Other blacks also ran into opposition from Douglass in this period. Ward reported soon after his arrival in Britain that he was "quickly followed by a paragraph in Mr. Frederick Douglass' Paper—the animus of which, was unmistakably characteristic." Brown also accused Douglass of writing letters to "distinguished Abolitionists in Great Britain" that were intended to hinder his efforts.[51] Although competition between leading black Americans bred conflict, it never led to the irreconcilable splits so characteristic of the larger movement. In this sense, blacks continued throughout the decade to present a united front in their efforts to maintain the moral cordon. These disputes may have changed some of its contours and may even have weakened it somewhat but they were never strong enough to breach it.

More black American leaders visited Britain between 1848 and 1854 than at any other period. They went for diverse reasons. Alexander Crummell went to raise money to build a church for his New York congregation, and J. W. C. Pennington, while attributing his visit to the presence of the Reverend John Miller of Maryland, an advocate of the American Colonization Society, also collected money to pay off debts incurred by his church. William Wells Brown went as a delegate to the Peace Congress in Paris and stayed five years in Britain. Josiah Henson was there raising funds for the Dawn Institute in Canada, and Samuel Ringgold Ward for the Canadian Anti-Slavery Society. William and Ellen Craft found refuge from slave catchers, and William G. Allen from the mob that had driven him out of Fulton, New York, for marrying one of his white students. Henry Highland Garnet, as we have seen, was invited to work as an agent of the FPM. Of these Brown and the Crafts had strong Garrisonian credentials, while Ward, Garnet, Pennington, Crummell, and Henson were supporters of political abolitionism. Allen, although influenced by Garnet while a student at Oneida Institute in upstate New York, seems to have moved easily between the two factions of the movement.

50. Pease to Dear Friend, March 25, 1851, in ASB.
51. *Frederick Douglass Paper*, March 16, 1855; *Provincial Freeman*, July 8, 1854.

More important for the cause, Brown, Pennington, and Crummell were there prior to the passage of the Fugitive Slave Law in 1850 and were able to capitalize on the increased sympathy for the slave generated by its passage. They were later joined by the Crafts, Henry "Box" Brown, Allen, Ward, and a host of lesser-known fugitives, all victims in one way or another of the new law. A London newspaper commenting on the importance of their agency at this juncture observed, "we can, at least, thank the Fugitive Slave Law for having sent amongst us a band of zealous and intelligent witnesses against slavery, who will not allow public feeling here to subside on the question. The slaveocracy could scarcely do themselves a worse injury than by driving forth from their country, on account of the colour of their skin a Pennington, a Brown and a Garnet, to proclaim the wrongs of their race throughout Europe."[52]

The law, part of the Compromise of 1850, both facilitated the recapture of fugitives settled in northern communities and, by denying the right of habeas corpus to suspected fugitives, threatened even free blacks with possible enslavement. Northern black communities were thrown into a panic by the law. From Boston, New York, Syracuse, Philadelphia, Cleveland, Detroit, and Pittsburgh, hundreds of blacks fled to the safety of Canada. Others held their ground, pledging to resist the law by any means. A meeting of Boston blacks, for example, formed the League of Freedom, which called on blacks to remain in the city and resist "this ungodly anti-republican law." The league proclaimed, "The liability of ourselves and families becoming its victims, at the caprice of Southern menstealers imperatively demanded an expression whether we will tamely submit to chains and slavery, or whether we will, at all and every hazard, *live* and *die* freemen."[53] But resistance, as the Crafts quickly found out, was fruitless in the face of government determination to enforce the law. Even though local resistance forced the slave catchers to flee Boston, when President Fillmore pledged the support of troops to enforce the law, the Crafts had no choice but to leave the country for the safety of Britain. They became the most famous of the many Ameri-

52. *Nonconformist*, n.d., in *Anti Slavery Reporter*, June 2, 1851.
53. *Liberator*, October 11, 1850.

can fugitives who found asylum in Britain in the decade before the Civil War.

The law gave a new impetus to the international movement. The abolition of the slave trade in Washington, D.C., one aspect of the compromise, was condemned as a ruse aimed at stemming the tide of foreign criticism and removing the glaring anomaly of clanking chains and "the groans of the wretched slaves" from a capital where "the tyranny and despotism of Europe [are] eloquently denounced and sympathy expressed for people struggling for liberty."[54] As they had done in the past, blacks led the opposition to the new law. Their warnings of growing southern power throughout the forties were confirmed by the clauses of the law. In the months leading up to its passage, they took every opportunity to explain and condemn its objectives: it was nothing more than a transparent attempt, they argued, to promote the system of slavery. More important, fugitives like William Wells Brown, Pennington, and Garnet symbolized both black potential and the destructiveness of slavery. To the middle classes they were the quintessential self-made men, who by industry and application had achieved self-respect in the face of overwhelming odds. Brown, like others, was willing to exploit these sentiments. He usually opened his lectures with apologies for his deficiencies, pointing out that they had resulted from an oppressive and dehumanizing system. He would then deliver an eloquent lecture that left his audience stunned and wondering how much potential was being destroyed by such a barbarous system of oppression. The working classes who continued to attend their lectures in large numbers saw in these fugitives examples of successful resistance to oppression and, as we have seen, in many instances demanded that the lecturers recognize the similarity between slavery and the exploitation of labor in Britain.

Slavery, which separated families, encouraged licentiousness, maimed and destroyed human life, was now further sanctioned by federal law. How, blacks asked, could a country that claimed to be free and civilized enact such a law in the middle of the nineteenth century? The question struck a responsive chord in a country pre-

54. *Anti Slavery Reporter*, November 1, 1850.

paring for the inauguration of the Great Exhibition at the Crystal Palace, that symbol of peace and civilization. The demonstration staged by William Wells Brown, the Crafts, and their British supporters that summer had some effect. Certainly, it embarrassed American visitors, who throughout the summer of 1851, complained of British interference in America's domestic concerns. Moreover, the presence of many American clergymen at the exhibition provided blacks and their British supporters with an opportunity to re-open the issue of the relationship of American churches to slavery. Although it never again assumed the centrality of the 1846 controversies, the issue remained an important weapon in the hands of abolitionists. On his first visit to Bristol in April, 1850, Brown called for a boycott of the American Tract Society, which, he pointed out, had "recently given a prize of £100 for the best essay against the 'vice' of dancing" but had "never published a word against the system of slavery—against the slave dancing at the end of a cowhide."[55] Brown and others had continued to attack American churches in their lectures, but it was not until the summer of 1851 that the issue once again became vital in the campaign to isolate proslavery American churches and clergymen.

At the annual meeting of the Congregational Union of England and Wales, the Reverend Joseph Fletcher called for a strong condemnation of American brethren who refused to advocate excommunication of proslavery clergymen and churches. In support, Garnet suggested that the union "unchristianize every American brother without regard to particular circumstances." The Reverend J. W. Chickering, a visiting American clergyman, opposed a resolution of such sweeping condemnation, associated in his view with "the worst form of Radicalism" in America. Peeved by continuing British criticism, Chickering suggested to his host that, if these churchmen were opposed to having American clergymen at their meetings, they should not invite them. Dismissing Chickering's remarks as largely irrelevant, the meeting resolved to refuse fellowship to slaveholders and to supporters of slavery and the Fugitive Slave Law.[56] It would

55. Bristol *Mercury*, April 20, 1850.
56. *Anti Slavery Reporter*, June 2, 1851; *Nonconformist*, May 25, 1851.

have been better for Chickering if he had kept quiet. Over the next few months a bitter transatlantic debate raged over his abolitionism. Lewis Tappan criticized him for keeping his abolitionism muted while he was in America. Tappan's main concern, as he told Scoble, was that "no one who goes from this country to England will acknowledge that he is favorable to the continuance of Slavery. Oh no!—They all consider Slavery an 'evil'—wish the country was rid of it—the gospel will effect it in due time—sorry the abolitionists are so rabid etc. etc." In his defense, Chickering argued that he was an abolitionist at heart even though he did not belong to any abolitionist party. Such a statement was not likely to satisfy his critics. The editor of the *British Banner* did come to Chickering's defense, but other American clergymen at the meeting only added fuel to the fire by arguing that the Fugitive Slave Law, however abhorrent, had to be obeyed. Garnet took great pleasure in denouncing these American clergymen who claimed to be antislavery.[57]

The relationship of churches to slavery was important only as it involved American churches. For example, when the existence of slavery in the Scottish United Presbyterian church's Old Calabar mission in west Africa was made public in 1854, it raised little protest from British abolitionists. Duncan Rice attributes this to a number of factors: the weakness of the GES, the absence of any American visitors, and the fact that many Glasgow "new" abolitionists were members of the United Presbyterian church. Finally, Rice claims, "church rivalries had on the whole softened" in the 1850s.[58] However, he overlooks the fact that Ward, the Crafts, and Allen were very active in Britain in 1854 and that none of them raised the issue of the Old Calabar mission. This silence can be explained in part by their and other abolitionists' acceptance of the importance of missionary activities. Both Crummell and Ward were convinced that

57. *Scottish Press*, November 29, 1851; *British Banner*, November 26, December 3, 1851, January 21, 28, February 11, April 14, 1852; Annie H. Abel and Frank J. Klingberg (eds.), *A Side-Light on Anglo-American Relations, 1839–1858: Furnished by the Correspondence of Lewis Tappan and Others with the British and Foreign Anti-Slavery Society* (Lancaster, Pa., 1927), 276–82.

58. C. Duncan Rice, *The Scots Abolitionists, 1833–1861* (Baton Rouge, 1981), 149.

Britain was "ordained" to carry Christianity to every corner of the world. Ward told the annual meeting of the Colonial Missionary Society in May, 1854, that "God had given to England these great provinces for the purpose of sending the Gospel to the distant parts of the earth, and to tell all the nations that this was her glorious privilege." Britain had a special obligation to spread the word of God throughout Africa because it "was a land the inhabitants of which had conferred upon Britain a very large portion of her literature and her art." Crummell went to Liberia as a missionary and teacher; Garnet went out to Jamaica as a Presbyterian missionary before the Old Calabar controversy broke; and Ward followed as a settler in 1855. Shortly after his arrival, Garnet reported that, "surely the wall is broken down, and the field is all grown over with thorns, and nettles cover the face thereof. This remark is true of our church, both in a temporal and spiritual point of view. Yet I think—ay, I know—that these walls can be raised again by God's help."[59] Here was classic missionary zeal and optimism: what mattered most was the spread of Christianity; other concerns seemed secondary. Where missionary activities were involved, one could expect silence on social problems.

However, abolitionists continued to attack American missionary groups that did not stand firm against slavery. The American Board of Commissioners for Foreign Missions had been under constant attack from American abolitionists since the late 1830s because it refused to expel slaveholders from its churches among the Choctaw and Cherokee nations or to question the sources of its financial support. The antislavery American Missionary Association was formed in 1846 to provide an alternative to the proslavery group. The board's missionaries argued that there was no alternative to slave labor available in the regions where they were working and that attempts to reform or destroy slavery, an integral institution of the Indian nations, would meet with vigorous opposition from local leaders and eventually lead to a cessation of missionary activities.

59. *Missionary Record*, May, 1853. See United Presbyterian Church Papers (7640–41), National Library of Scotland, Edinburgh, for correspondence around Garnet's mission. *British Banner*, July 20, 1853, May 10, 1854.

Confronted with the choice between abolitionism and the spread of Christianity, the board, like most other nineteenth-century missionary societies, opted for the latter.[60]

In February, 1854, the Reverend James Vincent appeared before the Congregational Union of England and Wales to ask its support for the American Reform Tract and Book Society. While praising the work of the society, the union declined to endorse it to avoid creating a precedent that might lead to difficulties in the future. Vincent accepted their arguments. In May, however, the Reverend Cuthbert Young appealed to the union to support the work of the Turkish Mission Aid Society (TMAS), a British arm of the Board of Commissioners for Foreign Missions. Young suggested that the union's support might influence the board to oppose slavery. Samuel Ringgold Ward discounted this idea. He had no confidence, he told the meeting, "respecting the probability of imparting to the Mission Board at New York Anti slavery feelings by any assistance which the Christians in this country might give to the Turkish Mission." Yet even though he viewed Young's hope as an "idle dream," he asked the union to aid the "good work" of the missionaries by supporting the TMAS.[61] The union agreed to support the new society.

The endorsement brought immediate condemnation from Vincent and his supporters in Bristol and from the BFASS. The *Anti Slavery Reporter* devoted three pages to an exposé of the board's views on slavery and its work among the Indian nations. It was, the paper concluded, "inexpedient and dangerous" for British abolitionists to give aid to the TMAS, offspring of the proslavery board.[62] Ward also found himself in an unenviable position. International efforts to isolate proslavery American churches had created one inviolable law to govern the activities of visiting American abolition-

---

60. Robert T. Lewit, "Indian Missions and Antislavery Sentiment: A Conflict of Evangelical and Humanitarian Ideas," *Mississippi Valley Historical Review*, L (1963), 42.

61. *British Banner*, May 17, 1854.

62. *Anti Slavery Reporter*, December 1, 1854; *Anti Slavery Advocate*, November, 1854.

ists: all attempts by proslavery churches to gain British endorsement must be opposed. The fact that Ward was black and a representative of his people only compounded his apostasy, and this issue was to haunt him for the rest of his visit to Britain.

It is entirely possible that Ward was influenced to approve the TMAS by Lord Shaftesbury, his British patron and the president of the new society. Ward was uniquely susceptible to the blandishments of the nobility. Other black men managed to maintain their equanimity despite the attentions of the British gentry, but Ward apparently could not. In his opinion, the Englishman of "good English society" had a knack of making visitors feel at home. "Really genteel people, of all ranks," he believed, "are perfectly alike; in that you cannot distinguish a nobleman from a commoner: but the most ridiculous blunders are made by those assuming it to whom it is not habitual, natural or educational." No doubt, he considered himself among the really genteel. He even attributed the differing treatment free blacks received in America to the social classes of the settlers in each region. New England, with the exception of Connecticut, treated blacks more humanely because of the better classes who had settled there. On the other hand, New Jersey, New York, and Pennsylvania, with their lower-class settlers, "out-American all Americans, save those of Connecticut, in their maltreatment of the free Negro." The best friends of the Negro in America "are persons generally of the superior classes, and of the best origin." It is no wonder that Ward was simply beside himself, "in a state of most excited delight" to be well received by British nobility.[63] Such was his admiration for the upper classes of Britain that some accused him of toadyism. The *British Friend*, in reviewing his narrative, wrote, "It would be a curious statistic how often the term 'I am *honoured*', by this or that gentleman or lady, appears in the volume." Pillsbury said that the references to "Esquires" were "*breaking out* in the book, as if it had measles or chicken pox."[64]

63. Samuel Ringgold Ward, *Autobiography of a Fugitive Negro: His Anti Slavery Labours in the United States, Canada, and England* (1855; rpr. Chicago, 1970), 209, 30–31, 170.

64. Parker Pillsbury to Samuel May, Jr., December 7, 1855, in ASB; *British Friend*, January, 1856.

Ward later defended his decision to support the TMAS to friends in Edinburgh: "I do not conceive that the wrong position of the Board ought to operate as a barrier to my contributing to the aid of converting Turks, who are labouring in connection with the Board. I do not see that such aid, *especially when accompanied with open and plain protests against the character of the Board*, is or can be candidly construed into approval, or a seeming approval, of the Board." However, he concluded, because Young continued to associate the two, he was left no choice but to "renounce all connection with and advocacy of the Turkish Mission Aid Society."[65] Ward's recantation is evidence of the force of abolitionist tradition and the resilience of the moral cordon. Had not the moral cordon been drawn around America, missionary zeal would probably have been enough to justify his endorsement. In the circumstances, however, a black man was expected to put the freeing of his fellow blacks ahead of other considerations.

The Fugitive Slave Law gave black visitors and their British supporters another opportunity to raise the issue of fellowshiping slaveholders, but it also raised thorny issues much nearer home. What was to be done, for example, with the thousands of fugitives and their families who had escaped to Canada in the months after the passage of the law? William Wells Brown suggested the establishment of schools, while missionary societies made plans to cater to the needs of the new settlers. Ward claimed that blacks in Canada were "as British and as loyal as any subjects Her Majesty has." Nevertheless, they met with widespread discrimination there. Ward argued that opposition to William King's Buxton Settlement, a black settlement in Ontario, came from "the lowest of the low, persons who were illiterate, and a disgrace to men of any colour," but this argument only skirted the issue. Because Ward, although persistently critical of Canadian racism, hoped that Canada would develop an integrated society free from the racism that haunted the United States, he opposed the establishment of exclusively black settlements and churches. In Canada where there were no legal re-

65. Edinburgh Ladies Emancipation Committee, *Turkish Mission: American Board of Commissioners for Foreign Missions. Reply of the Edinburgh Ladies Emancipation Committee, December 22nd, 1854* (Edinburgh, n.d.), 9–10.

strictions against them, blacks should "buy, build, live, die, and be buried, just where others of Her Majesty's subjects live." In such a country, "whose population must of necessity become more or less mixed, the maintaining of distinct nationalities is certainly exceptionable." Canada, he hoped, would avoid the pitfalls of American racism and take this opportunity to create a truly integrated society.[66]

Ward's optimism had little ground in reality. Not only was racism increasing, but Britain had consistently ignored abolitionists' petitions to clarify the extradition clause of the Webster-Ashburton Treaty signed in 1841, under which the United States theoretically could demand the return of fugitives from Canada. Black visitors became increasingly concerned to persuade the British government to take action against Canadian racism. Josiah Henson raised the issue at the annual meeting of the Congregational Union in 1852, where he explained that black settlers were not always welcome in Canada and that very few white ministers and churches, with the notable exception of the Reverend John Roaf, would minister to them. Henson's remarks raised immediate protests from a number of former British missionaries to Canada, and the debate was joined. John Scoble and Peter Bolton of the BFASS defended Henson— Scoble citing examples of discrimination he had witnessed while in Canada and Bolton quoting extracts from the *Voice of the Fugitive* that discussed opposition to the Buxton Settlement. Henson, in defense of his position, rejected the commonly held view that racism in Canada was attributable to a small group of Americans in frontier villages; it was, he wrote, to be found across Canada on boats and stages, in hotels, and in many churches and schools. The editor of the *British Banner*, wearied by the whole debate, flew in the face of abolitionist tradition to suggest that African colonization might be the answer to the growing problem.[67] The American Colonization Society must have rubbed its hands with satisfaction to find a leading British evangelical newspaper finally coming around to its view.

66. Samuel Ringgold Ward, *Autobiography*, 150–51, 143; *British Banner*, May 11, June 24, 1853.

67. For the entire debate, see *British Banner*, May 12, June 2, 30, August 1, 25, October 13, 1852.

Problems in Canada merely reflected larger and potentially more destructive developments in Britain. The period 1848–1854 produced even greater challenges to the international efforts of black Americans. The publication in 1849 of Thomas Carlyle's rabidly antiblack "Occasional Discourse on the Nigger Question" not only argued in favor of the primacy of the master-servant relationship in all successful societies but also condemned the activities of abolitionists, who in his view had seriously undermined the fabric of West Indian society. Carlyle argued that there existed a natural hierarchy among men; at the top was the "Wisest Man," followed by the "next-wisest," and so on "till we reached the Demerara Nigger from whom downwards, through the horse, etc." He dismissed the view that "all men be accounted equally wise and worthy" as sheer humbug, and productive of "Tyranny and Slavery."[68] Carlyle's views were especially disturbing to abolitionists and many black leaders, for many of them also subscribed to the notion of social hierarchies. William G. Allen, for instance, told a New York audience not only that the mind is the badge of distinction, the only measure of the man, "but it is also true that he who thinks the largest thoughts is the ruler of the world." These men of enlarged minds and profound intellect were equipped to rule, and like Beriah Green, his principal at Oneida Institute, he argued that true democracy would only be achieved when the wisest, the moral and intellectual giants of society, attained their "proper places" as leaders of men. These natural leaders of nations not only are superior to others in "the capacity to rule" but also "think the largest thoughts, perform the greatest deeds, and take good care that these thoughts and their deeds and the law of Rectitude shall be in perfect harmony." Carlyle may have violated Allen's "law of Rectitude," but his notion of social hierarchy obviously met with approval. Allen was not alone; in 1850 Wilson Armistead, the Leeds abolitionist, wrote, "I do not advocate the commingling of all ranks in society; I do not say that those in a situation of the educated and more wealthy classes, who necessarily move in a particular circle of their own, are to go and select individ-

68. Thomas Carlyle, "Occasional Discourse on the Nigger Question," in Carlyle, *Latter-Day Pamphlets* (London, 1858), 11–12.

uals from a different level for their associates, there is no necessity for this; the natural order of society may be preserved, and the distinctions of colour at the same time abolished."[69] This was the standard response to the views of Carlyle and others.

William Wells Brown attempted as best he could to refute Carlyle's theories, but he was a lone voice among visiting blacks. The variety and complexity of schemes devised by slaves to escape, he told a Leeds audience, showed their intelligence and ingenuity and refuted the "absurd doctrine" of Thomas Carlyle. Later Brown condemned Carlyle, a writer he had long admired, for "his recent attack upon the emancipated people of the West Indies, and his laborious article in favor of the reestablishment of the lash and slavery," but he paid for his boldness. His daughter Josephine reported that opposition to him grew following his attack on Carlyle.[70]

J. W. C. Pennington also joined the debate, but in a rather circuitous fashion. He argued that blacks had clearly shown progress over two centuries in spite of slavery and racial oppression. They had proved "that the race possessed vitality, and . . . proved too, that the law of progress was incorporated in its constitution. The law of vitality had stood the test of two centuries of trial and endurance on the American soil; the law of progress was now beginning to be developed." This was clearly shown in the efforts and successes of free blacks. Even blacks who were enslaved, Pennington observed, "were more enlightened more organised into families more sensitive to the ties of relationship and blood than were the wild inhabitants of Africa."[71]

This enlightenment was cold comfort indeed for an enslaved people, and while Pennington's argument may have struck a responsive chord among those eager to promote the Christianization of Africa, it did little to refute Carlyle's doctrines. Even so, many blacks

69. Jeremiah F. Asher, *Incidents in the Life of the Rev. J. Asher, Pastor of Shiloh (Coloured) Baptist Church, Philadelphia, United States* (London, 1850), 12; *Pennsylvania Freeman*, October 16, 1852.

70. Josephine Brown, *Biography of an American Bondsman* (Boston, 1856), 89–90; William Wells Brown, *Three Years in Europe; or, Places I Have Seen and People I Have Met* (London, 1852), 200–201; Leeds *Mercury*, January 19, 1850.

71. Bristol *Mercury*, October 19, 1850.

and their British supporters took the road of refutation by example. Blacks were held up as living proof of the enormity of Carlyle's error; the purer they were the more absurd was Carlyle. James McCune Smith observed that the foes of abolition in Britain had traditionally discounted the contributions and talents of blacks like himself by arguing that it was their white lineage that accounted for their intelligence. These people "denied the capacity of the pure negro for the higher branches of learning and science. The mouths of all such," he wrote, "were closed by the advent of Mr. Garnet. Here was a gentleman of splendid physique, polished manners, extensive learning, well up, especially in English poetry, ably filling the pulpits of their best divines, and bearing off the laurels in eloquence, wit, sarcasm, interlarded with soul-subduing pathos . . . and this gentleman an African of pure lineage, with no admixture of Saxon blood at the source of his unquestionable talent and genius." British newspapers agreed with Smith's analysis. One observed that "such appearances as that of Mr. Garnet among us furnish an admirable confutation of those who talk of the mental inferiority of the negro. He is decidedly above the mediocrity even of our own educated clergy." Others were surprised by his fluency and eloquence and concluded that he was "the best possible refutation of the idea that the negro belongs to an inferior grade of the creation."[72]

Opposing phrenologists and others who claimed that blacks were inferior, the *British Banner* argued that Douglass, Brown, Henson, Pennington, and Ward gave the lie to such ideas. Moreover, these were men who had had to labor under "every disadvantage, not having been trained in freedom, and enjoyed the opportunities of civilization for intellectual culture." What would they have achieved had they been "placed on an equality with white men?" Douglass, in spite of his experiences, was entitled to be ranked with "our CURRANS, our ERSKINS, our DENMANS, and our BROUGHAMS. Does the whole fraternity of Planters supply an individual his match, or that

72. Alloa *Advertiser*, March 20, 1852; Kilmarnock *Journal*, February 19, 1852; *North British Mail*, November 12, 1851; H. H. Garnet, *A Memorial Discourse, by Henry Highland Garnet, Delivered in the Hall of the House of Representatives, Washington City, D.C., on Sabbath, February 12, 1865, with an Introduction by James McCune Smith, M.D.* (Philadelphia, 1865), 54.

is capable of meeting him on the public platform?" But the editors did not absolve blacks from part of the responsibility for their own position. Their "fatal bequest"—affection, attachment, patience, and fidelity—added to their misfortune. If blacks could only add to their intellectual and physical power "the manly pride, the self-respect, the burning hatred of ruthless oppression, and its inhuman authors, which, under similar circumstances, would characterise the white," slave regions could become "a field of blood, or else the enslaved had been free."[73] Blacks and their British supporters, eschewing the simple and straightforward attack they had employed so extensively in America, substituted an ineffective mixture of nineteenth-century notions of racial characteristics and philanthropy in their response to Carlyle.

While Garnet, Crummell, Pennington, and other prominent blacks continued to win the praises of editors wherever they went, others, like the Georgia fugitive John Brown, found that there was "prejudice against colour in England, in some classes, as well as more generally in America."[74] Zilpha Elaw, the American fire-and-brimstone preacher, complained in the early 1840s that she found it difficult to get lodgings in Liverpool, but it appears that her experience was unique.[75] It is impossible to determine whether Elaw's problems were due more to her sex and avocation than to her race, but there were clear signs that racism did exist in Britain. Henry "Box" Brown found more than just minor prejudice; he was openly attacked by the editor of the Wolverhampton and Staffordshire *Herald*, who found Brown's popular panorama of American slavery a "gross and palpable exaggeration . . . a jumbled mass of contradictions and absurdities, assertions without proof, geography without boundary and horrors without parallel," which painted the slave states as "a series of inquisitorial chambers of horrors—a sort of Blue Beard, or a giant despair den, for the destruction, burning,

73. *British Banner*, March 22, 1854.
74. L. A. Chamerovzow (ed.), *Slave Life in Georgia: A Narrative of the Life, Sufferings, and Escape of John Brown, a Fugitive Slave Now in England* (London, 1855), 170.
75. Zilpha Elaw, *Memoirs of the Life, Religious Experience, Ministerial Travels, and Labours of Mrs. Zilpha Elaw, an American Female of Colour, Together with Some Accounts of the Great Religious Revivals in America* (London, 1846), 150.

branding, laceration, starving, and working of negroes" and slave-owners as a class of "demi-fiends, made of double distilled brim-stone." Both the panorama and Brown's speech, the editor con-cluded, were nothing more than amusement "in the richest nigger style." When Brown was asked by a member of the audience where the Dismal Swamp was located, the editor chose to report his reply in the most derogatory style: "He daint know; you might put it in Carolina, but he taut it was in Viginny." The *Herald* condemned other newspapers for giving support to the "bejewelled 'darkey' whose portly figure and overdressed appearance bespeak the gull-ibility of our most credulous age and country." The editor was not finished with Brown; in the next issue he reported that only the "shoeless daughters of the slums and alleys" were attending the showings. Brown, the "bejewelled and oily negro, whose obese and comfortable figure and easy *nonchalance*, reminds one of various good things and sumptuous living," performed his "nocturnal an-tics," the editor reported, with "ludicrous and semi-baboonish agil-ity" much to the delight of the "juvenile rag-a-muffins" who make up his audience. Brown sued the editor and was awarded one hun-dred pounds in damages. The *Times*, reporting on the trial, observed that although Brown's dress was "rather fine, and he displayed some jewellery about his person, his manner of giving his evidence was quiet and creditable; and his pronunciation altogether very correct."[76]

What is interesting is that not one of the prominent blacks in Britain came to Brown's defense—not even William Wells Brown, who also had a panorama on display at this time. It is quite possible that blacks may have decided that these new attacks were best dealt with by silence. Their objective—winning international support for the fight against American slavery and discrimination—may have dictated this approach, for to involve themselves in a debate on Brit-ish racism would have been to run the risk of alienating potential support. They had to tread a delicate path on the subject of racism in order to achieve their long-term objectives. In addition, the re-gard most blacks felt for Britain, which had long supported their

76. London *Times*, July 30, 1852; Wolverhampton and Staffordshire *Herald*, March 17, 24, 1852.

movement, may have further tempered their criticism of a phenomenon that by American standards was still very minor and that had
not seriously affected their efforts. This view dictated their actions
throughout the period.

The popular satirical journal, *Punch*, even during its radical days,
had a fair sampling of articles on "Nigger Peculiarities" that ridiculed blacks for their mimicry and antipathy to work. Later, blacks
would argue that minstrelsy was in some part responsible for the
growth of British racism. At the end of the Civil War, Sarah Parker
Remond observed that Ethiopian minstrels, those "vulgar men,"
were, like the proslavery British press, deliberately distorting the
character of blacks.[77] But throughout the antebellum period no black
visitor saw these performers as a problem, even though minstrel
groups were regular visitors to the towns and cities in which they
had their greatest successes. One of these groups visited Exeter
soon after a successful lecture by Douglass and Garrison. The *Western Times*, which had praised the visiting abolitionists, suggested
that its readers would not want to miss the minstrels' performance.
"The negroes of America, a light-hearted and joyous race, whenever they are treated with the least kindness, have a great love of
music," the newspaper reported; "songs, jest, and dance, beguile the
brief intervals of rest from the alloted toil! Their music is unsophis-
ticated, and their instruments simple and rude. Some of them have
fine voices, and their minstrelsy occasionally exhibits traces of deep-
feeling—but the grotesque and humorous are its chief characteristics."[78] These kinds of commentaries were not uncharacteristic, but
Douglass and others made no attempt to refute them while in Britain. Remond was right; although minstrels did not openly advocate
racism, they influenced the creation of racial stereotypes.

In spite of these growing trends, blacks continued to win popular acclaim in the 1850s. There appears to have been no abatement
in their popularity. Thousands continued to hear their lectures, purchase their narratives, and support their efforts. During a visit to a
Sheffield factory, the workers made a collection and presented Brown

77. *Freed-Man*, February 1, 1866; *Punch*, II (1841), 184.
78. *Western Times*, September 5, 1846.

with silver and electro plates "as a token of esteem, as well as an expression of their sympathy in the cause he advocates."[79] Garnet's supporters raised sufficient money to pay for his family's expenses to join him in Britain. Crummell's education at Cambridge University was paid for by his rich friends. William Wells Brown's two daughters were trained at schools in London and France and were later appointed teachers at British schools. Ward was offered a sizable portion of land by John Candler of Chelmsford when he agreed to go to Jamaica. Garnet was appointed a missionary to Jamaica by the United Presbyterian church of Scotland. The Crafts' schooling at Ockham was paid for by friends. Pennington and William Wells Brown were ransomed with money collected in Britain. For most black visitors, such support and popularity made Britain a paradise compared to America. Even when Douglass criticized the growth of racism in Britain and the "atmosphere of slavery" in Liverpool and Manchester during his second visit, he was careful to limit it to those with "large business connections with America," to men of science whose sole objective was "to prove the inferiority of the negro race," to clergymen who defend the system, and to Ethiopian serenaders who lampoon the slave.[80] Britain, in their eyes, remained a symbol of racial freedom and a supporter of black efforts in America. Signs of emerging racism there may have given some of them pause, but it was overshadowed by the real freedom they experienced and the continuing hospitality they received wherever they traveled. To paraphrase Douglass: blacks were still allowed there.

79. Sheffield *Independent*, February 9, 1850; *Liberator*, March 15, 1850.

80. Ayr *Observer*, April 3, 1860; Newcastle *Express*, February 24, 1860; *Douglass Monthly*, April, 1860.

Chapter 5

Making the Niger
the Mississippi
of Africa

In 1832 when Elliott Cresson was promoting the American Colonization Society in Britain, the *Eclectic Review* concluded that "colonization is like a pump to a leaky vessel." It was a commentary on both the shortcomings of American society and the inadequacy of the ACS' efforts to colonize Liberia with black Americans.[1] This view of colonization as a cure for America's racial troubles held sway among British abolitionists throughout the antebellum years, but Liberia itself, as a missionary base in an era of growing missionary activity in West Africa, was supported by those eager to promote the spread of Christianity. Despite the failure of Sir Fowell Buxton's ill-fated expedition up the Niger in the early 1840s, the majority of British humanitarians accepted Cresson's and Gurley's claims that the Liberian experiment held out the prospect for a reduction in slave trading, an increase in the availability of free-labor goods, and an augmentation of missionary activity. The support of Liberia, always separate and independent from the ACS, continued quietly and away from public scrutiny throughout the forties and fifties. It is no surprise, then, that British humanitarians were instrumental in their government's recognition of Liberian independence in 1847.

The rebirth of the Free Produce movement in the 1840s made Liberia an increasingly attractive prospect for those who argued that

1. *Eclectic Review*, November, 1832.

the availability of free-grown produce would ultimately lead to the destruction of slavery. This view was given wider currency and made more acceptable by black Americans like Garnet, Crummell, and Pennington, who actively promoted the cause throughout Britain. When four of these black advocates—Garnet, Crummell, and Ward in the fifties and William Craft in the sixties—went to either Africa or the West Indies from Britain, hopes were raised for an increased flow of free-labor goods into Britain. This confluence of expanding missionary activity, the search for tropical goods produced by free labor, and the long-held hope that thriving communities on the coast of Africa would ultimately destroy the slave trade, formed the backdrop of British humanitarian interest in Africa during the 1850s and 1860s.

By the late 1850s these objectives converged with those of Lancashire cotton men eager to find alternative sources to the cotton monopoly of the American South and so protect themselves from possible shortfalls in supply. This was also a period in which colonization and emigration were viewed by many as legitimate instruments of relieving the pressures of excess population. Advocates of Liberian colonization and selective black emigration employed the theories of Thomas Malthus in arguing that the pervasiveness of American racism made the free-black population in many respects an excess population. As we have seen, when the Reverend Josiah Henson complained to the *British Banner* about prejudice against blacks in Canada, the editor suggested that voluntary colonization would alleviate the problem. "We have never joined in the cry against this project [colonization]," the editorial ran. "Bad men, that is, slave-breeders, slave-dealers, and slaveholders, may see reason for promoting it which gives it to them a special recommendation; but it is quite possible the thing may be good in itself for all that." In the editor's view, emigration "lessens the sum of human misery, and, to that extent increases happiness." Periodic emigration to Liberia would be a "means of raising up a great community in Africa of civilised and Christian men of colour; and the two things in our view are perfectly compatible."[2] Similar views would have met with

2. *British Banner*, August 25, 1852.

immediate and vigorous condemnation in 1831 and 1841, but by 1852 the situation had changed.

Advocates of colonization learned from their defeats; no longer would there be the fanfare that accompanied the visits of Cresson and Gurley. When white American advocates toured Britain in the late 1840s and early 1850s, following the visit of Liberia's president J. J. Roberts in 1847 and the subsequent British recognition of Liberian independence, they made use of unofficial representatives and quiet diplomacy. For example, when the Reverend John Miller of Frederick, Maryland, made a private visit in 1849, he was asked to promote the interests of the ACS whenever the opportunity presented itself. Soon after his arrival in Liverpool, Miller set out, as Cresson had before him, to win support from influential editors, and like Cresson, he found himself up against a well-organized and determined opposition. Initial support from the Liverpool *Standard* soon disappeared in the face of opposition from local anticolonizationists. Unluckily for Miller, the Reverend Alexander Crummell happened to be in Liverpool at the same time. In private meetings, public lectures, and from the pulpit Crummell castigated the ACS for its racist policies. So too did the Reverend J. W. C. Pennington, who visited Britain in 1849 partly to undermine Miller's chances of success. Prior to William Wells Brown's departure for Europe, a farewell meeting adopted a series of resolutions calling on him to reassert free-black opposition to the ACS while abroad.[3]

Initially, Miller gained some exposure for the cause when he testified before a committee of the House of Lords investigating the degree to which settlements on the west coast of Africa hindered the slave trade. By the early summer, however, his efforts had been stymied by anticolonizationists. At a meeting with the Executive Committee of the BFASS, he was told that, although the committee was interested in Liberia, it could do nothing to promote the interests of the ACS. In republishing the "Protest" of 1833 the BFASS reiterated its stand against colonization. Continued black opposition

3. William E. Farrison, *William Wells Brown: Author and Reformer* (Chicago, 1969), 142–43; Liverpool *Standard*, February 20, 1849; John Cropper to [?], July 21, 1849, in BFASS.

to the ACS was partly instrumental in the defeat of Miller's efforts. But as in previous years, this opposition in no way hindered the flow of support to Liberia. Samuel Gurney, for instance, contributed a thousand pounds to the Liberian government's fund for the purchase of a coastal area known as the Gallinas.[4]

Two years later another attempt was made to expand British support for Liberia. This time the thrust came primarily from the Reverend Eli Stokes, bishop-elect of Liberia, who concentrated most of his efforts in northern Ireland, where he hoped to collect money for the building of a church. Stokes's timing was unfortunate—his visit came less than a year after the passage of the Fugitive Slave Law. Like Nathaniel Paul, who had earlier claimed that the establishment of the Wilberforce Settlement was the result of American racism, a racism fostered and utilized by the ACS for its devious scheme, black American visitors and their British supporters now argued with some justification that the society had done nothing to prevent the passage of the hated law and may even have encouraged it. James Stanfield of the Belfast Anti Slavery Society began working against the ACS even before Stokes held his first meeting, criticizing the Colonization Society and the Fugitive Slave Law and accusing the Liberian government of tolerating slavery. Stokes, like his predecessors, was forced onto the defensive. He avoided any discussion of the merits of the ACS and concentrated solely on the argument that Liberia was a country where blacks could develop, free from racism.[5]

Stokes's situation was not made any easier by the presence of Elliott Cresson, who was on his third visit to Britain. Although his visit was unofficial, Cresson's mere presence was sufficient to raise the hackles of anticolonizationists. Garnet took the lead at an antislavery soirée held in Freemasons Hall, London, in May. He devoted the greater part of his speech to an attack on colonization and Cresson, reemphasizing black opposition to the ACS. It should be added, though, that he did concede that Liberia "might do some good" in

4. *African Repository*, January, 1850, July, 1849; *Anti Slavery Reporter*, May 1, 1849; BFASS Minute Book 3, in BFASS.
5. *Banner of Ulster*, August 1, 1851.

Africa. In October, Garnet was in Belfast where he joined with local abolitionists in a condemnation of American slavery and the ACS reminiscent of the 1830s.[6] It is not clear what success, if any, Stokes had. But reaction to his visit testified to an abiding opposition to the society. Whenever necessary, anticolonizationists were capable of deploying an efficient mechanism to thwart the efforts of colonizationists.

The supporters of colonization learned from all these failures that black advocates, particularly Liberians, were more likely to meet with favorable responses in Britain. In the midst of Cresson's problems with anticolonizationists in the thirties, he and Hodgkin had called on the ACS to employ a black supporter, preferably John B. Russwurm, to counter the claims of Nathaniel Paul and Captain Charles Stuart. President Roberts' success in 1847 rather belatedly proved the efficacy of this approach. It should be noted, however, that it would have been difficult to find a black willing to advocate the cause of Liberia prior to its independence in 1847, such was the opposition of blacks to the ACS. Liberian independence was for many the severing of ties between the colony and the society. Although, as we shall see, many blacks remained sceptical, Liberia joined Haiti as a symbol of black independence and potential. This partly explains the modest success of the Reverend A. J. Wood's mission to Britain in 1852 just a few months after the bitter condemnation of Stokes and Cresson. Wood, reputedly a member of President Roberts' cabinet, was warmly received by both British humanitarians and black American visitors, who assisted him in his efforts to raise funds for Liberian development. Even Garnet used his wide circle of friends to aid Wood in his efforts. It was a reception that would have been impossible to hope for just a few months earlier.[7]

6. *Banner of Ulster*, October 21, 1851; *Anti Slavery Reporter*, June 2, 1851.

7. Henry Highland Garnet to John Scoble, August 10, 1852, in BFASS. There were reports that Wood was later charged in Hull with obtaining money under false pretences. According to one witness, who appeared for the prosecution, Wood claimed that Eliza Harris of *Uncle Tom's Cabin* was a member of his church and that Cassey died six weeks after her arrival in Liberia. I have seen only one reference to this and have not been able to confirm it. *Presbyterian*, January 15, 1853.

Liberian independence, however, only partly explains this new shift in the attitudes of black Americans; developments in America were equally influential. In the South the abolitionist movement had failed to bring about emancipation, and in the North the limited rights of the free-black population were being continually eroded. They were disenfranchised in Pennsylvania, banned from settling in Indiana, and generally denied many of the rights of citizenship. These policies were fueled by theories of "Negro inferiority" propounded by phrenologists and others who placed blacks very low on the Chain of Being. In addition, Egyptologists like the Englishman George Gliddon, who toured America in the late 1830s, and Americans like the Mobile physician Dr. Josiah Nott placed Egypt, the wellspring of modern learning, squarely in the lap of European civilization. To Nott the heads of Egyptian mummies showed beyond all doubt that they were Caucasians, and their relics depicted Negroes both as a separate race and as occupying the position of slaves. This American obsession with white superiority and its attendant fear of amalgamation produced some rather bizarre results. In a fictional tale published in New York in 1835, entitled *A Sojourn in the City of Amalgamation in the Year of our Lord 19———*, white men and women established the city of Amalgamation in which they were to do penance for the past wrongs inflicted on blacks. The aim was total racial equality, but the results, to the dismay of the white citizens, was "moral degeneration, indolence, and political and economic decline," brought about by assimilation. Previously virtuous and independent whites were corrupted by contact with "ignorant and irresponsible blacks."[8] Such nonsense, black Americans argued, was a clear sign that God had made America mad before he destroyed her. It is no wonder that many blacks advocated greater racial unity in the face of this growing antipathy.

The period witnessed a rekindling of interest in Africa among black Americans. They claimed Egypt as part of Africa and made much of the fact that, while Egypt was flourishing, Europe was in-

8. David M. Streifford, "The American Colonization Society: An Application of Republican Ideology to Early Antebellum Reform," *Journal of Southern History*, LXV (1979), 216; William Stanton, *The Leopard's Spots: Scientific Attitudes Toward Race in America, 1815–59* (Chicago, 1960), 49, 70.

habited by savages, the ancestors of present-day Europeans and white Americans. The Reverend Hosea Easton wondered how "modern philosophers, the descendants of this race of savages," could claim for "their race a superiority of intellect over those who, at that very time, were enjoying all the real benefits of civilized life." This "cloud of locusts," he maintained, had been directly responsible for the destruction of other civilizations with which they had made contact. Their present advanced state, he argued, was not the result of a "superior development of intellectual faculties" but was due entirely to the "nature of the circumstances into which they were drawn by their innate thirst for blood and plunder."[9]

While Easton undoubtedly set one standard for the discussion of the race issue among black Americans, others like William G. Allen, argued that America's future and potential rested on its ability to recognize the contributions of all of its different peoples to the development of its civilization. He believed that no successful nation was ever the result of a "pure" race; on the contrary, amalgamation was the indispensible prerequisite of nation building. Allen was not alone. As Leonard Sweet has pointed out, although the majority of nineteenth-century black leaders did not believe that racial blending was a precondition for black equality, "they considered miscegenation as ultimately destined to constitute a giant step in the progress of mankind." These debates, in part a reflection of a growing interest in Africa, prompted further discussion of African contributions to world civilization. Allen, for instance, found it necessary to publish a pamphlet, *Wheatley, Banneker, and Horton*, to accompany his popular lecture on the history, literature, and destiny of the African race. He told a Leeds audience in 1853, as he undoubtedly told many of his American audiences, that Egypt "carried to Greece the blessings of civilization . . . because they had a higher regard for the social and moral in man than the merely intellectual."[10] To Allen and others, this was a clear refutation of the Gliddons and Notts of the world.

9. Hosea Easton, "A Treatise on the Intellectual Character and Civil and Political Condition of the Colored People of the United States," in Dorothy Porter (ed.), *Negro Protest Pamphlets* (New York, 1969), 8–19.

10. Leeds *Intelligencer*, December 10, 1853; Leonard I. Sweet, *Black Images of*

Neither the contributions of blacks to American society nor their attempts to refute theories of racial inferiority, however, prevented the passage of the Fugitive Slave Law, which blacks rightly attributed to the reluctance or inability of white Americans to resolve the contradictions between the principles of the Declaration of Independence and the facts of slavery and racial discrimination. Not only were black communities thrown into turmoil by the law, but it also created problems for fugitives who were then in Britain. Under the new law, Garnet, William Wells Brown, Pennington, William and Ellen Craft, and Box Brown, all fugitive slaves, were likely to be hunted down with renewed vigor, if only because of their international fame, if they returned to America. Meanwhile, the number of fugitive slaves entering Britain increased dramatically in the early 1850s. William P. Powell, working in Liverpool, informed his friends in America that he alone had assisted five fugitives in as many months. The same was true in London where a new society, the Ladies' Society to Aid Fugitives from Slavery, was formed to give temporary assistance to fugitives and, in some cases, to resettle them in another country. Many were sent to Australia, Canada, Demerara, Barbados, New Zealand, and the west coast of Africa with the assistance of the Ladies' Society.[11] The years after 1850 also saw an increase in the number of black Americans visiting Britain in the hope of raising money to aid the significant number of fugitives who, fearing recapture, had moved to the safety of Canada. For many British abolitionists, these developments reopened the issue of emigration as an alternative for black Americans.

It was, however, much easier to settle destitute fugitives in distant parts of the empire and to support settlements in Canada than it was to persuade black leaders like Garnet, Crummell, Pennington, and William Wells Brown, who had been so critical of any form of colonization, that their future lay elsewhere than in America. Al-

America, 1784–1870 (New York, 1976), 100; *Frederick Douglass Paper*, May 20, June 10, 1852.

11. Report of the Ladies' Society to Aid Fugitives from Slavery, 1855, in BFASS. Francis Bishop informed Peter Bolton that he had found a number of jobs for fugitives who were in Liverpool. Francis Bishop to Peter Bolton, November 11, 1851, in BFASS; *National Anti Slavery Standard*, August 6, 1853.

though Brown supported some plans to improve Canadian settlements, he remained steadfastly opposed to colonization. But black fugitives in Britain were faced with unpleasant alternatives. Some of them accepted the help of their British friends in raising money to purchase their freedom. Some, like Box Brown and the Crafts, turned their backs on America; the Crafts did not return to the United States until 1869. Some, like Garnet and Crummell, chose to settle temporarily outside America. Some, like Ward, never returned. Every fugitive faced a difficult choice. William Wells Brown, as a Garrisonian, was ideologically opposed to paying slaveholders for the freedom of their slaves, especially those who had already escaped. He thought long and hard before allowing his friends to raise money for his ransom. Pennington seems to have had no such difficulty. He realized that the situation at home after 1850 clearly demanded a greater degree of flexibility and pragmatism. Crummell, who had so vigorously denounced Liberia, in the end chose that country as a temporary haven, but he and Garnet, who settled in Jamaica, had to wrestle with accusations that they were abandoning the cause for the relative comfort of another country.

Crummell's decision to go to Liberia clearly demonstrates the dilemma in which these men found themselves. He had visited Britain in 1848 to raise money to complete the building of his church in New York City. Soon after his arrival a number of his British friends raised enough money to pay his tuition at Cambridge University, from which he graduated in 1853. The irony of the fact that foreigners had supported his university education a few years after his own denomination had refused to accept him at its seminary was not lost on Crummell. He spent most of his time either at Cambridge or at Bath, where his friends were active in missionary activities. It is quite possible that these friends may have persuaded Crummell to devote himself to missionary work, for throughout his stay in Britain he actively participated in the meetings of West Country missionary groups. His experiences in America—the rejection of his application to attend an Episcopalian seminary, the continuing poverty that was the lot of most black ministers, and his poor health—may have made Crummell particularly amenable to his friends' suggestions. He tried to explain these concerns in a series of

long letters to his mentor John Jay. He told Jay that in spite of all he
had done for his people in Rhode Island, Philadelphia, and New
York, not a year passed "in which I have had sufficient money
to secure clothes to cover me, and to keep me decent. Many a time
my wife and myself have been so wretchedly poor that we have
not known where to get a morsel of food." His congregations, he
claimed, were never able to meet even half of his salary and many
even joined opponents to "abuse and crush" him. Crummell attributed his heart ailment to the continuing pressures under which he
lived in America. More important, he felt that his children should be
brought up and educated in a society that did not respect slavery. In
September, 1851, Crummell was still not certain where he would
go, but his doctors had recommended a warmer climate, and he was
determined to find a situation where he would not have to depend
on preaching for a livelihood and where he could open a school.[12]

His partiality for Africa seems to have been confirmed even before his letters to Jay. He told a BFASS soirée in May, 1851, that
Africa, as a missionary field, must be differentiated from Liberia, a
colony made up of "ignorant, degraded, benighted slaves fresh from
the slave-shambles and cotton plantations" of America. The hope of
Africa lay in it being evangelized through the Gospel. He called on
those interested in the future of Africa to instruct black American,
West Indian, and African youth for the work of evangelizing that
continent. Crummell placed great store in the role of missionaries.
Three years earlier at a Church Missionary Jubilee in Cheltenham,
he had praised the British, who had always struggled for the "poor
unprotected African," and the missionaries, those "simple-minded
men" who went out, "depending only on their faith, derived from
the simple truth of the Gospel, and relying on the fulness of God's
goodness," to defeat "the sins of satan, and win to his master the
souls of the poor ignorant, benighted heathen."[13] This was heady
stuff, indeed, of the sort that would later make many black missionaries and emigrationists the unwitting allies of European expansion
in Africa.

12. Crummell to Jay, September 12, 1851, in JF.
13. Cheltenham *Examiner*, November 8, 1848; *British Banner*, May 28, 1851; *Anti
Slavery Reporter*, June 2, 1851.

After many fruitless attempts to secure an appointment with other missionary boards, Crummell finally decided to apply to the Episcopal church of America for a position in Liberia. He told Jay that the choice was not easily arrived at, for he remained an opponent of colonization. His concern, however, was to be a missionary and educator to his race. At a meeting of the Ladies' Negro Education Society in Bristol, he condemned the ACS as a product of an "oppression principle" but praised Liberians for their "free government, independent, enlightened, enterprising and full of promise." On the eve of his departure Crummell told the editor of the *Slave* that he hoped his new home might "be the instrument, in part, for the destruction of slavery. She has the soil fully adapted to cotton and sugar growing; and all that is needed is enterprise on the part of the Liberians, and the favouring hand of God, and I believe that Liberia is blest with both."[14] In Liberia, he argued, was to be found the practical application of the principles of the Free Produce movement. In spite of his scrupulous attempts to differentiate between the ACS as a racist organization and Liberia as a field of missionary activity and a source of free-grown produce, the fact that one of Liberia's foremost critics had opted for settlement there raised its stock in the eyes of British humanitarians and stimulated further interest in Africa.

Emigration of a select group of skilled black Americans to the tropics, an obvious corollary of the Free Produce movement, was boosted even further by the settlement of Garnet and Ward in Jamaica. As we have seen, Garnet was invited to Britain in 1848 to promote the FPM. His success in establishing a significant number of local societies won for him a national reputation as one of black America's leading emissaries and for some time enhanced the image of the movement as a practical instrument of abolition. By 1851 Garnet had decided that his future activities should be centered around missionary work and the promotion of free-labor agriculture in the tropics. With the backing of his friends in the movement he was appointed a missionary to Jamaica by the United Presbyte-

14. *Slave*, July, 1853; Alexander Crummell to John Jay, December 27, 1852, in JF.

rian church of Scotland. At his station in Sterling, Jamaica, he and his wife established day and night schools for both males and females. Interestingly, they seem to have concentrated most of their energies on educating "native Africans" brought to the island in the hope of meeting the labor shortage caused by the refusal of former slaves to work on the plantations. It is quite possible that these contacts may have stimulated Garnet's later interest in African emigration. "Is it not wonderful," he told a friend in Britain, "that God should in his Providence have placed me in my present circumstances, where I find myself instructing some of the people from the nation to which my forefathers belonged? O how my heart leaped within me when some of them told me that they belonged to the Congo nation."[15] Although Garnet's stay in Jamaica lasted only a few years, it strengthened the argument that thriving communities in the tropics would ultimately undermine economies dependent on slave labor.

Samuel Ringgold Ward, unlike Garnet, was heavily involved in promoting the cause of black American emigrant communities even before his arrival in Britain in 1852. He had joined the exodus of black Americans to Canada in 1851, fearing that his participation in the famous rescue of the fugitive slave Jerry in Syracuse would lead to imprisonment. In Canada he became a leading figure in the Canadian Anti Slavery Society and it was this society in conjunction with the BFASS that arranged his tour of Britain to raise funds to aid the growing number of fugitives entering Canada. Ward's brilliant oratory won him such immediate success in Britain that he was able to complete his mission in a relatively short space of time. Although in his *Autobiography* Ward pointed out that he had contemplated going to Jamaica as early as 1839, it appears that his decision to settle there in 1854 was largely due to the widespread emigrationist, missionary, and free-labor sentiments among British abolitionists. These interests had been encouraged by Crummell's and Garnet's decisions and sanctioned by Harriet Beecher Stowe's call for Liberian colonization in her popular novel *Uncle Tom's Cabin.*[16]

15. *Slave*, June, 1854, September, November, 1853.
16. Samuel Ringgold Ward, *Autobiography of a Fugitive Negro: His Anti Slavery Labours in the United States, Canada, and England* (1855; rpr. Chicago, 1970), 38.

Many British abolitionists, while contributing extensively to fugitive settlements in Canada, viewed them mainly as temporary havens or way stations for permanent settlements in the tropics. In its application, the free-produce principle required the existence of economically viable colonies worked by skilled laborers producing tropical staples for metropolitan markets. As Ward told the 1854 annual meeting of the BFASS, merely boycotting slave goods would never destroy slavery; attempts had to be made to cultivate alternative sources on a large scale by developing resources in the West Indies and "sustaining fugitive slaves in Canada." He evidently shared the view that Canadian settlements were but temporary refuges for the skilled laborers who could work the land now available in Africa and the West Indies. In early 1854 a circular was issued in London calling on free blacks and fugitive slaves to emigrate to Jamaica where land was available at one pound an acre. Five thousand fugitives, "under the guidance and instruction of such a man as Mr. Ward," the circular claimed, could produce a number of crops there, and "4 or 5 acres of good land" could earn £130 to £140 annually. Following Garnet's path, Ward wanted to lead "industrious and skilled families" to Jamaica and hoped for the "final settlement there of many thousands of fugitives from the land in which they are now, not only enslaved, but treated as an inferior, and incapable people." In December, Ward told a Boston, Lincolnshire, audience that he aimed to raise funds to "establish sugar and cotton plantations" in Jamaica to compete with American slave-grown goods, and he repeated his plans during an antislavery lecture in Chelmsford, Essex. This time, John Candler, a local abolitionist who owned 150 acres in Portland, Jamaica, offered Ward 50 acres on which to conduct his experiment.[17] Ward accepted the offer, and although his experiment was stillborn, the idea behind it retained credence. There remained hope that such settlements could work, and the anticipation of successful free-produce settlements clearly contributed to an increased interest in emigration among British abolitionists.

17. Chelmsford *Chronicle*, December 15, 1854; Boston and Louth *Guardian and Lincolnshire Advertiser*, December 13, 1854; *Provincial Freeman*, July 1, 1854; *Anti Slavery Reporter*, June, 1854; *British Banner*, May 24, 1854.

These emigrationist efforts reached their zenith with the visit of Martin Delany and Robert Campbell in 1860. Their attempts to establish a colony of free blacks in Abeokuta, Nigeria, epitomized the whole complex of issues and problems associated with colonization and emigration schemes in the 1850s. Emigrationism—a black-inspired and black-led movement that blacks carefully differentiated from colonization, the scheme of the ACS—gained increasing currency in the 1850s. The Niger Valley Exploring Party, of which Delany and Campbell were commissioners, had visited Liberia, Lagos, and Abeokuta in 1859. On December 28, a treaty was signed between the commissioners and the Alake, the king or chief, of Abeokuta allowing for the settlement of a select group of black Americans in and around Abeokuta. The commissioners envisioned the colony as a base for the promotion of civilization and Christianity on the west coast of Africa. Cotton and other tropical crops produced there could compete with slave-grown cotton in the markets of Europe, undermining the profitability of American slavery and thus ultimately leading to its destruction.[18]

The exploring party was Delany's brainchild. As early as 1852, he had proposed an expedition to East Africa, but for the following six years had directed his efforts towards Central America and the Caribbean. Africa, associated with the work of the ACS, was studiously eschewed by most emigrationists in the early fifties. But growing American interest in Central America and Anglo-American conflicts over the Mosquito Coast, may have prompted Delany to seek an alternative site for his colony. The publication of the Reverend T. J. Bowen's *Central Africa* and David Livingstone's *Missionary Travels and Researches in South Africa* in 1857 rekindled an interest in Africa and awakened new hopes for African emigration. Sometime in 1857 or 1858 Delany began making plans for an exploration party to visit West Africa. The group was to consist of five members: Delany as chief commissioner; Robert Douglas as artist; Rob-

18. Martin R. Delany, "Report of the Niger Valley Exploring Party," in Howard H. Bell (ed.), *Search for a Place: Black Separatism and Africa, 1860* (Ann Arbor, Mich., 1970), 77, 248–50; treaty enclosed with African Aid Society to Foreign Office, February 7, 1861, in FOD.

ert Campbell, naturalist; Dr. Amos Aray, surgeon; and James W. Purnell, secretary and commercial reporter.[19] By the time the party sailed for Africa in the summer of 1859, however, Delany and Campbell were the only remaining commissioners.

Opposition by many prominent black Americans to any form of emigration, and fears by the ACS that a successful settlement in the area might undermine its efforts in West Africa made it next to impossible for the party to get the kind of financial backing it needed. The whole issue of black Americans growing cotton in Africa produced the most vitriolic debates among black leaders. George T. Downing attacked the African Civilization Society, a competitor of Delany that was headed by Garnet, as an offshoot of the ACS aimed at ridding the country of the free-black population. Emigrationists "have not succeeded in their attempts to stuff their ears and eyes with '*cotton in Yoruba*,'" wrote Frederick Douglass. "They think the *Ex*-ploring Expedition to Africa is not much to be *de*-plored, as it has not yet sailed, and will not probably, until the *spring—the first favorable spring*!" Another opponent, John T. Gaines, saw in the Civilization Society "the same old Colonization *coon*." Ralph Gurley of the ACS openly expressed his fears that a settlement of black Americans near Lagos "if under special British protection might obtain some aid from Englishmen, but it would be very unfortunate for the character and destiny of such a settlement either to ask or receive such protection." It would be much better, he thought, "to have it connected with Liberia" or totally independent.[20]

It is no wonder that Delany found little support in America. It was partly in the hope of receiving some form of financial backing that Campbell left for England in April, 1859. In May he issued a circular calling for support from abolitionists and industrialists, especially Lancashire cotton manufacturers. A successful colony producing cotton for the English market, it proclaimed, would relieve English dependence on the South. This was a promising approach,

19. Delany, "Report of the Niger Valley Exploring Party," 39; Martin R. Delany, *The Condition, Elevation, Emigration, and Destiny of the Colored People of the United States Politically Considered* (1852; rpr. New York, 1968), 209–15.

20. R. R. Gurley to Theodore Bourne, March 3, 1859, in ACS; New York *Tribune*, December 10, 1858; *Douglass Monthly*, January, 1859.

for Lancashire textile producers were concerned about their almost total dependence on southern cotton. There were widespread fears that bad harvests or slave uprisings would destroy cotton supplies, and Campbell was listened to with much interest. Thomas Clegg, a Manchester cotton spinner involved in promoting cotton cultivation in Africa since 1850, gave Campbell letters of introduction to a number of prominent philanthropists. Clegg had been aware of the efforts among black Americans to establish a colony in Africa. A letter signed by Delany and two blacks from Wisconsin, J. J. Myers and Ambrose Dudley, had been sent to Clegg in 1858, requesting information on the most suitable place for the location of a colony. The original letter on the stationery of the "Mercantile Line of the Free Colored People of North America" was sent via an English professor of history at Wisconsin State University to the Royal Geographical Society in London. Campbell also had meetings with the BFASS, which gave its support to the expedition and the proposed colony. Through the efforts of Edmund Ashworth, a prominent cotton manufacturer from Bolton and a member of the Manchester Cotton Supply Association, Campbell was given a free passage by the British government on the packet sailing in June from Liverpool and letters of introduction by Lord Malmesbury, minister for foreign affairs to the acting consul in Lagos. In his brief visit Campbell raised two hundred pounds for the exploring party.[21]

By the time Delany and Campbell arrived in England in May, 1860, abolitionists and cotton manufacturers were aware of their successes in Africa. On May 18, two days after their arrival in London, they were invited to a meeting held at the London residence of Dr. Thomas Hodgkin, who had written the response to the earlier letter from Myers, Dudley, and Delany. Hodgkin was the leading

21. Henry Christy to Lord Russell, July 29, 1859, Edmund Ashworth to Foreign Office, May 20, 1859, both in FOD; Robert Campbell, "A Pilgrimage to My Motherland: An Account of a Journey Among the Egbas and Yorubas of Central Africa in 1859–1860," in Bell (ed.), *Search for a Place*, 162; Manchester *Weekly Advertiser*, July 17, 1858; Joseph Hobbins to Secretary, Royal Geographical Society, June 7, 1858, Jonathan Myers, Ambrose Dudley, and Martin R. Delany to Hobbins, May 31, 1858, both in Royal Geographical Society Papers, Royal Geographical Society Archives, London; *Anti Slavery Reporter*, June 1, 1859; Circular, May 13, 1859, in BFASS; Delany, "Report of the Niger Valley Exploring Party," 43–44.

English supporter of Garnet's African Civilization Society, and it
was this organization, through its agent in Britain, the Reverend
Theodore Bourne, that had called the meeting. Actually, many British abolitionists erroneously believed that the Niger Valley Exploring Party was operating under the auspices of the Civilization Society. Since his arrival in England as agent of the society, Bourne
had worked diligently to foster this belief. He told a Bolton meeting
in September, 1859, that several of the society's members were
"upon the West Coast of Africa and others at Yoruba, pioneering
the way for those who were to follow." Garnet himself had helped
to create this false impression. In an open letter to English supporters of the cause he wrote, "some members of the Society have already gone there [Yoruba], and have made an agreement with the
Kings and Chiefs of the Egba country." Although Campbell had associated briefly with Bourne and the society before leaving for England, both he and Delany continually declared their independence
from the society.[22]

Bourne had been hard at work since August, 1858, creating support for the society among British abolitionists. In August he attended a meeting chaired by Lord Brougham at which the aims of
the society were introduced by George Thompson. Throughout
September, Bourne worked on winning the support of Manchester
cotton men. At a meeting held in the mayor's parlor on September 21 and chaired by the president of the Manchester Chamber of
Commerce a resolution was adopted approving the objects of the
Civilization Society and a committee formed to raise money for its

22. Henry Venn of the Church Missionary Society told the Reverend Henry
Townsend, head of the CMS mission in Abeokuta, that in a meeting with Bourne
the agent was unable to show a link between the Civilization Society and Delany
and Campbell "except that if Mr. Campbell succeeded in establishing friendly relations with the Chiefs and obtained territory (!) the Society would be glad to avail
themselves of his position." G. F. Buhler, a former missionary in Africa, told Venn,
"The Americans, Mr. Campbell and Dr. Delany go ahead without us, they are in-
deed not the white man's friend though they will take his money; they rail against
Rev. Theodore Bourne . . . who collected funds in England." G. F. Buhler to Henry
Venn, February 24, 1860, Venn to Henry Townsend, October 23, 1859, both in
CMS; Bolton *Chronicle*, October 1, 1859; African Civilization Society, Circular, in
BFASS; *Weekly Anglo African*, March 31, 1860.

efforts. Bourne proudly informed the meeting that the society had already won the endorsements of the BFASS and the Congregational Union. But Bourne's progress was not all clear sailing; he had to contend with opposition from Sarah Parker Remond. At a Bolton meeting she condemned Bourne for giving the false impression that free blacks wished to return to Africa to civilize the natives and raise cotton. The idea was as ludicrous, she told her audience, as thinking that the Pilgrims wished to return to England to civilize the natives. As she told a Manchester audience a few days later "there is nothing the free colored people of the United States hate like colonization in the concrete. They are attached to their homes and their country; for America not Africa is their country; and they have no more idea of leaving it than the oppressed Italian people have of leaving Italy."[23]

The debate echoed the controversies surrounding the visits of Cresson and Gurley in the 1830s and 1840s, but there was one crucial difference. There were now strong proslavery feelings in Liverpool and Manchester especially attributable, Remond believed, to concern about the cotton supply. For precisely this reason Bourne succeeded in 1860 where Cresson and Gurley had failed earlier. His chances of success were further enhanced by the growth of emigrationist sentiment among British abolitionists, fostered by the FPM. The play of these two factors is seen in the endorsement given the Civilization Society by the London Emancipation Society, a Garrisonian group the majority of whose members would have viewed the proposal as utter heresy ten years earlier. By the time Bourne returned to America for a short stay at the end of November, he had effectively established the Civilization Society as the agent of Yoruba colonization in the eyes of British abolitionists and cotton manufacturers.[24]

On his return to England, Bourne continued to promote the society. He wrote A. A. Constantine, corresponding secretary of the society, that Lord Churchill, who would later become chairman of

23. *Anti Slavery Advocate*, November, 1859; Bolton *Chronicle*, October 1, 1859.

24. *Weekly Anglo African*, September 3, 1859; Manchester *Guardian*, September 5, 21, 1859; Bolton *Chronicle*, October 1, 1859; *Anti Slavery Reporter*, November 1, 1859; New York *Colonization Journal*, December, 1859; Bourne to Louis Chamerovzow, March 2, 1860, in BFASS; *Anti Slavery Advocate*, December, 1859.

the African Aid Society, had developed a plan for the formation of a large joint-stock company to assist in implementing the scheme of the Civilization Society. Sir Culling Eardly, a leader of the Evangelical movement, had promised one million pounds to support this effort. A circular issued by Bourne in April called for the formation of a British society with branches throughout the United Kingdom to aid the society "to carry out the objects of promoting the Christian Civilization of Africa, by means of Christian colored settlers from America and to instruct the natives in improved modes of art, manufactures and the cultivation of the soil." He proposed the creation of the Central African Commercial Company to purchase, collect, and forward African goods—especially cotton—to Britain and to sell British goods to Africa. The circular was issued on the authority of a recently formed committee that would later organize itself into the African Aid Society (AAS). Among its members were Churchill, Eardly, Dr. Cummings, Minton, Richardson, Hale, McLeod, and Dr. Hodgkin. All but Hodgkin would sit on the Executive Committee of the AAS.[25]

The existence of an organization allied to the Civilization Society posed a particularly thorny problem for Delany, still smarting as he was from his failure to win substantial support in America. Now that he had succeeded in Africa he saw no reason to give ground to his competitors. It is also possible that news of the continuing bitter dispute between the Civilization Society and its black opponents in New York had reached Delany in London. He used the first meeting at Hodgkin's home to undermine Bourne's position and reestablish himself as the dominant force in African emigration. Bourne's position was made even more difficult because of British partiality for blacks promoting their own cause. Delany, noted for his racial pride and his insistence that blacks should act independently of whites—American whites at least—capitalized on this British proclivity. At a meeting called by the society at Clayland Chapel, London, on May 30, he told his audience exactly how black he was and assured them that his personal success was the surest vindication of his race's "superior intellectual gifts."[26]

25. *Anti Slavery Reporter*, April 2, June 1, 1860; New York *Colonization Journal*, May, 1860.

26. New York *Colonization Journal*, July, 1860; Delany, "Report of the Niger Val-

Delany continued to employ this strategy throughout his stay in Britain. By June he had effectively destroyed Bourne's credibility with many abolitionists. "Our friend Bourne is still labouring in the cause which brought him here," Hodgkin told a friend, "but I fear that the presence of the travellers to which he looked for help in his advocacy may rather prove to have been an incumbrance. He has succeeded in exciting an interest in various quarters but I see that he is tried by a variety of unfortunate coincidences which may occasion him considerable annoyances." In a later letter to Garnet, Hodgkin explained exactly what he meant; "No man can rely more than I on our friend Bourne's integrity, zeal, knowledge of the subject and perseverance. I think him far beyond Delany and in most respects they will not bear comparison yet Delany is courted for his color and I fear that flattered by this he may stay to the injury of the cause." Although Bourne attended the founding meeting of the AAS in July and was given a loan by the society, by September he had lost his influence. The Civilization Society ended his mission rather abruptly toward the end of September. Constantine explained the termination in the most guarded language. The society's supporters in England, he wrote, were so well acquainted with their plans and objectives that it was no longer necessary to continue Bourne's agency. But the fact remained that Delany had replaced Bourne as the leading promoter of emigration and was causing the society considerable concern. By the end of the year those who had abandoned Bourne attempted to salve their consciences by giving him a number of testimonials at which his efforts were lauded. Both Hodgkin and Bourne also attempted to soften the blow by suggesting that his agency ended only after the formation of the British African Civilization Society. The evidence suggests, however, that this organization was never really operative.[27]

Delany and Campbell arrived in England at a time when textile manufacturers were openly expressing their concern about the con-

ley Exploring Party," 122–23.

27. New York *Colonization Journal*, March, May, 1861; Bourne to George Whipple, December 1860, in AMA; *Anti Slavery Reporter*, October 1, 1860; A. A. Constantine to Chamerovzow, September 1, 1860, in BFASS; Thomas Hodgkin to William Coppinger, June 30, 1860, Hodgkin to Garnet, August 29, 1860, both in HP.

tinued supply of cotton from the South as their dependence on American cotton grew. The depression of 1857 only increased their anxieties. The weekly consumption of British cotton mills rose from 30,000 to 45,000 bales between 1850 and 1856. Meanwhile, American production fell temporarily, resulting in heavy price increases between 1856 and 1857. By 1859 British mills were consuming five-sevenths of American production at a cost of £732 million, textile exports were valued at one half of all exports, and almost £25 million were expended on wages for the employment of some 1.5 million operatives. It was estimated that £150 million was invested in mills and machinery, and roughly 2 million tons of shipping was used in the trade with a marine force of some ten thousand seamen.[28]

The fear created by this dependence led to the formation of the Cotton Supply Association (CSA) in April, 1857. The association was not to undertake the cultivation of cotton but "to obtain as full and reliable information as possible respecting the extent and capabilities of cotton cultivation in every country where it could be grown." Unlike the economists of the Manchester school, the CSA envisaged government involvement in paving the way for their efforts, a view in many respects similar to Prime Minister Palmerston's. Although Palmerston was critical of the textile manufacturers' failure to procure alternative sources of cotton, he instructed British representatives in cotton-growing areas to cooperate with the CSA. In September, 1858, Benjamin Campbell, consul at Lagos, visited Manchester to brief the CSA on cotton growing in West Africa. Although the CSA's main interest was India, West Africa's potential was not ignored. In 1857 exports of palm oil, cotton, ivory, and cotton clothes from the Bight of Benin were valued at £1,062,800. Consul Campbell was instrumental in the increased exports of cotton from Lagos and Abeokuta. Between March, 1858, and March, 1859, Liverpool and London imported a total of 1,800 bales from West Africa; between 1859 and 1860, Liverpool imported 1,600 and

28. *Anti Slavery Reporter*, April 2, 1860; Frank L. Owsley, *King Cotton Diplomacy: Foreign Relations of the Confederate States of America* (Chicago, 1969), 3; Arthur Silver, *Manchester Men and Indian Cotton, 1847–72* (Manchester, 1966), 77–79; Cotton Supply Association, *Third Annual Report* (Manchester, 1860).

London 1,847 bales—an increase of nearly 100 percent in twelve months. As the first report of the association said, "Africa bids fair in a very few years to rival our best sources of supply."[29]

Interest in Africa was in large measure promoted and sustained by Thomas Clegg. Clegg, who employed about fifteen hundred workers in his mills on the outskirts of Manchester, had become involved in West African cotton in 1850 when he joined forces with the Church Missionary Society to encourage Africans to increase their cotton production for export to Britain. Under their joint efforts industrial institutions were established at Abeokuta and later at Onitsha and Lokojo to encourage the cultivation of cotton for export. Like Henry Venn of the CMS, Clegg was concerned to create a local indigenous middle class as an agency for the promotion of commerce, Christianity, and civilization. He feared that, "if Europeans took up the cultivation of cotton, or dealing in the interior, it would, in all probability, result in the revival of slave labour, or merely in a spasmodic effort or two, and then a sickening off, a failure and relinquishing the effort, after destroying, in all probability, the self-reliance the native formally had." In order to achieve his objective Clegg, with the help of the CMS, brought to his mills in Manchester two Sierra Leonians, Henry Robbins and Josiah Crowther, to teach them the skills of processing and packing cotton. It is no wonder that Clegg followed Delany and Campbell's efforts in Africa with a keen interest. A colony of black Americans could form part of his proposed native agency. When Clegg said "Africa for the Africans, Europe for the white man," he was articulating the sentiments of Delany.[30]

By 1858 English cotton manufacturers, abolitionists, and the government were becoming increasingly involved in West African de-

29. Cotton Supply Association, *First Annual Report* (Manchester, 1858), 11, 8–9; *Anti Slavery Reporter*, March 1, 1858; BFASS to Foreign Office, June 22, 1861, in FOD; Isaac Watts, *The Cotton Supply Association: Its Origin and Progress* (Manchester, 1861), 98, 10; W. O. Anderson, "The Cotton Supply Association, 1857–1872," *Empire Cotton Growing Review*, IX (1932), 133.

30. *Anti Slavery Reporter*, May 1, 1858; James A. Mann, *The Cotton Trade of Great Britain* (London, 1860), 84; *Douglass Monthly*, August, 1859; J. F. A. Ajayi, *Christian Missions in Nigeria, 1841–1891: The Making of a New Elite* (London, 1965), 156.

velopments. The cotton manufacturers sanctioned Delany's scheme in the hope that it would provide an alternative source of cotton, and abolitionists supported it on free-labor grounds. Delany, therefore, found an alert and responsive audience for his plans. His ideas of economic development corresponded very closely to the conventional wisdom of laissez-faire economic organization. Land was available and free, labor was plentiful, and black Americans could provide the necessary expertise. Throughout England and Scotland, Delany preached the theory of what he later called the triple alliance: with capital from Britain large profits would be made and divided equally among colonists, capitalists, and the African owners of the land.[31] It was a rather simplistic analysis of economic development that played into the hands of British cotton manufacturers and capitalists.

After a series of meetings in May and June, the AAS was formed on July 17, 1860. According to its first report, formation of the society was stimulated by the African emigrationist movement among black Americans. Its development was in large measure due to the activities of the Reverend Theodore Bourne and to the interest of cotton manufacturers and merchants in West Africa. Bourne had attracted most of the society's leading figures to the cause of African emigration even before the arrival of Delany and Campbell. In addition, both Churchill and J. Lyons McLeod, leading officers of the society, were actively involved with the CSA as early as 1859. With the removal of Bourne, Delany became the prominent American involved in the promotion of emigration and cotton cultivation in West Africa. It is quite clear that the formation of the AAS was a product of economic exigencies created by dependence on southern cotton, rather than the work of philanthropists and abolitionists, although many supported the effort. The society aimed to develop the resources of Africa, Madagascar, and the adjacent islands and to promote the Christian civilization of the African races, which would ultimately result in the destruction of the slave trade. This was to be achieved by encouraging the production of tropical crops through

31. Glasgow *Merchantile Advertiser*, October 30, 1860; *Cotton Supply Reporter*, November 2, 1860.

the introduction of skilled black or white labor "into those parts of the earth which are inhabited by the African race." It would assist by means of loans all blacks willing to leave Canada and the United States for the West Indies, Liberia, Natal, and "such countries as may seem to offer a suitable field of labor." These emigrants were to form industrial missions and join with those already in existence for the extension of Christianity. The society in its turn would supply mechanical tools and get samples of native products to the manufacturing community in Great Britain "with a view to the promotion of legitimate commerce."[32]

In his relations with the AAS, Delany continued to insist that decisions affecting the proposed black settlement were to be self-generated. All loans made to the settlers were to be repaid in "produce or otherwise." He saw the role of the society as mainly aiding "the *voluntary* emigration of colored people from America in general, and our movement as originated by colored people in particular."[33] However, it is doubtful whether a colony of this nature could have maintained its independence in light of the interest of British capital. The composition of the society reflected its interest. A few members of its Executive Council were clergymen and ministers, but most were businessmen. The Glasgow Branch Committee and the Birmingham Auxiliary Committee had a similar composition, while the proposed Manchester Branch Committee was to include a large representation from the CSA and the Manchester Chamber of Commerce. In memorials sent to the Foreign Office by the AAS requesting the establishment of a consulate at Abeokuta, 110 of the 167 signatories were businessmen. A letter addressed to the Foreign Office by the Manchester Committee suggesting that a commissioner be sent to the king of Dahomey was signed by 45 people of which 39 were manufacturers, merchants, and agents associated with cotton.[34]

Following the formation of the AAS, Delany spent five months

32. African Aid Society, *First Report, from July, 1860, to the 31st March, 1862* (London, n.d.), 2–3; *Cotton Supply Reporter*, November 16, 1860.

33. Delany, "Report of the Niger Valley Exploring Party," 124–25.

34. African Aid Society to Foreign Office, March 23, February 8, 1861, both in FOD; African Aid Society, *First Report*, 31–32.

on tour of Britain to promote his scheme. Wherever he went his views were favorably received. On his way to Glasgow to attend the Social Science Congress he gave a series of lectures in Newcastle entitled "Africa and the African Race" on the prospects for development through commerce. On the issue of African commerce one local newspaper observed that the "subject is one of vast importance to England and we must trust that we may witness ere long a proper appreciation of it." In Glasgow, Delany continued in the same vein. In his lecture on October 9, he called on Scottish businessmen to increase their involvement in West African trade for, he argued, "although there were 1,500 civilized blacks in Lagos, who were raised in the missionary schools, there was not much commercial ability about them, and a higher degree of intelligence was wanted there," which would be provided by the skilled American black emigrant. He was not above pandering to the greed of his audience; white men, he told them, stood to make ten thousand pounds yearly from business investments in Lagos. Of course he repeated the old theory that the expansion of commerce and the spread of Christianity would lead to the civilization of backward Africa. Three hundred pounds was needed immediately for the transportation and temporary assistance of the ten or twelve people whom he intended to take to Abeokuta the following spring. By the end of the month a committee was formed to raise funds to help him "carry out his mission in Central Africa."[35]

Throughout his stay in Britain, Delany's efforts to procure a market for the products of his African colony were based on the rather naïve assumption that his proposed alliance between British capital, African labor, and black American expertise was an alliance of equal parts, in which profits would be shared equally. He established commercial relations with some of the leading firms in Glasgow "for an immediate, active and practical prosecution of our enterprise, and whose agency in Europe for any or all of our produce, may be fully relied on." In Leeds he promised to provide that city's chamber of commerce with all the facts he had gathered in Africa in

35. Glasgow *Examiner*, October 13, 27, 1860; *Daily Chronicle and Northern Counties Advertiser*, September 17, 1860; Newcastle *Chronicle*, September 22, 1860.

the hope of stimulating interest in his plans.[36] Given the clearly stated and limited objectives of commercial interests involved in his plans, it is highly unlikely that Delany or his proposed colony could have maintained independence. Apparently, these cotton manufacturers and merchants saw the Abeokuta colony as an easy way of establishing their presence and influence in the area.

When the Alake, under pressure from the Reverend Henry Townsend of the Church Missionary Society, rescinded his agreement with Delany and Campbell, the AAS promptly proposed to shift the site of the colony to Ambas Bay. When that proposal also proved unsuccessful because the blacks from Canada who were to have emigrated decided to join the Union army instead, the AAS quickly abandoned all idea of a colony and instead moved to pressure the British government to extend its sphere of influence in West Africa. It called for the occupation of the fort at Whydah, Dahomey, if the king of Dahomey failed to accede to demands to stop human torture. Inasmuch as William Craft was summarily dismissed by the Company of African Merchants, whose secretary was F. Fitzgerald, secretary of the AAS, however, it seems likely that concern about torture was nothing more than a fig leaf to hide the society's commercial designs. The company had appointed Craft its agent in Whydah during his second trip to Dahomey in 1863. But by 1867 it had seen fit to discontinue the relationship, leaving Craft little to show for the association. Like Delany, Craft found himself shunted aside by commercial interests. It is no wonder that at the height of the cotton famine the *African Times*, organ of the society, could call for making the Niger the Mississippi of Africa "as regards cotton and other valuable produce."[37]

But there is one other curious aspect in all of this. In spite of the fact that rising interest in emigration coincided with the quickening of racist views in Britain typified by men like Carlyle and Knox, black American visitors, all of whom expressed a deep interest in

36. Leeds *Mercury*, December 8, 1860; Delany, "Report of the Niger Valley Exploring Party," 139–42.

37. *African Times*, February 23, 1862; Company of African Merchants to Foreign Office, December 16, 1863, in FOD.

Africa and all of whom condemned American racism in no uncertain terms, ignored British racism. With the exception of William Wells Brown's rather tepid condemnation of Carlyle's "Occasional Discourse on the Nigger Question," not a single black abolitionist attempted a sustained refutation of British advocates of white superiority. Indeed, only one black newspaper in North America, the *Provincial Freeman*, saw any possible relationship between the growth in support of Jamaican emigration and British racism. But the editors of the *Provincial Freeman* had their own axe to grind, for they were leading advocates of Canadian settlements. In opposing the 1854 circular that proposed Ward as the leader of emigrants from Canada to Jamaica, they claimed that land was much cheaper in Canada and that the scheme had been devised by the Jamaican planter class to ensure a supply of labor and so "perpetuate the peasant class." Some men in England, they observed, were promoting Jamaican emigration solely because they wanted to keep North America "for the 'white races' alone."[38] But the *Provincial Freeman* remained a lone voice in a silence that continued, with a few minor exceptions, throughout the fifties. Ward's and Delany's continuous reiteration of pride in their blackness may have been meant as refutation, and William G. Allen's lectures, which concentrated on antiquity and the contributions of Africa to European civilization, may also be viewed as indirect refutation of white supremacists, but by and large, blacks were silent. They concentrated their attention on redeeming their less fortunate brethren in Africa.

Delany delivered a series of lectures entitled "Africa and the African Race" throughout Britain in 1860. He spoke of the economic potential of West Africa and his prescription for its development and "civilization." Like most other African emigrationists, he argued that successful commerce and the spread of Christianity would ultimately civilize the African continent. The "new world" emigrants were to be harbingers of African redemption, creating in their new home a moral order that—through Christianity, economic strength, and social balance, the prerequisites of cultural development—

38. *Provincial Freeman*, July 1, 1854; William Wells Brown, *Three Years in Europe; or, Places I Have Seen and People I Have Met* (London, 1852), 200–201.

would lead to the removal of inequalities and the march of African societies toward "perfection." This moral order was to be achieved through hard work, seriousness of character, respectability, and self-help, or as Crummell put it, "forecast, wakefulness, industry, thrift, probity and tireless, sweatful toil." Crummell would have accepted Matthew Arnold's differentiation between "'cultivation' [culture], which was difficult to nurture, and 'civilization', which just grew," but would not have agreed with Arnold that the nurturing of culture was the work of people "in every class of society who were endowed with an honest curiosity about their best selves." Crummell was no nineteenth-century liberal. To him, the all-powerful and regulating hand of God had placed the emigrant in Liberia to be "the guardian, the protector, and the teacher of our heathen tribes." The untutored natives, like adolescent children, were to be wards of superior talent and wiser heads until such time as they acquired all the necessary skills and sophistication. This maturation would only be achieved through careful guidance and the judicious use of authority. "All historical fact," Crummell boldly argued, "shows that force, that is authority, must be used in the exercise of guardianship over heathen tribes."[39]

Here was the emigrationists' variant of Manifest Destiny. Unlike Charles Dickens' Mr. Dombey, they aimed to deal in both hides and hearts. Every African emigrationist saw the "hand of God" directing him towards the task of African redemption. "Industrious, enterprising and carrying with them, one here and another there, a knowledge of some of the useful arts," the recaptured slaves returning from Sierra Leone to Abeokuta and Lagos, Robert Campbell argued, "have doubtless been the means of inaugurating a mighty work, which, now that it has accomplished its utmost" should be continued to "a higher form by the more civilized of the same race, who for a thousand reasons, are best adapted to its successful prose-

39. Alexander Crummell, *Africa and America* (1891; rpr. New York, 1969), 185; Asa Briggs, *The Age of Improvement, 1783–1867* (London, 1959), 475–78; Wilson J. Moses, "Civilizing Missionary: A Study of Alexander Crummell," *Journal of Negro History*, LX (1975), 229–51; Alexander Crummell, *The Future of Africa* (1862; rpr. New York, 1969), 233. Although these quotations are from a later period in Crummell's life, he first expressed these views while in England.

cution." To emigrationists, slavery and the slave trade were the crucibles in which blacks acquired the skills and talents for the work of African redemption. God had trained blacks in the New World, wrote Crummell, echoing the early colonizationists, for "His own great work in Africa." The exile in slavery had given blacks the opportunity to acquire the "Anglo-Saxon tongue," a language that instilled concepts of freedom, ordered and systematic reform, and through the Bible, a sense of justice. Having acquired the language of the Magna Carta, blacks from the New World, Crummell argued, were to be the agents for shedding "light" on "benighted" Africa. The mission of this vanguard was not to produce "intelligent heathens" or "intellectual paganism" but natives trained "to the spirit, moral sentiments, and practical genius of the language."[40] This new moral order, based on the precepts of Christianity, would be the bedrock of civilization and perfection.

All these attitudes and their propagation in the 1850s played directly, if unwittingly, into the hands of a growing and aggressive Anglo-Saxonism. If, as Douglas Lorimer has suggested, attempts by abolitionists to win British sympathy for the African paradoxically intensified Victorian race consciousness, then the position of many black American emigrationists must have contributed, albeit unconsciously, to the confirmed belief in African inferiority.[41] The failure to criticize men like Carlyle and Knox in the 1850s could be attributed in part to the almost unanimously favorable treatment black Americans received from their hosts, in part to a desire to win support for their many schemes, and in part to the fact that emigrationists held many views in common with mid-century Britain about Africa and the African. It would have been surprising, in any case, if black American criticism had been any more strident or sustained in the 1850s, for there was no appreciable change in British hospitality. Aside from Zilpha Elaw, John Brown, and Box Brown, not one visitor felt it necessary to comment, privately or publicly, on racism in

40. Crummell, *The Future of Africa*, 47–48; Crummell, *Hope for Africa: A Sermon on Behalf of the Ladies' Negro Education Society* (London, 1853), 42; Campbell, "A Pilgrimage to My Motherland," 201.

41. Douglas A. Lorimer, "British Attitudes to the Negro, 1850–1870" (Ph.D. dissertation, University of British Columbia, 1972), 86.

Britain. In fact, throughout the 1850s blacks continued to comment on the lack of racism in Britain compared to America. The shifts we can now discern in British racial attitudes during the decade before the Civil War were never clearly defined to the visitors themselves. They continued to be warmly received wherever they went, and this hospitality contrasted so markedly with their experiences in America that it could not have failed to impress even the least sensitive of the black American visitors. Not until the end of the decade did they have cause to rebuke Britain for her views on race. Frederick Douglass, for example, during his second tour of Britain, in 1860, called on British humanitarians to condemn both growing racism in their midst and the popular minstrel shows that mocked black American culture.[42]

By 1863 racist theories began to gain some currency, and abolitionists became increasingly concerned that these views could provide a justification for recognition and support of the South. William Craft, who had recently returned from a mission to Dahomey but who could in no way be considered an emigrationist, launched an attack on the growing body of race theories. Craft had been invited to report on his trip to the annual meeting of the British Association for the Advancement of Science. In a contretemps that threatened to disrupt the otherwise staid proceedings, Craft launched blistering attacks on the presidents of the Ethnological and Anthropological Societies, John Crawfund and James Hunt, both of whom read papers that argued for African inferiority and European superiority. Crawfund, in his paper on August 28 entitled "The Comixture of the Races of Man as Affecting the Progress of Civilization," argued that in situations where superior races had mixed with races inferior to themselves their civilizations had declined. Nature, he observed, had endowed the various races with widely different qualities both physical and mental, and where there was a great disparity between the races, antipathy rather than amalgamation was the natu-

42. Ayr *Observer*, April 3, 1860. Rehin has argued that there is little evidence to suggest that racism fostered minstrelsy or that the popular art form pandered to growing racism in Victorian society. George Rehin, "Harlequin Jim Crow: Continuity and Convergence in Blackface Clowning," *Journal of Popular Culture*, IX (1975), 682–701.

ral consequence. To him the Americas epitomized the purest expression of this law, for neither the freedmen in the Caribbean nor slaves in areas where they were a majority in the United States had assumed dominant positions over whites. The existence of racist laws in the South testified, he thought, to black inferiority, and he concluded that it was "the presence of the African race, too prone to live and labour in slavery or in special degradation, and utterly incapable of rising to an equality with the higher race among whom it has been unhappily planted, that has caused the present distracted state of the North American continent." Craft countered Crawfund's contention of natural antipathy between races by pointing out that a considerable portion of the black population in America was in fact mixed, in spite of the laws that banned interracial marriages. The general degraded state of the black population was due, he observed, not to any inherent racial characteristics but to social oppression. Whenever blacks had been given an equal opportunity "they had shown that they possessed considerable intellectual ability, and many of them had risen to very high positions, in society." He concluded with the remark that he had lived in England for thirteen years but had only managed to find one Shakespeare among the Anglo-Saxons. The session was thrown into a heated round of discussion in which "science" and "scientific data" were quickly abandoned, finally forcing the chairman to end the meeting early.

By the time Dr. Hunt presented his paper, "On the Physical and Mental Character of the Negro," the conference was eagerly awaiting a confrontation. They were not to be disappointed. Hunt mustered all the past experts of racial history and the science of races to assert that the African races were "intermediate between the highest and lowest existing races of Man." Examinations of facial angles, weight and thickness of bones, size of thorax and skull, gait, and many more characteristics showed, in Hunt's view, that the Negro was inferior to the European and that no amount of civilization could change that fact. Negroes who had managed to advance in the scale of civilization all had European blood. Those who opposed these scientific laws and continued to plead for and give support to Negro equality were either ignorant or stupid men. "From all the evidence we have examined," he concluded, "we see no reason to believe that the pure Negro even advances further in intellect than an intelligent European boy of fourteen years of age."

Craft replied to Hunt's paper with sarcasm and ridicule. He apologized for his own racial mixture but insisted that he was black enough to oppose Hunt's position. Countering Hunt's claim that the African's thick skull was ample evidence of his smaller brain and intelligence, Craft suggested that the skull's thickness "had been wisely arranged by Providence to defend the brain from the tropical climate in which he lived. If God had not given them thick skulls their brains would probably have become very much like those of many scientific gentlemen of the present day." After repeating many of the points he had made against Crawfund's paper, Craft said that the opinions of men like Hunt and Crawfund went beyond the mere expression of "scientific fact" and were being developed and used as justifications for the continued oppression of blacks.[43] In defense of his position, Hunt argued for the primacy of scientific evidence, which could only be refuted by contrary scientific evidence and not by what he called "poetical clap-trap, or by gratuitous and worthless assumptions." A correspondent for the Newcastle *Chronicle* captured the bitterness of the encounter: "The tone of these unenviable anthropologists on the Negro anatomy was an outrage to every kindly feeling, and an insult to humanity. . . . Mr. Craft's clear, open generous and manly countenance contrasted most successfully with that of his bitter opponent."[44]

While Delany and other emigrationists understandably placed unbending faith in commerce—the "handmaiden of religion," to use Crummell's phrase—as the foundation of African redemption and the destroyer of American slavery, many of those who came to their assistance were interested only in commerce. As products of their time, very few black emigrationists saw the possible consequences of their arguments and proposals. From their standpoint, black Americans and West Indians were to lead the "benighted" African out of darkness into the light of Christian civilization through

43. London *Times*, August 31, 29, 1863.
44. James Hunt, letter to *Anthropological Review*, I (1863); Newcastle *Chronicle*, September 19, 1863.

commercially viable settlements. By the late 1850s this cultural "arrogance" and their determination to employ all possible means to destroy slavery played into the hands of British cotton interests and unintentionally gave some credence to the views of Carlyle and his ilk. Where Buxton and Venn had previously envisaged the creation of an African elite as a conduit of "civilization," Lancashire cotton men saw a colony of skilled American blacks as the means of procuring an alternative source of cotton for their mills. Throughout the 1850s, commercial interests slowly but perceptibly replaced the sort of "telescopic philanthropy" directed toward the natives of Borrioboola-Gha by Charles Dickens' Mrs. Jellyby. Delany's scheme was doomed to failure given the economic foundations of the colony and its relationship to British commercial interests; the "triple alliance" was just not feasible in the mid–nineteenth century.

Conclusion

The building of the antislavery cordon and its preservation for over thirty years demanded skill, determination, and consummate diplomacy on the part of black Americans. As products of American slavery and discrimination, they brought an authenticity, a legitimacy, to the international movement that their white co-workers could never claim. They were the bona fide representatives of millions of oppressed human beings whom they successfully portrayed as the pariahs of American society. Unlike white American abolitionists, blacks were constrained neither by the niceties of ideology nor by competition within the movement. They brought to the task a pragmatism—some said a cynical expediency—that appealed to all factions of the international movement. This ensured relatively free movement between competing factions at a time when schisms threatened the international alliance. Abolitionist affiliations in America, although never totally rejected, were shelved whenever they endangered the existence of the cordon. Garrisonian abolitionists Charles L. Remond, Frederick Douglass, and William Wells Brown moved relatively freely between competing groups in the interest of unity. J. W. C. Pennington, Henry H. Garnet, and other supporters of political abolitionism had a harder time convincing British Garrisonians that their aims transcended narrow sectarian objectives. But they persisted, working together particularly in the early 1850s to plug the breaches in the antislavery wall brought on by divisions in the movement. This catholic approach initially helped keep the movement alive and vibrant when threatened by schisms, but ultimately it created a third alternative that further split the movement. From the arrival of McCune Smith in 1831 to the visit of Martin Delany, Douglass, and Sarah Parker Remond in 1860, blacks worked to persuade the British public that American slavery and discrimination violated human rights and threatened the moral order. They did not seek to overthrow the American government, nor were they concerned to promote British government intervention in American politics. Rather they aimed to inform the British public about the nature of American slavery and discrimination and to let America know that the world was aware of and watching her actions toward her black "citizens." It is not easy to evaluate the success of these efforts; it is never easy to gauge the intangible effects of the international appeals of oppressed groups. The fact that the Free Church refused to return the money it had collected in the South distressed Douglass, but he took comfort in the assurance that the controversy provided abolitionists with an opportunity to extend the debate over American slavery and to increase British public awareness about the nature of the system. The failure in 1846 of the Evangelical Alliance and of later efforts to reactivate it in the 1850s provided evidence of success that even Douglass may have overlooked. But while these victories were important, they should be viewed as by-products of the primary effort, which aimed at informing British public opinion. Certainly, this effort was successful though impossible to quantify with any certainty. Perhaps, black Americans influenced British policy at the outbreak of the Civil War, for governments cannot ignore an informed public, and the British public was informed.

The objective—building a moral cordon—dictated tactics. Displaying the "faculty of easy anger," as Walter Bagehot called it, the lectures, pamphlets, narratives, panoramas, and personal contacts of blacks exhorted the British to support the victims and their representatives. Personal contacts broadened support even among those who were ideologically antagonistic. Elizabeth Pease's insistence that she found Garnet charming and intelligent in spite of the attempts of Douglass and the British Garrisonians to discredit him is a case in point. John Cropper of Liverpool, initially a partisan of the ACS, attributed his change of mind to an interview with Alexander Crummell. Thomas Clarkson's rejection of the ACS was, in Garrison's view, directly attributable to his interview with Nathaniel Paul. Of course it is next to impossible to determine the extent to which these personal contacts influenced those who were not already partial to the cause, but thirty years of communication, given the popularity of blacks, must have made inroads into the ranks of the uncommitted.

Few areas of Britain remained untouched by their lectures. Thousands heard their eloquent and stirring pleas for the slave. Local editors continually expressed amazement at the talent displayed. A Charles Remond lecture on slavery and prejudice contained, according to a Dublin editor, "some of the finest bursts of natural, trembling, heart-stirring eloquence it has ever been our lot to witness." Remond was no exception; Douglass' wit and eloquence were legendary. His mimicry of the southern planter and clergyman added a touch of entertainment to his lectures. Listeners in Alloa were genuinely surprised at Garnet's fluency and eloquence, which one newspaper thought was "the best possible refutation of the idea that the negro belongs to an inferior grade in the creation." British abolitionists were convinced that these lectures contributed greatly to the isolation of proslavery America. When he heard that the Crafts and Box Brown were on their way to Britain, Webb wrote his American friends: "if they do come they will excite a hearty interest for American slaves and an increasing contempt and repugnance for their republican masters. There is no truer saying than 'by their fruits ye shall know them'—and a troupe of fugitive slaves—true heroes—lecturing through England must diffuse strange ideas of the peculiar institution."[1]

British abolitionists were not to be disappointed. These lectures, combining condemnation with analyses of slavery and prejudice, were meant to inform the listeners as well as to prod them to support the movement. Wherever an opportunity presented itself—from pulpits, church halls, sabbath schools, mechanics institutes, soirées, tea parties, and street corners—blacks lectured against American oppression. They never restricted themselves to purely

1. *National Anti Slavery Standard*, December 26, 1850; Alloa *Advertiser*, March 20, 1852; *Freeman's Journal*, n.d., in *Liberator*, September 10, 1841.

abolitionist meetings. William Wells Brown and Pennington used the occasion of the Paris Peace Congress to attack slavery as part of the "war element." Pennington and Garnet did the same in Germany. Brown, arguing that slaves "derived great advantage through teetotalism" and that there existed a commonality of benevolence, called on a Christian Temperance Union meeting to condemn American slavery.[2] Almost every other visitor worked with British temperance societies, too, and some, like Ward and Crummell, used meetings of missionary societies and Sabbath unions to promote the cause.

These efforts were supported by the publication of slave narratives, which sold as fast as they were printed. From the appearance of Moses Roper's in 1837 to that of the Crafts' in 1860, these narratives lent further authenticity and support to the effort to isolate proslavery America. In the decade before the war roughly one dozen major and minor narratives were published in Britain, all going through multiple editions. These were supplemented by a number of autobiographical pamphlets like William G. Allen's *The American Prejudice Against Colour* that also exposed American oppression. Brown's travelogues and his novel *Clotel*, in spite of its shortcomings, testified to the stifling and stirrings of black talent. They captured the imagination of nineteenth-century Britain and America because they were so much a part of that period's fascination with tales of rags to riches. The narratives told of successful resistance to oppression and were avidly read, therefore, by the British working classes. They were the precursors of *Uncle Tom's Cabin*, which in eight short months sold over one million copies in England. In turn, Stowe's novel increased interest in the narratives. British workers seized on the ideas presented in the narratives and in *Uncle Tom's Cabin*, for implicit in the argument for the emancipation of the black slave were principles that would also free the wage slave. William Wells Brown, who recognized this fact, undertook a lecture tour in the months preceding Stowe's visit to Britain. He called his lecture

2. *National Temperance Chronicle*, January, 1850; Peace Congress, *Report of the Proceedings of the Second General Peace Congress Held in Paris on the 22nd, 23rd, and 24th of August, 1849* (London, 1850), 77–78.

"American Slavery and Uncle Tom's Cabin." It was a rousing success; hundreds attended to hear the fugitive confirm Stowe's claims.[3]

These were the bricks and mortar of the antislavery wall; its foundation was the brotherhood of man or what Pennington called the "universal law of morals" that made all forms of oppression the concern of true-hearted Christians. Charles Remond put it in laymen's terms: all oppression, he warned, had to be fought, for while "it existed in the world, it must mar the sacred cause of freedom elsewhere." These were not just idle words. During their stay in Britain, many black visitors associated with European exiles. Emerick Szabad, the Hungarian refugee, attended the farewell soirée for Pennington in Edinburgh; Sarah Remond met with Neapolitan exiles; and Delany was very proud that he had the opportunity to meet Victor Hugo.[4] Blacks came to see their struggle as part of the wider resistance to all forms of oppression.

Their views would not allow blacks to avoid the issue of working-class poverty and oppression in Britain. Nor would the British working classes who attended their lectures in large numbers allow them to circumvent the issue. Richard Oastler, a Yorkshireman, had reopened the issue in 1830 when he castigated British abolitionists for ignoring the existence of wage slavery in their midst. It was not the first condemnation of its kind, but it set the tone for subsequent debate.

> Thousands of our fellow-creatures and fellow-subjects, both male and female, the miserable inhabitants of a *Yorkshire town* . . . are this very moment existing in a state of slavery, more horrid than are the victims of that hellish system "*colonial slavery.*" These innocent creatures drawl out, unpitied, their short existence, in a place famed for its profession of religious zeal, . . . and are compelled, not by the cart-whip of the negro slave-driver, but by the dread of the equally appalling thong or strap of the overlooker, to hasten half-dressed, *but not half-fed*, to those

3. *Hampshire Independent*, February 5, 1853; Hereford *Times*, December 10, 1853.

4. *Scottish Press*, July 2, 1851; *National Anti Slavery Standard*, April 30, 1859; *British India Advocate*, August 16, 1841.

magazines of British infantile slavery—*the worsted mills in the town and neighbourhood of Bradford.*

Like the inhabitants of Muggleton, British abolitionists and philanthropists seemed more interested in raising subscriptions to send "flannel waistcoats and moral-handkerchiefs" to the West Indies, than in stemming the excesses of the factory system at home.[5]

Oastler and Dickens were not alone in their criticism; abolitionist meetings were disrupted by Chartists and their supporters, determined to force British abolitionists to recognize and commit themselves to the elimination of wage slavery. In November, 1837, James Beaumont, editor of the *Northern Journal*, speaking on behalf of the North of England Working Men's Association and determined to force the local Newcastle antislavery society to adopt a more radical position, called on the meeting to unite the antislavery cause "to the movement of working men and radicals in Newcastle." Workingmen demonstrated their opposition to the local middle-class leadership of the society at the end of the meeting. The dispute grew increasingly strident, so much so that in 1840 the leadership of the society decided to disband rather than resolve their differences with local Chartists. When Garrison dismissed the claims of a Glasgow Chartist leaflet that slavery existed in Britain and abolitionists did little to alleviate it, its author, Charles M'Ewan, countered, "a bloated Aristocracy, supported by our admirers, and the minions of a lawless faction, have gorged upon the life-springs of the indigent, until penury has filled the land with paupers, crime and degradation; our political horizon is daily darkened . . . the poor man's fireside is hourly becoming a scene of desolation, and yet our sapient lovers of freedom look cooly on, with perfect indifference to the claims of suffering humanity."[6]

Black visitors ran into no similar opposition from their working-class audiences. On many occasions these audiences did insist that

5. Charles Dickens, *Pickwick Papers* (1837; rpr. New York, 1964), 408; Quoted in J. T. Ward, *Chartism* (London, 1973), 57.
6. Quoted in Marcus Cunliffe, *Chattel Slavery and Wage Slavery* (Athens, Ga., 1979), 17, and discussed in I. E. Melvir's paper on abolitionist activity in Newcastle prepared for Dr. R. C. Reinders' undergraduate seminar at Nottingham University.

blacks address the similarities between American slavery and British wage slavery, but at no time were they denounced, even when their views were not as sympathetic as some would have liked. At a Newcastle meeting in February, 1841, Remond was asked by a local Chartist to suggest some concrete ways in which the British could aid American abolitionists. Remond recommended memorials, and abstaining from slave produce, among others. When it became clear that the Chartist would demand some reciprocity for the British worker, he was promptly silenced by the chairman. Although the situation grew tense, the meeting was not disrupted. Local Chartists were courteous to Remond; their dispute was not with him, but with local middle-class opponents. Remond confronted similar situations in Ipswich and throughout his tour of Scotland and in all instances was allowed to express his views without interruption. This may be accounted for in part by the fact that Remond, like most other black visitors, seems not to have accepted the polarity between liberty and slavery. Their experiences as free blacks in the North belied such a view. They believed—and this is the point they all reiterated in their lectures—that black slavery was the worst of all forms of oppression and, therefore, had to be destroyed if all were to be free. As Brown told a Faneuil Hall meeting before his departure for Europe, labor—whether white or black—could never be free while slavery existed.[7] In the war against oppression, British workers fighting their own battles at home must also lend support to the destruction of slavery if their own freedom was to be assured.

Blacks were also well received by British workers because they symbolized successful resistance to oppression. While the analogy of slavery was employed by British labor to condemn the excesses of industrialism, it also provided a useful mechanism for comparing and attacking both systems. In his poem "The White Slave" Henry Mence compared the "wretched seamstress" living in a slum where "balmy zephyr ne'er came nigh" to the black slave:

> The Afric maid, poor child of woe!
> Who bound in fetters droops her head,

7. William E. Farrison, *William Wells Brown: Author and Reformer* (Chicago, 1969), 122; Gateshead *Observer*, February 6, 1841.

May envy not a paler slave,
Whose grief-worn heart so oft had bled.[8]

Both types of slaves were oppressed and should be free. On more than one occasion local working-class leaders used the visit of black Americans to condemn middle-class indifference to the plight of the poor and to recommit themselves to the removal of inequalities. Following Douglass' farewell visit to Sheffield, Samuel Roberts wrote to protest against those who opposed American slavery but ignored the plight of "hundreds of poor ulcerated, crippled, little black-looking, half-naked, shivering" chimney sweeps, who were sold by their parents and "attired in that full sable undress in which they are sent out by 4 o'clock through the snow, in the keenest frost of winter, probably for miles, to be employed in tasks more horrible, maiming, demoralizing and destructive than ever America enforced on even adult slaves."[9] Roberts and others rarely missed an opportunity to use the sympathy for American slaves to rouse the moral indignation of the British middle class against wage slavery. But none of these working-class spokesmen ever attacked the views and efforts of black American visitors, even when they argued, as Douglass frequently did, that there was a fundamental difference between chattel slavery and wage slavery. That fact was accepted from black Americans but not from their British supporters or white Americans. Labor spokesmen were always careful to point out that their comparisons were never intended to imply support for American slavery.

It would be wrong, however, to suggest that black visitors involved themselves seriously in the conflict between contending classes in Britain. They stayed clear of the issue as much as they could. This was sound strategy, for their concern was to win British opposition to American slavery, not to become embroiled in domestic disputes. Douglass did attend one meeting of the Metropolitan Complete Suffrage Association, after which he wrote Garrison, "in the triumph of complete suffrage in this country, aristocratic rule must end—class legislation must cease—the law of primogeniture

8. Henry Mince, "White Slave," *Truth Seeker*, III (1848), 207.
9. Sheffield and Rotterham *Independent*, April 3, 1847.

and entail, the game laws, etc., will be utterly swept from the statute book. When people and not property shall govern, people will cease to be subordinated to property."[10] But this was an exception; generally blacks shied away from organizational affiliation with the working-class movement although they continued to express sympathy with its aims. Their principal concern was the spread of abolitionist sentiment, and where other issues, such as Wright's antisabbatarianism, threatened to deflect attention away from the cause, they avoided them.

Avoiding British domestic issues was not only politically sound, it was also dictated by the imperatives of the moral crusade. These activities took place in an era of national jealousies between Britain and America, which blacks cautiously exploited. They held up their country to international scorn for its refusal to abolish slavery and stem racial discrimination, but they generally stopped short of total condemnation. America, if it could but eradicate slavery and discrimination, could offer the world a great deal. In this context their business was to make America ashamed of her inequalities before her greatest rival. This to some extent explains why each visitor wrote home of his reception in Britain, the support of its abolitionists and philanthropists, and the sense of freedom produced by the absence of racial discrimination.

In an international moral crusade, set in an atmosphere of national jealousies, representatives of an oppressed minority who have little or no political power at home are almost compelled to avoid issues of larger political significance. The same applied to the efforts of white American abolitionists in the Atlantic movement. No visitor to Britain could have afforded to present opponents at home with concrete evidence of political machinations. As it stood they were already accused of abandoning their country and promoting foreign interference in America's domestic affairs. This may explain why the imprisonment of foreign black seamen remained a tangential issue in the international movement. Southerners viewed the protests that greeted the first case tried under the Negro Seamen's

10. Philip Foner (ed.), *The Life and Writings of Frederick Douglass* (6 vols.; New York, 1950–78), I, 167.

Act in 1823, almost a decade before Paul and Garrison visited Britain, as a sinister collaboration between American and British abolitionists. When the BFASS called on Lord Palmerston in 1846 to protest the imprisonment of British subjects in southern ports few other abolitionists vigorously supported their demands. What is even more interesting is that black visitors virtually ignored the issue until Samuel Ringgold Ward questioned British policy in 1854. He rejected American arguments that the Seamen's Acts fell under state jurisdiction and therefore could not be affected by federal law. The British, he said, were "culpably negligent of their duty" when they accepted this position, especially since they had paid compensation, under pressure from the federal government, to American slaveholders for slaves who had escaped to British territories in the Caribbean. The British government would go to the aid of the Turks, he argued, "but when the wrongs of the British negro demanded redress, the same lion became a very harmless creature, and suddenly became destitute of every particle of power, and without either teeth or claw." The seamen were being ignored because they were black and because the British were fearful of disrupting trade with the South. "What was the negro made for," he thundered, "but to be oppressed and trodden under foot, that trade may go on, and white men make fortunes."[11] Ward remained the one exception among black visitors in the antebellum period.

Avoiding discussion of issues that touched on relations between America and Britain proved ticklish at times. At a Cork meeting, for instance, Douglass openly condemned British policy on Texas, asserting that when America rattled her saber Britain quickly retreated from open support of the independent republic. America, he told his listeners, in spite of its breast beating, could not afford to go to war with Britain with "3 millions of slaves in their bosom, only looking for the first favorable opportunity of lifting their arms in open rebellion." He repeated this position at a subsequent meeting in Dundee. Disclaiming all attempts to foster a spirit of war, he nonetheless observed, "let England, in her claim of Oregon, decry slavery,

11. *Anti Slavery Reporter*, June 1, 1854; *British Banner*, May 24, 1854; Manchester *Examiner and Times*, August 2, 1854.

and their slaves would flock to her banner. Were this done there would be no war. America had enough on hand in governing her own population."[12] The infrequency of these comments in comparison with his other views suggests that Douglass never saw this as a reasonable proposition. More important, blacks in America were convinced that these views compounded, rather than alleviated their problem. When Thomas Van Rensselaer suggested in 1841 that blacks refuse to join America in any future wars with Britain because of America's refusal to recognize their contributions in the War of Independence and the War of 1812 and to accord them the rights of citizenship, he was condemned by other blacks in no uncertain terms. Charles Ray and others accused him of being a traitor and argued that, having fought for America, blacks will "ultimately reap benefits."[13] Blacks could hardly afford to carry this additional burden, and little was heard of this issue again.

Refusal or reluctance to comment on social inequities in Britain were to a significant degree the product of the favorable reception blacks were given. For the first time in their lives, they were able to move about all walks of society free from racial restrictions. They were lionized, feted, and patronized by British aristocracy and men of wealth. Working-class audiences greeted them enthusiastically wherever they went. Crummell, for instance, who had so much trouble with his own denomination in America, was offered a temporary position as a curate when he was short of money. He was well received and met with "no fainting fits, no consternation, no fierce and fretful anger" because of his color. In fact he was convinced that his color was an asset. William G. Allen, who was forced to flee Fulton, New York, by a mob opposed to his proposed marriage to one of his white students, was invited to read his paper on "American Poets" to a conversazione organized by the Literary and Philosophical Society of Leeds. William Wells Brown was made an honorary member of the Whittington Club, whose membership included such literary and political luminaries as Dickens, Henry Brougham, and Douglas Jerrold. Garrison reported that Remond

12. Dundee, Perth, and Cuper *Advertiser,* January 30, 1846; Cork *Examiner,* November 7, 1845.

13. *Colored American,* January 23, February 6, 13, March 27, 1841.

was a favorite of the duchess of Sutherland, Lord Morpeth, Lady Byron, and Samuel Gurney. Elizabeth Greenfield, a singer who was known as the "Black Swan," was patronized by the duchesses of Sutherland, Norfolk, Beaufort, and Argyll.[14] Like many of their white American co-workers, blacks were very impressed by and enjoyed fraternizing with British aristocracy.

It would have been startling if this kind of treatment had not made these blacks into anglophiles who particularly revered the British philanthropists. They were all, with the possible exception of Moses Roper, warmly greeted and openly endorsed in the period before the Civil War. Even Roper's problems with the Reverend Thomas Price of London can be explained by the fact that he reneged on a commitment to complete his education and undertake missionary work in Africa. Price took it upon himself to publicly condemn Roper as he had publicly supported him when he first arrived in England.[15] Britain was criticized rarely and then only mildly. Even the blatantly racist views of men like Carlyle elicited few comments from black Americans in Britain. It was not until the 1860s that they actively began a sustained attack on such views. Only after the failure of his London school in 1869 following five years of resisting local jealousies and competition from fellow schoolmasters, could William G. Allen bring himself to believe that racism was a factor in his failure. "Certain schoolmasters in this locality," he wrote a friend, "not influenced by a spirit of honorable competition, but by a spirit not usually supposed to exist among Englishmen, resolved to put the school out of the house, and after I had gone to such expense fitting up the house for school purposes."[16]

Acceptance by the British was also used as a device to expose inequalities in American society. This is precisely what Garrison intended in his comments on Remond's acceptance by members of the British aristocracy. "Surely," he concluded, "if Dukes, Lords, Duch-

14. James M. Trotter, *Music and Some Highly Musical People* (1881; rpr. New York, 1968), 84–85; *Liberator*, July 31, May 5, 1840; William Wells Brown, *Three Years in Europe; or, Places I Have Seen and People I Have Met* (London, 1852), xlv; Alexander Crummell to John Jay, September 12, 1851, in JF.

15. *Patriot*, November 16, 23, 26, 1840.

16. William G. Allen to Dear Madame, April 21, 1869, in BFASS.

esses, and the like, are not ashamed to eat, sit, walk and talk with colored Americans, the *democrats* of our country need not deem it a vulgar or odious thing to do likewise." Remond employed similar arguments during his testimony before the Massachusetts legislature on Jim Crow transportation soon after his return home. This partiality toward Britain did not blind them to the existence of oppression; they chose, as a matter of policy, to avoid discussion of it. Soon after his arrival in Britain, McCune Smith wrote of the "miserable beggars, with whom the streets are occasionally disgraced, and whose crafty display of putrescent sores, is fearfully disgusting."[17] There were other comments on poverty in Britain, but they were few. Nor did blacks ally themselves too closely with aristocratic circles, as some have suggested. Support from this quarter, while flattering, was cherished, as Garrison implied, for its symbolic value. What mattered was acceptance by all walks of British society. In an Atlantic community with expanding cultural, trading, religious, and scientific links, blacks were now able to claim that the dominant partner had openly welcomed those whom America refused to grant the full rights of citizenship. Half the task was completed; with this meed of approval they were at least recognized as members of the Atlantic community. All that was now left was to pressure America to remove slavery and discrimination from her otherwise sound republican system.

It is clear that black Americans were active workers in the construction of the antislavery *cordon sanitaire*. They also manned its defences. Whenever it was breached, they rallied to hold the line against opponents. Victories were consistently recorded against the American Colonization Society whenever it attempted to present itself as an antislavery society. Blacks were able to distinguish the society from Liberia, which most saw as an important vehicle for the spread of Christianity and a producer of free-labor goods, and they convinced their listeners to support the colony but not the society. However, with the spread of missionary activity in the 1850s, which coincided with an increased demand for alternative sources of cotton to meet the needs of British manufacturers, many blacks, who

---

17. *Colored American*, July 21, 1838; *Liberator*, July 31, 1840, October 21, 1842.

by 1855 had adopted emigrationism with its strong missionary dimensions, found themselves unwitting tools of British colonial expansion. Some, especially missionary proponents like Crummell
and Ward, even argued that Britain was somehow providentially ordered to lead the advance of Christianity through "benighted" Africa.

There were some failures, the most notable of which was the
refusal of the Free Church to return the money it had collected in
the South. But even here there was a measure of success. Not only
did the controversy provide abolitionists with an opportunity to
carry their message to all parts of Britain, but it also made it virtually impossible for proponents of increased transatlantic evangelical contacts to formalize their plans without first addressing the issue of American slavery. The Evangelical Alliance fell prey to this
new attitude, and repeated attempts to reactivate it during the 1850s
were unsuccessful. Blacks and their British supporters were vigilant
in exposing any such schemes if they included American churches
that had not refused fellowship with slaveholders. The Turkish Mission Aid Society, an associate of the proslavery American Board of
Commissions for Foreign Missions, won support, however, because
of its missionary objectives, of which blacks like Ward could approve.

Blacks brought to their task an independence that kept the international movement alive at a time when it appeared that it might
founder on the rocks of sectarian dispute. They were no one's "ebony
echo" or "loving shadow," as one author described Remond's relationship with Garrison.[18] On the contrary, they were fiercely independent men and women and on more than one occasion dismayed
their supporters. Their desire to act independently ultimately led to
the creation of a third alternative in an already badly divided Atlantic movement that at the time sorely needed consolidation. The
thirty years of black involvement in the movement were the foundation and the precedent for black activism in the twentieth century.

---

18. Mirian L. Usrey, "Charles Lenox Remond: Garrison's Ebony Echo at the
World Anti-Slavery Convention, 1840," *Essex Institute Historical Collections*, CVI
(1970), 120.

Craft, William and Ellen.

By far the most famous of America's fugitive slaves, the Crafts settled in England in 1851 after attempts were made to recapture them
in Boston and return them to slavery in Georgia. During nineteen
years in Britain, the Crafts played an active role in the international
antislavery movement. William also spent five years in Dahomey
where he ran a school and merchant business. The Crafts returned
to America in 1869 and purchased a plantation in their home state
that they hoped to cultivate as a cooperative farm.

Crummell, Alexander.

Like James McCune Smith, Crummell was also denied admittance
to an American college because of his race. In his case it was his
own denomination that rejected his application to its seminary.
Crummell left for England in the late 1840s hoping to raise money
to build a church for his congregation, which had been meeting in
rented accommodations. After he had achieved his objective, Crummell's English friends subscribed to a fund to pay his expenses while
he attended Queen's College, Cambridge. After graduation Crummell went to Liberia as a missionary where he spent many years
before returning to America.

Delany, Martin R.

Better known as the "father of black nationalism," Delany was the
leading theoretician and mover of black American emigrationism in
the 1850s. He toured West Africa with Robert Campbell in 1859–
1860, signing an agreement with the authorities at Abeokuta for the
establishment of a colony of black Americans there. On his way
home he toured Britain in an effort to win financial support for his
plans. Although he gained substantial support from cotton interests
and philanthropists, the settlement failed to materialize mainly because of opposition from English missionaries at Abeokuta.

Douglas, Robert.

A member of a well-known Philadelphia family, Douglas attended classes at the Royal Academy of Arts during the early 1840s. On his return home, he quickly established himself as a fine artist and daguerreotypist. He emigrated to Jamaica in the mid-1840s but returned home after only a few months.

Douglass, Frederick.

Volumes have been written about the life and labors of Frederick Douglass, by far the most prominent black American of the nineteenth century. A fugitive slave from Maryland, Douglass quickly made his mark on American abolitionism. During his visit to Britain in 1845, he led the protests against the Free Church of Scotland for receiving money from southern proslavery churches and was instrumental in forcing the Evangelical Alliance and the World Temperance Congress to condemn American slavery. During this visit, friends raised money to purchase his freedom. By the time he returned to America in 1847, Douglass had already established himself as one of the leading figures in the international antislavery movement. Douglass made a second brief tour of Britain in 1859–1860.

Elaw, Zilpha.

Born in the 1780s outside Philadelphia, Elaw was already a well-established preacher before she took her ministry to Britain in 1840. She seems to have had her greatest success among the small Primitive Baptist and Methodist churches in the provinces. She was still an active preacher in Britain when she published her memoirs in 1846.

Garnet, Henry Highland.

A fugitive slave from Maryland, Garnet has been described as the most radical of the group of black Americans who led the fight against slavery and discrimination during the nineteenth century. In 1848 he was invited to lecture in Britain by the leaders of the British Free Produce Association. Four years later he went out to Jamaica as a missionary of the United Presbyterian church of Scotland. After his return to America, around 1856, Garnet became a leading proponent of African emigration.

Henson, Josiah.

Erroneously believed to be the person on whom Harriet Beecher Stowe modeled Uncle Tom, Henson, following his escape from slavery, settled in Canada where he became a leading figure among the communities of black Americans in exile. Henson visited Britain around 1850, hoping to raise money for the Dawn community. Difficulties dogged his path throughout his stay in Britain, but Henson did manage to raise considerable support for Dawn among British philanthropists.

Paul, Nathaniel.

A Baptist minister from Albany, New York, Paul and his brother Benjamin joined the fledgling settlement of Wilberforce in Ontario, Canada, soon after it was established by blacks fleeing the racial laws of Ohio. Paul left for Britain in 1832 to raise money for the settlement and for a college that blacks and their white supporters hoped to open in New Haven, Connecticut. While in Britain, Paul vigorously opposed the mission of Elliott Cresson, representative of the ACS. He also testified before a parliamentary committee on slavery. During his four years in Britain, Paul raised a considerable sum of money, none of which actually reached the struggling settlers at Wilberforce.

Pennington, J. W. C.

Pennington escaped from slavery in Maryland about 1828. Largely self-educated, he later taught school in New York. After years of studying for the ministry, he was ordained in the late 1830s and took charge of a black Congregational church in Hartford, Connecticut. Pennington made three visits to Britain, in 1843, 1849–1852, and 1861. During his first visit, he attended the first Peace Congress and the second World Anti-Slavery Convention. On his second visit friends in Scotland raised sufficient money to buy his freedom. In December, 1849, Pennington was awarded an honorary degree of Doctor of Divinity from the German University of Heidelberg. By the mid-1850s, however, Pennington's continuing problem with alcohol led to his fall from favor among abolitionists.

Powell, William.

Powell is best known for his extensive work among the community of seamen, particularly black seamen, who lived in New York. For many years he ran a home for black seamen who could find no other accommodation while in the city. Powell took his family to England after the passage of the Fugitive Slave Law in 1850, determined that his children would grow up in an atmosphere free from racial oppression. One of his children read medicine at London University. Powell returned to America during the Civil War.

Remond, Charles Lenox.

One of the most prominent black Americans of the nineteenth century, Remond was a leading advocate of Garrisonian abolitionism. In the summer of 1840, he was a member of the American delegation attending the World Anti-Slavery Convention in London. When women were not recognized as delegates to the Convention, Remond, Garrison, and others protested by joining the women who were forced to sit in the galleries. It was Remond who was largely responsible for maintaining communications between "old" and "new" organizationists when it appeared that the split in the ranks of abolitionists would destroy the movement in Britain. American abolitionists were well aware that an irreconcilable division of the movement in Britain would seriously undermine their efforts at home.

Remond, Sarah Parker.

Sister of Charles Lenox Remond, Sarah Remond emerged as a prominent Garrisonian abolitionist in the 1850s. She left America on an antislavery tour of Britain toward the end of the decade. During her long sojourn in Britain, she was an active member of the British Freedman Aid movement, at the same time attending classes at Bedford College, London, and following a grueling antislavery lecture schedule. After a short visit to America, Sarah left for Florence, Italy, where she studied and practiced medicine.

Roper, Moses.

Roper was a towering man, six feet, five inches, tall. He escaped from slavery in the 1830s and later moved to England where he became a regular feature on the antislavery lecture circuit. With the aid of a number of London philanthropists, Roper was able to attend school. His benefactors hoped that on completion of his studies Roper would go to Africa as a missionary, but he seems to have spent the rest of his life in England.

Smith, James McCune.

After graduation from the African Free School in New York, Smith was denied admittance to a number of colleges because he was black. He then left for Scotland where he enrolled at the University of Glasgow, from which he received his baccalaureate and medical degrees. Smith was a founding member of the Glasgow Emancipation Society and remained an honorary member after his return to America. Not long after his return to New York Smith established a successful practice that made him a leading figure in the city. He was an active member of the Negro Convention Movement and national and local abolitionist societies.

Ward, Samuel Ringgold.

A fugitive slave from Maryland, Ward was considered one of the great orators of his time. He edited a number of newspapers in America before he moved to Toronto following the famous rescue of the fugitive slave Jerry. While in Canada, Ward worked among the growing fugitive communities. He toured Britain in the early 1850s to raise money for the efforts of the Canadian Anti Slavery Society. He left England for Jamaica in 1855 where he spent the rest of his life.

Watkins, James.

A fugitive slave from Maryland, Watkins was a great success in Britain during the 1840s and 1850s. Unlike most of his contemporaries, the major part of his antislavery work was confined to small villages and towns in the provinces where he always drew large crowds. Nothing is known of his later life.

Selected Bibliography

CONTEMPORARY MATERIALS

Manuscripts

American Anti-Slavery Society Papers. Boston Public Library. Used by courtesy of the Trustees of the Boston Public Library.

American Colonization Society Papers. Manuscript Division, Library of Congress.

American Missionary Association Papers. Amistad Research Center, New Orleans.

Anti Slavery Papers. Cornell University, Ithaca, N.Y.

Birmingham British and Foreign Anti-Slavery Society Papers. Birmingham Public Libraries, Birmingham, England.

Birmingham Ladies Negroes' Friend Society Minute Book, 1837–59. Birmingham Public Libraries, Birmingham, England. Reproduced by permission of the Reference Library, Local Studies Department, Birmingham, England.

British and Foreign Anti-Slavery Society Papers. Rhodes House Library, Oxford University, Oxford.

British Foreign Office Documents. Public Record Office, London.

Brougham Papers. University College, London.

James Buchanan Collection. Historical Society of Pennsylvania, Philadelphia.

Lydia Maria Child Papers. Personal Miscellaneous. Rare Books and Manuscripts Division. The New York Public Library, Astor, Lenox, and Tilden Foundations.

Church Missionary Society Papers. Church Missionary Society Archives, London.
Thomas Clarkson Papers. British Library, London.
James Cropper Papers. In possession of Cropper family, Kendal, England.
George M. Dallas Collection. Historical Society of Pennsylvania, Philadelphia.
Frederick Douglass Papers. Microfilm. Library of Congress.
Raymond English Deposit. John Rylands University Library of Manchester, Manchester, England.
English, Irish, and Scottish Letters Addressed to Henry C. Wright, 1843–47. Houghton Library, Harvard University, Cambridge. Used by permission of the Houghton Library.
Estlin Papers. Dr. Williams's Library, London.
Leon Gardiner Collection. Historical Society of Pennsylvania, Philadelphia.
Sydney Howard Gay Papers. Rare Book and Manuscript Library. Columbia University, New York.
Glasgow Emancipation Society Papers. Smeal Collection. The Mitchell Library, Glasgow.
Simon Gratz Collection. Historical Society of Pennsylvania, Philadelphia.
Thomas Hodgkin Papers. In possession of Hodgkin family, Warwickshire.
Jay Family Papers, etc. Rare Book and Manuscript Library. Columbia University, New York.
Harriet Martineau Letters. Cumbria Record Office, Kendal, England.
Rawson Papers. John Rylands University Library of Manchester, Manchester, England.
Royal Geographical Society Papers. Royal Geographical Society Archives, London.
Gerrit Smith Papers. Syracuse University, Syracuse, N.Y.
Department of State Diplomatic Instructions. National Archives, Washington.
United Presbyterian Church Papers. National Library of Scotland, Edinburgh.

Books and Pamphlets

Abel, Annie H., and Frank J. Klingberg, eds. *A Side-Light on Anglo-American Relations, 1839–1858: Furnished by the Correspondence of Lewis Tappan and Others with the British and Foreign Anti-Slavery Society.* Lancaster, Pa., 1927.
Adams, F. C. *Manuel Periera; or, The Sovereign Rule of South Carolina.* London, 1852.

Adams, H. G. *God's Image in Ebony*. London, 1854.

African Aid Society. *First Report, from July, 1860, to the 31st March, 1862*. London, n.d.

Africa Redeemed; or, The Means of Her Relief Illustrated by the Growth and Prospects of Liberia. London, 1851.

Allen, William G. *The American Prejudice Against Colour: An Authentic Narrative*. London, 1853.

————. *A Short Personal Narrative*. Dublin, 1860.

An American. *American and English Oppression and British and American Abolitionists: A Letter Addressed to R. D. Webb, Esq*. London, 1853.

Anti-Slavery Songs. Edinburgh, 1847.

Aptheker, Herbert, ed. *A Documentary History of the Negro People in the United States*. 2 vols. Secaucus, N.J., 1951.

Armistead, Wilson. *A 'Cloud of Witnesses' Against Slavery and Oppression: Containing the Acts, Opinions, and Sentiments of Individuals and Societies in All Ages*. London, 1853.

————. *Memoirs of Paul Cuffee: A Man of Colour*. London, 1840.

————. *A Tribute to the Negro: Being a Vindication of the Intellectual and Religious Capabilities of the Coloured Portion of Mankind*. Manchester, 1848.

Asher, Jeremiah F. *Incidents in the Life of Rev. J. Asher, Pastor of Shiloh (Coloured) Baptist Church, Philadelphia, United States*. London, 1850.

Bell, Howard H., ed. *Search for a Place: Black Separatism and Africa, 1860*. Ann Arbor, Mich., 1970.

Birmingham British and Foreign Anti Slavery Society. *Report for 1843*. Birmingham, 1844.

Birmingham Ladies Negroes' Friend Society. *Twenty Fourth Report*. Birmingham, 1849.

————. *Twenty Ninth Report*. Birmingham, 1854.

Birney, James G. *The American Churches, the Bulwarks of American Slavery*. London, 1840.

Blassingame, John, ed. *The Frederick Douglass Papers*. New Haven, 1979.

————. *Slave Testimony: Two Centuries of Letters, Speeches, Interviews, and Autobiographies*. Baton Rouge, 1977.

Brent, Linda. *Incidents in the Life of a Slave Girl: Written by Herself*. London, 1862.

Bristol and Clifton Ladies Anti-Slavery Society. *Special Report of the Bristol and Clifton Ladies Anti-Slavery Society: During Eighteen Months, from January, 1851, to June, 1853; with a Statement of the Reasons of Its Separation from the British and Foreign Anti-Slavery Society*. London, 1852.

British and Foreign Anti-Slavery Society, *First Annual Report.* London, 1840.

———. *Second Annual Report.* London, 1841.

———. *Fourth Annual Report.* London, 1843.

———. *Sixth Annual Report.* London, 1845.

———. *Seventh Annual Report.* London, 1846.

———. *Eighth Annual Report.* London, 1847.

———. *Tenth Annual Report.* London, 1849.

———. *Eleventh Annual Report.* London, 1850.

———. *Twelfth Annual Report.* London, 1851.

———. *Minutes of the Proceedings of the General Anti-Slavery Convention of the British and Foreign Anti-Slavery Society, Held in London, 12 of June, 1840, and Continued by Adjournments to the 23rd of the Same Month.* London, 1841.

British Association for the Advancement of Science. *Report of the Thirty Third Meeting, Held at Newcastle-upon-Tyne in August and September, 1863.* London, 1864.

British India Society. *Proceedings of a Public Meeting for the Formation of the British India Society Held at the Corn Exchange, Manchester, on Wednesday Evening, August 26th, 1840.* Manchester, 1840.

Brown, Henry "Box." *Narrative of the Life of Henry "Box" Brown: Written by Himself.* Manchester, 1851.

Brown, Josephine. *Biography of an American Bondsman.* Boston, 1856.

Brown, William Wells. *The Anti Slavery Harp: A Collection of Songs for Anti Slavery Meetings.* Newcastle, 1850.

———. *Clotel, the President's Daughter: A Narrative of Slave Life in the United States.* London, 1853.

———. *A Description of William Wells Brown's Original Panoramic Views of the Scenes in the Life of an American Slave.* London, 1850.

———. *Narrative of William Wells Brown: An American Slave.* London, 1850.

———. *Three Years in Europe; or, Places I Have Seen and People I Have Met.* London, 1852.

Canadian Anti Slavery Society. *First Annual Report.* Toronto, 1852.

Carey, M. *Letters on the Colonization Society and on the Probable Results.* Philadelphia, 1832.

Carlyle, Thomas. *Latter-Day Pamphlets.* London, 1858.

Chamerovzow, L. A., ed. *Slave Life in Georgia: A Narrative of the Life, Sufferings, and Escape of John Brown, a Fugitive Slave Now in England.* London, 1855.

Clogher Anti Slavery Association. *Second Annual Report.* Clogher, 1857.

Collins, John A. *Right and Wrong Among the Abolitionists of the United States.* Glasgow, 1841.

Cotton Supply Association. *First Annual Report.* Manchester, 1858.

———. *Third Annual Report.* Manchester, 1860.

Craft, William. *Running a Thousand Miles for Freedom.* London, 1860.

Cresson, Elliott. *Report of the Board of Managers of the Pennsylvania Colonization Society.* London, 1831.

Cropper, James. *The Extinction of the American Colonization Society: The First Step to the Abolition of American Slavery.* London, 1833.

Crummell, Alexander. *The Duty of a Rising Christian State to Contribute to the World's Well-Being and Civilization and the Means by Which It May Reform the Same.* London, 1856.

———. *Hope for Africa: A Sermon on Behalf of the Ladies' Negro Education Society.* London, 1853.

———. *The Man, the Hero, the Christian: A Eulogium on the Life and Character of Thomas Clarkson Delivered in New York, December, 1846.* London, 1849.

———. *The Negro Race Not Under a Curse: An Examination of Genesis IX: 25.* London, n.d.

Denman, Lord. *Uncle Tom's Cabin, Bleak House, Slavery, and the Slave Trade.* London, 1853.

Douglass, Frederick. *The Constitution of the United States: Is It Pro Slavery or Anti Slavery?* London, 1860.

———. *Narrative of the Life of Frederick Douglass.* Cambridge, Mass., 1960.

———. *The Nature, Character, and History of the Anti Slavery Movement.* Glasgow, 1855.

Dumond, Dwight L., ed. *Letters of James Gillespie Birney, 1831–1857.* 2 vols. New York, 1938.

Edinburgh Ladies Emancipation Society. *Annual Report of 1846.* Edinburgh, 1847.

———. *Annual Report of 1847.* Edinburgh, 1848.

———. *Annual Report of 1850.* Edinburgh, 1851.

———. *Annual Report of 1851.* Edinburgh, 1852.

———. *Annual Report of 1852.* Edinburgh, 1853.

———. *Annual Report of 1859.* Edinburgh, 1859.

———. *Annual Report of 1860.* Edinburgh, 1860.

———. *Report of the Proceedings at a Public Meeting of the Edinburgh Ladies Emancipation Society Held at Queen's St. Hall, Friday, the 28th December, 1849.* Edinburgh, n.d.

Elaw, Zilpha. *Memoirs of the Life, Religious Experience, Ministerial Travels, and*

Labours of Mrs. Zilpha Elaw, an American Female of Colour, Together with Some Accounts of the Great Religious Revivals in America. London, 1846.

Estlin, John. *A Brief Notice of American Slavery and the Abolitionist Movement.* London, 1855.

Evangelical Alliance. *British Organization: Abstract of the Proceedings of the Second Annual Conference, Held in Bristol, June, 1848, with the Annual Report.* London, 1848.

———. *Report of the Proceedings of the Conference, Held at Freemason's Hall, London, from August 19th to September 2nd Inclusive, 1846.* London, 1847.

Fedric, Francis. *Life and Sufferings of Francis Fedric, While in Slavery: An Escaped Slave After Fifty One Years in Bondage. A True Tale Founded on Facts Showing the Horrors of the Slave System.* Birmingham, 1859.

Foner, Philip, ed. *The Life and Writings of Frederick Douglass.* 6 vols. New York, 1950–78.

Free Church Alliance with Menstealers: Send Back the Money. Great Anti Slavery Meeting in the City Hall, Glasgow. Glasgow, 1846.

Free Church Anti Slavery Society. *An Address to the Office-Bearers and Members of the Free Church of Scotland on Her Present Connection with the Slave-Holding Churches of America.* Edinburgh, 1847.

Free Churchman. *A Word to the Members of the Free Church: In Reference to the Proceedings of the General Assembly of 1847, on the Question of Communion with Slave-Holding Churches.* Edinburgh, n.d.

Free Church of Scotland. *Report of the Proceedings of the General Assembly on Saturday, May 30, and Monday, June 1, 1846, Regarding the Relations of the Free Church of Scotland and the Presbyterian Churches of America.* Edinburgh, 1846.

Gaffie, G. *The Nature, Character, and History of the Anti Slavery Movement.* Glasgow, 1855.

Garrison, William Lloyd. *Thoughts on African Colonization.* 1832; rpr. New York, 1969.

Glasgow Emancipation Society. *First Annual Report.* Glasgow, 1835.

———. *Second Annual Report.* Glasgow, 1836.

———. *Third Annual Report.* Glasgow, 1837.

———. *Sixth Annual Report.* Glasgow, 1840.

———. *Seventh Annual Report.* Glasgow, 1842.

———. *Tenth Annual Report.* Glasgow, 1845.

———. *Eleventh Annual Report.* Glasgow, 1846.

————. *Twelfth Annual Report.* Glasgow, 1847.

————. *Thirteenth Annual Report.* Glasgow, 1851.

————. *Resolution of the Public Meeting of the Members and Friends of the Glasgow Emancipation Society; Correspondence of the Secretaries; and Minutes of the Committee of the Said Society, Since the Arrival in Glasgow of Mr. John A. Collins, the Representative of the American Anti-Slavery Society in Reference to the Divisions Among American Abolitionists.* Glasgow, 1841.

Glasgow Female Anti Slavery Society. *First Annual Report.* Glasgow, 1842.

————. *Second Annual Report.* Glasgow, 1843.

————. *Fifth Annual Report.* Glasgow, 1846.

————. *Sixth Annual Report.* Glasgow, 1847.

————. *An Appeal to the Ladies of Great Britain in Behalf of the American Slave. By the Committee of the Glasgow Female Anti Slavery Society.* Glasgow, 1841.

Glasgow Female Association for the Abolition of Slavery. *A Defence of the Glasgow Female Association for the Abolition of Slavery from the Misrepresentations of Revs. Messrs. Jeffrey and Scott and Mr. W. Smeal.* Glasgow, 1851.

Glasgow New Association for the Abolition of Slavery. *Eighth Annual Report.* Glasgow, 1859.

Grandy, Moses. *Narrative of the Life of Moses Grandy, Late a Slave in the United States of America.* Boston, 1844.

Grant, James. *Sketches in London.* London, 1850.

Greeley, Horace. *Glances at Europe: In a Series of Letters from Great Britain, France, Italy, and Switzerland, etc., During the Summer of 1851.* New York, 1851.

Gurley, Ralph R. *Letter to the Hon. Henry Clay, President of the American Colonization Society and Sir Thomas Fowell Buxton, . . . on the Colonization and Civilization of Africa.* London, 1841.

————. *Mission to England in Behalf of the American Colonization Society.* Washington, D.C., 1841.

Halifax Ladies Anti Slavery Society. *Third Annual Report.* Halifax, 1860.

Henson, Josiah. *The Life of Josiah Henson, Formerly a Slave, Now an Inhabitant of Canada: Narrated by Himself.* Boston, 1849.

Hodgkin, Thomas. *On the British African Colonization Society.* London, 1834.

————. *An Inquiry into the Merits of the American Colonization Society: And a Reply to Charges Brought Against It. With an Account of the British African Colonization Society.* London, 1833.

————. *On Negro Emancipation and American Colonization.* London, 1833.

Howitt, William. *A Sermon Addressed to the Members of the Anti Slavery Society on Its Present Position and Prospects.* London, 1843.

Hutchinson, John W. *Story of the Hutchinsons (Tribe of Jesse).* 2 Vols. Boston, 1896.

Innes, William. *Liberia; or, The Early History and Signal Preservation of the American Colony of Free Negroes on the Coast of Africa.* Edinburgh, 1832.

Irish Metropolitan Anti Slavery Association. *Formation of the Irish Metropolitan Anti Slavery Association: With a Report on the Irish Contributions of 1856 to the Rochester Anti Slavery Bazaar.* Dublin, 1857.

Johnson, J. F. *Proceedings of the General Anti-Slavery Convention Called by the Committee of the British and Foreign Anti-Slavery Society Held in London From Tuesday, June 13th, to Tuesday, June 20th, 1843.* London, 1844.

Leeds Anti Slavery Association. *First Annual Report.* Leeds, 1854.

A Letter to Those Ladies Who Met at Stafford House in Particular and to the Women of England in General on Slavery at Home. London, 1853.

Liberia Unmasked; or, The Incompatibility of the Views and Schemes of the American Colonization Society with Those of the Real Friends of the Immediate Abolition of Slavery, Proved by Facts. Edinburgh, 1833.

London Emancipation Committee. *Proceedings of an Anti Slavery Meeting Held at Spafields Chapel on Friday, 14th October, 1859.* London, n.d.

Mackenzie, Alexander, ed. *The History of the Highland Clearances.* Inverness, 1883.

Mayhew, Henry. *London Labour and the London Poor.* 4 vols. 1851–64; rpr. London, 1967.

Moore, Archy. *The Slave; or, Memoirs of Archy Moore.* Leeds, 1847.

Mott, James. *Three Months in Great Britain.* Philadelphia, 1841.

Osofsky, Gilbert, ed. *Puttin' on Ole Massa.* New York, 1969.

Peace Congress. *Report of the Proceedings of the First General Peace Convention Held in London, June 22nd, 1843, and the Two Following Days.* London, 1843.

————. *Report of the Proceedings of the Second General Peace Congress Held in Paris on the 22nd, 23rd, and 24th of August, 1849.* London, 1850.

————. *Report of the Proceedings of the Third General Peace Congress, Held in Frankfort on the 22nd, 23rd, and 24th of August, 1850.* London, 1851.

————. *Report of the Proceedings of the Fourth General Peace Congress, Held in Exeter Hall, London, on the 22nd, 23rd, and 24th of July, 1851.* London, 1851.

Pennington, J. W. C. *The Fugitive Blacksmith; or, Events in the History of*

J. W. C. Pennington, Pastor of a Presbyterian Church, New York, Formerly a Slave in the State of Maryland, United States. London, 1849.

————. *A Lecture Delivered Before the Glasgow Young Men's Christian Association: And Also Before the St. George's Biblical, Literary, and Scientific Institute, London.* Edinburgh, n.d.

————, ed. *A Narrative of Events in the Life of J. H. Banks, an Escaped Slave from the Cotton State, Alabama, in America.* Liverpool, 1861.

Quincy, Edmund. *An Examination of the Charges of Mr. John Scoble and Mr. Lewis Tappan Against the American Anti Slavery Society.* London, 1852.

Randolph, J. Thornton. *The Cabin and Parlour; or, Slaves and Masters.* London, 1852.

Rodwell, James. *Queen Cora; or, Slavery and Its Downfall.* London, 1856.

Roper, Moses. *A Narrative of the Adventures and Escape of Moses Roper from American Slavery.* London, 1837.

Steward, Austin. *Twenty-Two Years a Slave and Forty Years a Freeman.* 1856; rpr. New York, 1968.

Stowe, Harriet Beecher. *The Key to Uncle Tom's Cabin.* London, n.d.

————. *Sunny Memories of Foreign Lands.* 2 Vols. Boston, 1854.

————. *Uncle Tom's Cabin.* London, 1852.

Strictures on Dr. Hodgkin's Pamphlet on Negro Emancipation and American Colonization. London, 1833.

Stuart, Charles. *The American Colonization Scheme Further Unravelled.* Bath, 1833.

————. *A Letter to Thomas Clarkson, by James Cropper and Prejudice Vincible; or, The Practicability of Conquering Prejudice by Better Means Than by Slavery and Exile; in Relation to the American Colonization Society.* Liverpool, 1832.

————. *Remarks on the Colony of Liberia and the American Colonization Society: With Some Account of the Settlement of Coloured People, at Wilberforce, Upper Canada.* London, 1832.

Tappan, Lewis. *Reply to Charges Brought Against the American and Foreign Anti Slavery Society.* London, 1852.

Taylor, Clare, ed. *British and American Abolitionists.* Edinburgh, 1974.

Thompson, George, and Henry C. Wright. *The Free Church of Scotland and American Slavery: Substance of Speeches Delivered in the Music Hall, Edinburgh, During May and June, 1846.* Edinburgh, 1846.

Tremble, William. *The Liberian Crusade.* Louth, 1833.

Twelvetrees, Harper. *The Story of the Life of John Anderson, the Fugitive Slave.* London, 1863.

Wallace, Sarah A., and Frances E. Gillespie, eds. *The Journal of Benjamin Moran, 1857–1865.* 2 vols. Chicago, 1948.

Walvin, James, ed. *Black and White: The Negro and English Society, 1555–1945.* London, 1973.

Ward, Samuel Ringgold. *Autobiography of a Fugitive Negro: His Anti Slavery Labours in the United States, Canada, and England.* 1855; rpr. Chicago, 1970.

Watkins, James. *Narrative of the Life of James Watkins, Formerly a Slave in Maryland, United States.* Manchester, 1859.

Webb, Richard D. *The National Anti Slavery Societies in England and the United States.* Dublin, 1852.

Williams, John. *Narrative of John Williams, a Negro: Showing How He Made His Escape from New Orleans, in America, and Came to England,— Where He Was Instructed in the Saving Truths of Christianity.* Chatham, 1855.

Woodson, Carter G., ed. *The Mind of the Negro as Reflected in Letters Written During the Crisis.* Washington, D.C., 1926.

Wright, Henry C. *American Slavery Proved to Be Theft and Robbery: With a Letter to Dr. Cunningham.* Edinburgh, 1845.

———. *The Dissolution of the American Union: . . . With a Letter to Rev. Drs. Chalmers, Cunningham, and Candlish . . . and a Letter to the Members of the Free Church.* Glasgow, 1845.

Newspapers and Periodicals

Abolitionist, 1833–35
African Repository, 1831–60
African Times, 1860
American and Foreign Anti Slavery Reporter, 1840–46
Anti Slavery Bugle, 1845–60
Anti Slavery Reporter, 1840–60
Anti Slavery Watchman, November, 1853–January, 1854
Bond of Brotherhood, 1859–61
British Banner, 1848–58
British Emancipator, 1837–40
British Friend, 1843–61
British India Advocate, 1841–42
Christian Witness, 1844–60
Colonization Herald, 1859–60
Colored American, 1837–41
Douglass Monthly, 1859–61

Eclectic Review, 1832–33
Freedom's Journal, 1827–29
Irish Friend, 1837–42
Liberator, 1831–60
National Anti Slavery Standard, 1840–60
New York *Colonization Journal*, 1859–60
Nonconformist, 1841–61
Non-Slaveholder, 1846–54
North Star/Frederick Douglass Paper, 1848–60
Patriot, 1831–53
Pennsylvania Freeman, 1852–60
Provincial Freeman, 1853–57
Rights of All, 1829
Slave, 1850–55
Weekly Anglo African, 1860

SECONDARY MATERIALS

Books

Adams, Ephraim D. *Great Britain and the American Civil War*. 2 vols. New York, 1925.
Ajayi, J. F. A. *Christian Missions in Nigeria, 1841–1891: The Making of a New Elite*. London, 1965.
Barnes, Gilbert. *The Anti Slavery Impulse, 1830–1844*. New York, 1964.
Briggs, Asa. *The Age of Improvement, 1783–1867*. London, 1959.
———. *Victorian People*. London, 1965.
Burn, William L. *Emancipation and Apprenticeship in the British West Indies*. London, 1937.
Coupland, Sir Reginald. *The British Anti Slavery Movement*. London, 1933.
Cunliffe, Marcus. *Chattel Slavery and Wage Slavery*. Athens, Ga., 1979.
Curti, Merle E. *The American Peace Crusade, 1815–1860*. Durham, N.C., 1929.
Curtin, Philip D. *The Image of Africa: British Ideas and Action, 1780–1850*. Madison, Wis., 1964.
Davis, David Brion. *The Problem of Slavery in the Age of Revolution, 1770–1823*. Ithaca, N.Y., 1975.
———. *The Slave Power Conspiracy and the Paranoid Style*. Baton Rouge, 1969.
Douglas, Ann. *The Feminization of American Culture*. New York, 1977.

Ellul, Jacques. *Propaganda: The Formation of Men's Attitudes.* New York, 1965.

Ellison, Mary. *Support for Secession: Lancashire and the American Civil War.* Chicago, 1972.

Farrison, William E. *William Wells Brown: Author and Reformer.* Chicago, 1969.

Fladeland, Betty. *Men and Brothers: Anglo-American Cooperation.* Urbana, Ill., 1972.

Fredrickson, George M. *The Black Image in the White Mind: The Debate on Afro-American Character and Destiny.* New York, 1971.

Hollis, Patricia, ed. *Pressure from Without in Early Victorian England.* London, 1974.

Little, K. L. *Negroes in Britain: A Study of Racial Relations in English Society.* London, 1947.

Mathews, Donald G. *Religion in the Old South.* Chicago, 1977.

Miller, Floyd J. *The Search for a Black Nationality: Black Colonization and Emigration, 1787–1863.* Urbana, Ill., 1975.

Nevins, Allan, ed. *America Through British Eyes.* New York, 1948.

Nichols, Charles A. *Many Thousands Gone: The Ex-Slaves' Account of Their Bondage and Freedom.* Leiden, Germany, 1963.

Nuermberger, Ruth K. *The Free Produce Movement: A Quaker Protest Against Slavery.* Durham, N.C., 1942.

Owsley, Frank L. *King Cotton Diplomacy: Foreign Relations of the Confederate States of America.* Chicago, 1969.

Pease, William H., and Jane H. Pease. *Black Utopia: Negro Communal Experiments in America.* Madison, Wis., 1972.

Quarles, Benjamin. *Black Abolitionists.* New York, 1969.

———. *Frederick Douglass.* Washington, D.C., 1948.

Richards, Leonard L. *Gentlemen of Property and Standing: Anti-Abolition Mobs in Jacksonian America.* London, 1970.

Schor, Joel. *Henry Highland Garnet: A Voice of Black Radicalism in the Nineteenth Century.* Westport, Conn., 1977.

Silver, Arthur. *Manchester Men and Indian Cotton, 1842–72.* Manchester, 1966.

Stanton, William. *The Leopard's Spots: Scientific Attitudes Toward Race in America, 1815–59.* Chicago, 1960.

Sweet, Leonard I. *Black Images of America, 1784–1870.* New York, 1976.

Temperley, Howard. *British Anti Slavery, 1833–1870.* Columbia, S.C., 1972.

Ward, J. T. *Chartism.* London, 1973.

Winks, Robin W. *The Black in Canada: A History.* New Haven, 1971.

Wyatt-Brown, Bertram. *Lewis Tappan and the Evangelical War Against Slavery*. Cleveland, 1969.

Articles

Billington, Louis. "British Humanitarians and American Cotton, 1840–1860." *Journal of American Studies*, XI, 313–34.

Brogin, Ruth. "Sarah Parker Remond: Black Abolitionist from Salem." *Essex Institute Historical Collections*, CX, 120–50.

Crawford, Martin. "British Travellers and Anglo-American Relations in the 1850s." *Journal of American Studies*, XII, 203–19.

Curti, Merle E. "Young America." *American Historical Review*, XXII, 23–55.

Donovan, Theresa A. "Difficulties of a Diplomat: George Mifflin Dallas in London." *Pennsylvania Magazine of History and Biography*, XCII, 412–40.

Enkvist, Nils E. "The Octoroon and English Opinions of American Slavery." *American Quarterly*, VIII, 166–70.

Hamer, Philip M. "Great Britain, the United States, and the Negro Seamen's Acts, 1822–1848." *Journal of Southern History*, I, 3–28.

Harrison, Brian. "Philanthropy and the Victorians." *Victorian Studies*, IX, 353–74.

Harrison, Roydon. "British Labor and American Slavery." *Science and Society*, XXV, 291–319.

Kirk-Green, A. H. M. "America in the Niger Valley: A Colonization Centenary." *Phylon*, XXIII, 225–39.

Klingberg, Frank J. "Harriet Beecher Stowe and Social Reform in England." *American Historical Review*, XLIII, 542–52.

Levy, David W. "Racial Stereotypes in Anti Slavery Fiction." *Phylon*, XXXI, 265–79.

Maynard, Douglas H. "The World's Anti Slavery Convention of 1840." *Mississippi Valley Historical Review*, XLVII, 452–71.

Moses, Wilson J. "Civilizing Missionary: A Study of Alexander Crummell." *Journal of Negro History*, LX, 229–51.

Osofsky, Gilbert. "Abolitionists, Irish Immigrants, and the Dilemmas of Romantic Nationalism." *American Historical Review*, LXXX, 889–912.

Quarles, Benjamin. "Ministers Without Portfolio." *Journal of Negro History*, XXXIX, 27–42.

Rehin, George. "Harlequin Jim Crow: Continuity and Convergence in Blackface Clowning." *Journal of Popular Culture*, IX, 682–701.

Reinders, R. C. "Anglo-Canadian Abolitionism: The John Anderson Case, 1860–1861." *Renaissance and Modern Studies*, XIX, 72–79.

Riach, Douglas C. "Blacks and Blackfaces on the Irish Stage, 1830–1860." *Journal of American Studies*, VII, 231–41.

———. "Daniel O'Connell and American Anti Slavery." *Irish Historical Studies*, XX, 3–25.

Rice, C. Duncan. "The Anti Slavery Mission of George Thompson to the United States, 1834–1835." *Journal of American Studies*, II, 13–31.

Shepperson, George. "Frederick Douglass and Scotland." *Journal of Negro History*, XXXVIII, 307–21.

———. "The Free Church and American Slavery." *Scottish Historical Review*, XXX, 126–143.

———. "Harriet Beecher Stowe and Scotland, 1852–1853." *Scottish Historical Review*, XXXII, 40–46.

Striefford, David M. "The American Colonization Society: An Application of Republican Ideology to Early Antebellum Reform." *Journal of Southern History*, LXV, 201–20.

Usrey, Mirian L. "Charles Lenox Remond: Garrison's Ebony Echo at the World Anti-Slavery Convention, 1840." *Essex Institute Historical Collections*, CVI, 112–25.

Walters, Ronald G. "The Erotic South: Civilization and Sexuality in American Abolitionism." *American Quarterly*, XXV, 177–201.

Zanger, Jules. "The 'Tragic Octoroon' in Pre–Civil War Fiction." *American Quarterly*, XVIII, 63–70.

Theses and Dissertations

Billington, Louis. "Some Connections Between British and American Reform Movements, 1830–1860. With Special Reference to the Anti Slavery Movement." M.A. thesis, University of Bristol, 1966.

Bingham, Robert LeBaron. "The Glasgow Emancipation Society, 1833–1876." M.Litt. thesis, University of Glasgow, 1973.

Dixon, Edward. "The American Negro in Nineteenth Century Scotland." M.Litt. thesis, University of Edinburgh, 1969.

Harwood, Thomas F. "Great Britain and American Anti Slavery." Ph.D. dissertation, University of Texas, 1959.

Lorimer, Douglas A. "British Attitudes to the Negro, 1850–1870." Ph.D. dissertation, University of British Columbia, 1972.

Murray, Alexander Lowell, "Canada and the Anglo-American Anti Slavery Movement: A Study in International Philanthropy." Ph.D. dissertation, University of Pennsylvania, 1960.

Owen, Gwynne E. "Welsh Anti Slavery Sentiments, 1795–1865: A Survey of Public Opinion." M.A. thesis, University of Wales, 1964.

Pilgrim, Elsie I., "Anti Slavery Sentiment in Great Britain, 1841–1854: Its Nature and Its Decline, with Special Reference to Its Influence upon British Policy Towards the Former Slave Colonies." Ph.D. dissertation, University of Cambridge, 1952.

Riach, Douglas C., "Ireland and the Campaign Against American Slavery." Ph.D. dissertation, University of Edinburgh, 1975.

Rice, C. Duncan, "The Scottish Factor in the Fight Against American Slavery." Ph.D. dissertation, University of Edinburgh, 1969.

Taylor, G. Clare. "Some American Reformers and Their Influence on Reform Movements in Great Britain from 1830 to 1860." Ph.D. dissertation, University of Edinburgh, 1960.

Index